"I want credit for discovering . . . Garga's Pasta Magnifico. pasta you'll ever taste. It doesn't taste Italian. It doesn't taste American. It tastes like a celebration. It's so outrageous you will want to have it as a main course and then you will want to have it as a dessert. Learn to cook it and you will be applauded at your dinner parties for the rest of your days."

—**Alan Richman**, foreword, *The Best American Recipes 2003/2004*

"I had a wild night at Garga's. . . . I'll remember it forever."

—**Jeff Bridges**, actor and director

"I first tasted the goodies in Garga in 1997, and have since made the place my mainstay in Florence. . . . Not only is the cuisine deliciously original and terrific (dig the veal with avocados and the best cheesecake in this life or the next), but from the family to the service to the wild walls and laughter out of the kitchen from Giuliano, the restaurant feels like home."

—**Peter Weller**, actor and director

"The aromatic steam coming up from the plate gave me a shudder of pleasure and also some fear—this was something one might never get enough of."

—**Sarah Lydon**, "New Year's Eve in Florence," *Saveur*

"For a late dinner, [James Ferragamo] favors Garga. . . . 'The spaghetti alla bottarga (with sundried fish roe) is delicious,'. . . and buttery, tender veal is prepared in various delectable sauces."

—**Mimi Murphy**, "Their Own Private Tuscany," *Town & Country*

"Nowhere have I been better able to enjoy my daily respite from the rigors of modern life than at Trattoria Garga. . . . But there is more to Garga than good food. A big part of its appeal comes from an almost surreal ambience. . . . I love this place."

—**Lori De Mori**, "Florence: An Insider's Guide to All That's Delicious," *Bon Appétit*

"If you want colorful surroundings, Trattoria Garga is the place. Every square inch is covered with murals, and the arugula salad is perfection, as is the pasta with mint, lemon zest, and cream. Best of all, if the proprietor's in the mood, he'll sing a bit of opera."

—**Richard Lambertson** and **John Truex**, "Feeding Firenze," *Elle Décor*

"Trattoria Garga, with its . . . international clientele, epitomizes new-wave Florentine."

—**Faith Heller Willinger**, "Florence: A Restaurant Renaissance," *Gourmet*

"What seems like anarchy is Garga's road to perfection, as fragrant and beautifully prepared dishes appear from the kitchen."

—*Events in Italy*

"We thought we had discovered one of Florence's best kept secrets, only to learn that Trattoria Garga is an establishment of international acclaim . . . on everyone's 'best' listings for Florentine eateries. . . . The memory will last forever."

—**Frederica Hopper**, "A Class Act in the Kitchen," *Italy*

ONCE UPON A TUSCAN TABLE

Tales and Recipes from Trattoria Garga

SHARON ODDSON GARGANI

with
Rena Bulkin

Camino Books, Inc.
Philadelphia

Manufactured in the United States of America

1 2 3 4 5 09 08 07 06

Library of Congress Cataloging-in-Publication Data

Gargani, Sharon Oddson, 1950-
  Once upon a Tuscan table : tales and recipes from Trattoria Garga / Sharon
Oddson Gargani with Rena Bulkin.
    p. cm.
  ISBN 0-940159-90-2 (alk. paper)
 1. Gargani, Sharon Oddson, 1950- 2. Restaurateurs—Italy—Florence—
Biography. 3. Cookery, Italian—Tuscan style. 4. Trattoria Garga (Restaurant)
5. Tuscany (Italy)—Social life and customs. I. Bulkin, Rena. II. Title.

  TX910.5.G33G37 2005
  647.95'092--dc22   2004030673

ISBN-13: 978-0-940159-90-7
ISBN-10: 0-940159-90-2

Cover and interior design: Jerilyn Bockorick
Cover photograph: Courtesy of Antonio Sferlazzo.
Photographs on pages 1, 25, 39, 112, 160, and 175 courtesy of Nancy Rica
Schiff.

This book is available at a special discount on bulk purchases for
promotional, business, and educational use.

Publisher
Camino Books, Inc.
P.O. Box 59026
Philadelphia, PA 19102

www.caminobooks.com

This book is dedicated to Zoe,
who inspired so many of its stories

Contents

Acknowledgments   *ix*

Racconti
TALES   1

1.   The Girl from the Frozen North   *3*
2.   Swiss Cheese and a Story Full of Holes   *11*
3.   The Relative Discomfort of Denmark   *18*
4.   Woodstock on the Arno   *23*
5.   Life with Zoe   *36*
6.   Andrea   *51*
7.   How Giuliano Saved Our Marriage   *62*
8.   *Après le Déluge, le Dîner:* The Drowned Chicken Party   *71*
9.   Rocks Ahead / Chickens Redux   *77*
10. Our First Trattoria: Hosts Serving Hosts   *84*
11. You Talkin' to Me?   *92*
12. Via delle Bombarde Redux   *98*
13. Heaven Help Us   *106*
14. *Putto* among the Pigeons   *110*
15. The Year of the Sunflower   *117*
16. Giuliano Falls Down, Andrea Steps Up   *125*
17. Arm Wrestling   *131*
18. Dinner with Nancy   *137*
19. Going Underground   *142*
20. Renewal   *147*
21. Alessandro Defends His Country   *152*
22. Magrittings—La Cucina del Garga   *159*
23. Celebrating the Birthdays of Giuliano and Jesus   *167*
24. Looking Back, Looking Ahead   *174*

Ricette

RECIPES   181

Antipasti ℭ℈ Hor d'Oeuvres   *187*
  Bruschette, Crostini, and *Fettunte*   *198*

Primi Piatti ℭ℈ First Courses   *207*
  Zuppe Soups   *208*
  Crespelle Crêpes   *214*
  Polente Polentas   *216*
  Risotti   *218*
  Gnocchi and *Gnudi*   *223*
  Paste Pastas   *228*

Secondi Piatti ℭ℈ Second (Main) Courses   *251*
  Secondi di Mare Fish and Seafood Entrées   *252*
  Secondi di Pollo, Anatra, Coniglio, e Quaglie Chicken, Duck,
    Rabbit, and Quail Entrées   *260*
  Secondi di Carne Beef, Lamb, Pork, and Veal Entrées   *269*

Contorni ℭ℈ Side Dishes   *285*

Dolci ℭ℈ Desserts   *295*

Index   *319*

ACKNOWLEDGMENTS

This book was a slow-moving project that underwent a metamorphosis. Over the years, old friends and new acquaintances alike gave me encouragement and helped me persevere, and I would like to thank them.

Special mention must go to Rena Bulkin, my co-writer, for her patience and her trust in this work.

Warmest thanks to:

My three dear friends, Janet Lansill, Nancy Rica Schiff (her tenacity in bringing out her own book, *Odd Jobs*, has been an example for me), and Mims Walbridge, for her priceless collaboration with La Cucina del Garga.

Samuel Limor and Rosemary Espanol, for getting the ball rolling by introducing me to my publisher. I will never be able to thank them enough.

Edward Jutkowitz, my publisher, for believing in my book.

Barbara Gibbons from Camino Books for her astute and caring editing.

All the staff members, past and present, of Trattoria Garga, but a particular thank you must go to *mio fratellino*, Elio Cotza, our partner and chef.

Giuliano, for his unique means of understanding. It has helped me continue onward.

Mille baci for Andrea, Ginevra, and little Fiammetta.

Un abbraccio stretto for Alessandro and Elizabeth; thank you for being there for me.

Grazie to those who are held in my heart. You all know who you are.

Racconti'

Sharon and Giuliano. Courtesy of Nancy Rica Schiff

TALES

Chapter 1

THE GIRL FROM
THE FROZEN NORTH

My twin sister, Karen, and I entered the world on a thirty-below January day in Barrie, Ontario, where the winters are long and brutal. My mother was a first-generation Canadian of Danish parentage; my father's family, in northern Iceland, was descended from Vikings. As far back as my ancestors can be traced on either side, we've always lived amid howling winds and raging storms.

Early on, I was aware that my parents' marriage was as chilly as their climatic ancestry. In 1954, when Karen and I were four, Mummy took us on a trip to Denmark, where we stayed with various relatives for six months. She thought a little time away from home would provide some perspective on her marital problems, and she hoped my father would miss his family. Evidently, he didn't. They divorced a few years later, and we moved to Winnipeg to share a home with my mother's parents and her younger brother, Brian, then eleven. I seldom saw my father again. In 1982, he won half-a-million dollars in the Canadian lottery and took all his brothers and sisters on a trip back to Iceland.

By the time we moved to Winnipeg, Karen and I were seasoned travelers. In addition to our flight to Denmark, my father, an aeronautical engineer in the Royal Canadian Air Force, had been relocated three times since we were born. Every time he was assigned a new post, we all packed up our belongings and went along with him—to Air Force bases

The Oddson twins in Canada, Sharon, *left*

in Ottawa, Calgary, and Alberta. Already strongly bonded as twins, Karen and I became especially close as we banded together to confront ever-changing environments. Unlike most siblings, we never fought.

Though, like many twins, we were dressed alike, we weren't identical and had markedly different personalities. Karen was gentle and timid, very pretty, with long blond ringlets. I was a rambunctious red-head, something of a ham, avid for adventure. With my stick-straight hair, I coveted Karen's fat curls. Mummy and Grandma Gerda would tightly tie my hair around rags (low-tech curlers) to achieve the desired effect, but, alas, my short-lived waves would soon wave goodbye.

In 1959, our extended family moved, yet again, to a house on the Red River, where we kept a rowboat and a canoe. Poor Karen was terrified of the water, sure she was going to drown. Grandpa would tie ropes, secured from the dock, around our waists and toss us—me ecstatic, Karen apprehensive but resigned to life's exigencies—into the river, then sit on the dock reading the paper while we frolicked. In addition to the rope, Karen always insisted on an air float. Finally, exasperated by her fearfulness, Grandpa surreptitiously opened the valve one day. As he expected, Karen didn't notice her deflated float until we were out of the water, and she was finally shamed into giving it up.

Winters, when cross-country skiing replaced water sports, provided no respite for Karen. She always lagged behind everyone else, sinking down into the slush and calling out plaintively for help. She would so much have preferred to stay peacefully at home by the fireplace, her nose buried in a book.

At school, Karen and I always felt like outsiders, not only because our parents were divorced—a rarity in the 1950s—but also because of the exotic food we ate. Mummy's only concession to Canadian food was her fervor for breakfast porridge, a steaming bowl of which was forced upon us daily during the winter months. The first two bites, with the milk poured on top still cold and the brown sugar still crunchy, were palatable. Choking down the rest took sheer willpower. But after the morning meal, Mummy and Grandma Gerda returned to their Danish culinary roots.

Our classmates, whose white-bread lunches daily ran the gamut from Velveeta to peanut butter and jelly, gazed on in histrionic horror as we unpacked sandwiches on homemade rye stuffed with pickled herring, pungent Danish blue cheese, or liver sausage and red beets. Every noon, we ate to a taunting chorus of "yecchs!" and exaggerated gagging noises. Throughout our school years, the joke of the Oddson twins' lunches never paled.

We shrugged it off, taking refuge in feelings of superiority. In our minds, and only ours, we comprised a culinary elite of two. While other kids' after-church Sunday meals centered on prosaic roast beef, ours was a bountiful smorgasbord, with four or five kinds of anchovies in different sauces, Black Forest and smoked hams, smoked and pickled herring, sweet-and sour squash pickles, hard-boiled eggs, an array of cheeses and cold cuts, and, of course, Grandma Gerda's fresh-baked rye. The grown-ups washed it all down with shots of schnapps and beer chasers.

At Christmas, in lieu of the traditional Canadian turkey or ham, we dined on crisp-skinned roast goose stuffed with apples, onions, and prunes. It was followed by a delicious rice pudding, one portion of which contained an almond. The lucky recipient of the almond got a special present, usually a marzipan pig.

These lavish meals sparked—or perhaps I should say nurtured—my lifelong love affair with food; a passion for food is something you're born with. By the time I was three, Grandma Gerda had already nicknamed me the *gryde licker*, Danish for "pot licker," because I always begged to lick clean (well, not actually lick; I'd be given a spoon) her cooking pots and bowls. On our trip to Denmark, at the home of my Tante Johanna, I devised my first actual recipe, mixing salty Danish licorice and water over a Bunsen burner. This experiment ended in disaster when, in my haste to sample the "soup," I burned my mouth and upset the pot, spilling its inky contents all over her fine Persian rug! Kindly Tante Johanna showed only loving concern. I wasn't even scolded.

My other great love, for as long as I can remember, has been art. Mummy, quite a talented painter in her own right (her watercolors of local landscapes were coveted Christmas gifts), had purchased a series of big soft-cover books filled with prints by famous artists, and I spent many hours of my childhood sprawled on the floor in front of a blazing fire, entranced by their contents. Picasso's effeminate harlequins; Gauguin's serene, semiclad Tahitian women; Van Gogh's besmirched, potato-eating coal miners; Degas's ballet dancers; and Toulouse-Lautrec's prostitutes, chorus girls, and demimondaines—all of them as real to me as the flesh-and-blood people who inhabited my life—provided my first foray into a world beyond Winnipeg.

Drawing and painting were my favorite childhood activities, and I covered hundreds of sheets of big white butcher paper with my creations. Pictures of trees were my specialty, developed on blissful outings alone with my mother. We'd sit on rocks and paint watercolors of the lake and forest. She'd exclaim enthusiastically over my masterpieces, frame them herself, and display them proudly to friends and family. I felt immensely important and talented when one of my watercolors, of birch trees in winter, was sent around the world to be exhibited in a collection of schoolchildren's art. When I was taken to a Van Gogh exhibition at the age of twelve, I was so moved—overwhelmed really—that I decided I'd be an artist when I grew up.

In 1964, my mother, who entertained romantic ideas about the Wild West, decided we should move to Texas. Her younger brother, Lloyd, who lived in Houston and worked as a plastic surgeon, found her a job as a medical secretary. Karen and I hated it from day one and complained constantly. Everything was so big and new; we missed the coziness of home dreadfully. Chili dogs were the only thing we actually liked about the Lone Star State.

Though Lutheran, we were sent to Sacred Heart, a private Catholic School, where diligent students received a coveted blue sash for learning doctrine. Though Karen and I always made perfect grades on catechism tests, because we weren't Catholics, we were never rewarded with the sash. It was unfair.

We made no friends. To our insular classmates, the Oddson twins were odder than ever. And the heat was unbearable. We had come from the frozen north (where, in our nostalgic memories, the climate had been invigoratingly brisk) to a fiery furnace. After two years, Mummy, who'd never gotten along with her brother Lloyd anyway (they fought constantly), had had enough of Texas. To our great relief, we moved back to our grandparents' house in Winnipeg.

In hindsight, I can see that being constantly uprooted as a child set the psychological stage for my later life as an expatriate. Because I never fit in anywhere, I'm most comfortable in the role of an outsider.

After high school, I briefly studied painting and art history at the University of Manitoba. But Canada—especially stolid, provincial Winnipeg, an isolated frontier town characterized by its stockyards and grain elevators—seemed too stifling a setting for my youthful artistic yearnings. Winnipeg has its own variety of natural beauty: crystalline forests brought into being by winter ice storms, vast Wyeth-like wheat fields punctuated by lonely farmhouses, and clear, starry nighttime skies providing captivating glimpses of the aurora borealis. But in the way of art, save for bronze images of deer and polar bears, it left a lot to be desired.

And it wasn't just Winnipeg. I was going through a tough time with Mummy, who, alarmed by the cultural upheaval making its way north from the States along with American draft dodgers, was constantly grilling me about my comings and goings. She'd pore over lurid newspaper accounts of the Manson family, and picture me spiraling downwards into a sordid abyss of drugs, sex, and revolution. The more I asserted my independence, the more she clamped down on my activities, and we were very much on each other's nerves. When I wanted to do something she'd forbidden, I'd lie, and because I wasn't especially good at covering my tracks, she'd usually find out, further fueling her distrust. We argued constantly. Karen wisely kept a lower profile, slipping under the parental radar.

I was ready to leave home. Had I been an American, I probably would have headed to New York, but as a Canadian, I looked to Europe as the fount of bohemianism and sophistication.

GRANDMA GERDA'S ROAST STUFFED GOOSE

3 large Golden Delicious apples

12 dried prunes (pitted)

$1/2$ yellow onion, sliced paper thin

Salt

1 goose (6 to 7 pounds)

Fresh-ground black pepper

$1/2$ cup cognac

Cider vinegar

2 tablespoons flour

2 cups canned vegetable stock

2 tablespoons tart jelly, such as crabapple or currant

2 tablespoons heavy cream

1. Preheat oven to 500 degrees. Peel, core, and slice apples, length-ways, into strips approximately $1 1/2$ inches by $1/4$ inch. Cut prunes in half. Place fruit and onion slices in a bowl, mix, and sprinkle lightly with salt.

2. Pull fat out of cavity of goose (at same time removing any organs or other pieces stored there). Discard gizzard; heart and liver can be cut into $1/4$-inch cubes and added to your stuffing. Chop fat into very fine pieces (approximately $1/4$ inch), and place in bottom of a large, deep roasting pan. Rub salt and pepper on inside of cavity, and stuff with onion/fruit mixture.

3. Sew up cavity (or skewer it closed), and tie goose legs together with string. Remove tips of wings. Wrap entire goose with string to tie wings to body (alternatively, you can use skewers to fasten wings).

4. Rub salt and pepper into skin of entire bird. Prick goose skin all over, approximately every 2 inches, with a 2-pronged cooking fork.

5. Put a rack in your roasting pan, and place goose on it, breast side down. Bake for 30 minutes.

6. Remove goose from pan, pour off fat, and reserve it in a bowl in your refrigerator (you won't need it for this recipe, but it's great for frying potatoes). Reduce oven temperature to 350 degrees. Place goose in pan, breast side up. Pour cognac over it, and continue roasting for 30 minutes more. Baste goose with pan juices, and bake for another 30 minutes, or until juices from thigh run clear. Boil water for next step.

7. Brush goose with cider vinegar, and bake another 5 minutes. Remove goose from roasting pan, and set on a large platter. Add $\frac{1}{2}$ cup boiling water to roasting pan, and scrape up brown bits with a spatula. Transfer pan juices, along with brown bits, to a saucepan, add flour, and cook on medium heat for 3 minutes, stirring continuously.

8. Add vegetable stock, and cook for 5 minutes, still stirring continuously, until thickened. Add jelly and cream. Continue stirring as gravy cooks for another 5 minutes. Strain, and transfer to a gravy boat.

9. Remove stuffing from cavity, and place in a large serving bowl. Slice off legs and wings, then carve slices from breast. Serve with Grandma Gerda's Red Cabbage and boiled redskin potatoes.

GRANDMA GERDA'S RED CABBAGE

2 pounds red cabbage
$^3/_8$ cup cider vinegar
$^3/_8$ cup sugar
1 teaspoon salt

1. Chop cabbage into large strips, and place in a colander under running water. Rinse and drain.
2. Place cabbage in a large stockpot, cover with water, and cook on low heat for 30 minutes, or until tender.
3. Add cider vinegar, sugar, and salt, and simmer for another 10 minutes.

DANISH RICE PUDDING

Don't forget the present (marzipan pig or other) for the person who finds the almond in his or her serving.

1 cup white rice
$^1/_2$ teaspoon salt
5 cups milk
$^1/_2$ cup sugar
1 whole almond
1 teaspoon almond (or vanilla) extract
Cinnamon

1. Combine rice, salt, and milk in top of a double boiler. Cover and cook over simmering water for 2 hours or until thickened, stirring often.
2. Stir in sugar and cook for 10 minutes over low heat.
3. Add whole almond and almond (or vanilla) extract.
4. Serve in individual bowls. Sprinkle each serving with cinnamon.

Chapter 2

SWISS CHEESE AND A STORY FULL OF HOLES

The day after my twentieth birthday, my friend, Andrea Kristof, and I made our break for freedom. Her family was Hungarian (they'd escaped during the 1956 revolution) and, like me, she was straining at the parental leash, especially at odds with her father, a stern paterfamilias in the Old World tradition. When I'd rail against my mother, she'd scoff, "Sharon, you have no idea; I'm living in the Victorian era."

Still young enough to require parental permission for our trip abroad—especially as we needed our families to fund it—Andrea and I selected Switzerland as our initial destination; it sounded less threatening than any other European country. Also, the Kristofs had friends (fellow refugees) in Zurich, a Dr. and Mrs. Szabo, who'd promised to keep an eye on us. Andrea and I planned to ditch the Szabos after a perfunctory lunch.

As we boarded the plane to Europe and a future filled with limitless possibilities, I experienced an exhilarating rush. Adult life—which I imagined, contrary to all empirical evidence, would be a soul-stirring adventure—was about to begin.

Then, horrible surprise, the Szabos showed up at the Zurich airport, beaming welcoming smiles, full of plans for our visit. Certain—though it was the first we'd heard of it—that we'd stay at their house, they brushed aside our protests about "not wanting to put them to any trouble." Bowing to the inevitable, we piled into the back seat of their car like a pair of docile children, as Mrs. Szabo chattered gaily about places with such implausible-sounding names as the Schweizerisches Landesmuseum and the Grossmünster. "Don't worry, dahlings," she assured us. "I make plenty time to show you around."

No sooner did we cross the threshold of their house than the phone rang. It was Andrea's parents, calling to make sure we'd arrived safely. Their call, and the Szabos' kindly concern and hospitality, exasperated us. We felt ourselves the victims of an adult conspiracy to control our every movement.

But though both Andrea and I were very much annoyed at finding ourselves caught up once again in the parental cocoon (she signaled her frustration to me with grimaces and raised eyebrows when our hosts weren't looking), secretly, I was also a little relieved. We'd arrived late in the afternoon on a bitterly cold January day, and it was already dark outside. Exhausted from the long flight, and encumbered by heavy luggage, I'd dreaded combing strange streets for a cheap hotel. I've never been one for roughing it. Nor, evidently, were the Szabos. Having escaped Hungary with little more than their lives, they'd risen phoenixlike from the ashes of their precarious past to create a haven of suburban comfort. Their rambling house was filled with a clutter of plush upholstered sofas and clunky Victorian furniture, and firelight from the hearth shone warmly on dark oak floors.

Mrs. Szabo sat us down at a massive mahogany dining table and brought out "a few things" she'd prepared for us—veal in a rich cream sauce, crêpes stuffed with chicken mousse, candied carrots, homemade noodles with walnuts swimming in butter, potato rosti, and fresh-baked apple strudel. She must have been cooking for days.

As we ate, the Szabos, who hadn't seen Andrea since she was six, barraged her, in Hungarian, with questions about life in Canada. They had a lot of catching up to do, and their interest in me, tepid to begin with, now completely subsided. This suited me perfectly, since I tend to be shy around new people. Also, I like to give my full concentration to really delicious food, and I ate happily away in silence. Mrs. Szabo was a first-rate cook.

Surfeited at last, and drifting off, I excused myself and went upstairs to bed, nestled under down covers, and immediately fell into a deep sleep. Downstairs, the Szabos continued questioning Andrea about various Laszlos, Istvans, and Anikos whom they'd last seen in Budapest.

The next few days were spent sightseeing, an activity that frustrated both Andrea and me for different reasons. I love visiting museums and cathedrals, but Mrs. Szabo, basking in the comfort of her native language, occupied Andrea with endless conversation in Hungarian. I soon tired of my isolation, while Andrea, bored to distraction with endless questions about her parents—and their many refugee friends and relatives—would have much preferred shopping and nightclubs to sightseeing.

We stayed a few more nights, then, with effusive, and actually heartfelt, thanks (after all, they had been very kind), insisted that we had to move on. After breakfast the next morning, the Szabos drove us to the station. As we kissed them goodbye and boarded the train, all we could think was "free at last!"

I've done a lot of traveling since, but I'll never forget the thrill of arriving in Geneva that day. Andrea and I were immediately captivated by the city's pristine beauty. Encountering a foreign city for the first time (I don't count Zurich, where our enthusiasm was dampened by constant chaperonage) is a singular experience, never to be recaptured, much like your first time making love.

Geneva, framed by the sheltering grandeur of the Alps, is idyllically set on a vast Alpine lake that glitters like a blue jewel, its surface dotted with sailboats and yachts. Its shores, bordered by ancient gnarled trees, are home to an array of aquatic birds. Geneva is a city of parks and promenades, flower-filled squares, and picturesque old cathedrals.

European accommodations were wonderfully cheap in 1970. We found a *pensione* that charged only a few dollars a night and settled in. Having left Canada in January, we'd arrived in Geneva during an unseasonably warm spell, which, without further inquiry, we concluded was typical Swiss weather. In a burst of youthful enthusiasm, we packed up all our heavy Canadian gear—down-lined winter coats, woolen hats with earflaps, and fleece-lined boots and gloves—and mailed them back to our parents in big cardboard boxes. We emerged from the *bureau de poste* giggling maniacally, feeling lighter in luggage and spirit. Symbolically, we'd put our cumbersome Canadian past behind us. The next day it snowed, and the temperature plummeted. Unable to afford new winter clothes, and too proud, or fearful of recrimination, to ask our parents to send ours back, we shivered until spring in light jackets.

Our stated intention in traveling—the one we had, with disingenuously earnest faces, presented to our parents—was to find jobs as *au pairs* with French families and improve our command of the language. But as long as our money held out, the search for employment was shelved. Instead, we hung out in Old City cafés, chain-smoking Gauloises and sipping espressos, striking up intense but fleeting friendships with American and European kids who, like us, were drifting aimlessly about the continent in search of adventure. Many were students, but our itinerant crowd also included models in Europe for the collections, expatriate jazz musicians, druggy disciples of Timothy Leary, even exiled Black Panthers whose unsmiling revolutionary stance scared me to death. Museum visits and excursions to nearby towns provided culturally correct fodder for letters home.

Both Andrea and I reveled in the exoticism of continental cuisine. Like me, she'd been raised on European food and had a more sophisticated palate than the average Canadian. Early on, we found the Café de Paris, near the train station, where the *spécialité de la maison* was a superb entrecôte with herbed butter and crunchy pommes frites. Peeking through its lace-curtained windows, we were lured in by an air of distinctly European coziness—a mélange of lovingly prepared food and aesthetically pleasing décor. Deft professional waiters, attired in black jackets and long white aprons, proudly bore their platters (on large chafing dishes warmed by candles) like ensigns carrying flags onto a battlefield. A *boulangerie* across the street sold fabulous fresh-baked croissants; we'd buy ten at a time and eat five each, savoring every buttery bite. And between meals, we'd binge on chocolate truffles and marzipan from Swiss pastry shops.

This decadent life of leisure went on for two months. Then, with money running low, we could no longer postpone the inevitable. I found an *au-pair* position with the Vigiers, a French family living in a ritzy apartment building on the shore of Lac Léman. Most of its residents were people working for the United Nations or foreigners conducting business or politics in Switzerland. Monsieur, I was informed by his proud wife "was in the higher echelons of the French government."

M. Vigier, a dapper little man with a thin moustache, didn't conform to my mental conception of a political VIP. I hardly ever saw him without a Gauloise dangling from his lips. Madame, still a little heavy from a recent pregnancy, was more imposing, though her good looks were slightly marred by a tightness about her mouth. Her chestnut hair was pulled back in a flawless chignon, her coiffure set off by the large pearl earrings she wore with every outfit. I thought she was wonderfully chic. My Canadian wardrobe leaving everything to be desired, I envied her Chanel suits and Hermès silk scarves.

I worked days only, continuing to reside at the *pensione.* Nights, I still frequented the cafés of the Old City, except when Andrea, who loved to dance, dragged me to *caves*, below-ground clubs that predated discos in Europe. She was much more the party girl than I.

My job was a breeze. I had to keep Fabrice, a darling little four-year-old, amused, taking him for walks, playing with him in the park by the lake shore, and teaching him a few words of English. My only other task was the grocery shopping with Madame, which I relished. On these daily excursions, I discovered the joy of fresh vegetables (in Canada we ate only frozen or canned), which Madame would lightly sauté in butter; European cheeses like tangy chèvre, creamy fromage frais avec fines herbes, and Swiss blue; lettuces other than iceberg; and salads other than the Canadian lettuce, tomato, and cucumber mortared with mayonnaise. Of the latter, my favorite was Madame's warm celery root with blue cheese vinaigrette.

One day at the *charcuterie*, Madame Vigier was fishing around in her handbag for money to pay the bill, when she looked over at me, distraught.

"Shar-on (accent on the *ON*)," she practically whispered, "I left my wallet at home. You don't happen to have some cash on you?"

"*Bien sûr, madame,*" was my immediate reply. I handed her a wad of francs and also paid for the wine at our next stop. When I left the flat that afternoon, she'd made no mention of the loan, and I was too shy to bring it up.

We had our daily midday meal together—Madame, Monsieur, little Fabrice, and I—in the flat's small dining room, its table placed in front of French windows overlooking Lac Léman. Monsieur would read *Le Figaro* and comment on the news while Madame and I prepared lunch. My school French was quickly becoming conversational, and, at first, I felt flattered, and very grown up, when M. Vigier, who turned out to be an impassioned left-winger, engaged me in political discussions. I'd read Marx and Engels in college and was pleased to air my views. Soon noticing, though, that my employer grew irritated whenever I expressed an opinion that differed from his own, I began to agree wholeheartedly with everything he said. It was much easier, anyway, to nod knowingly and murmur, "*Oui, oui,*" than to struggle along in French. Madame Vigier, who'd no doubt heard all of her husband's theories thousands of times, always turned a deaf ear to these conversations.

Andrea took a job in the same building, working for the Giussanis, a family of straitlaced Italian Jehovah's Witnesses, who relentlessly tried to convert her. One weekend, she took off to the mountains for a ski weekend with her boyfriend, Karl, the son of a

Swiss–German banker she'd met at a dance club. Somehow, Signora Giussani found out. She fired off an indignant letter to the Kristofs, informing them that their daughter was "walking the broad road to eternal damnation." Further fanning the infernal flames of parental panic, she penned dire warnings about the perils of Alpine avalanches.

The Kristofs' reaction was all Signora Giussani could have wished. It was only via an impassioned campaign of contrite persuasion—and because of the difficulties involved in actually extracting a wayward child from Europe—that Andrea wasn't immediately whisked home to Canada's safer shores. Having, however, worn out her welcome among the Witnesses—they prayed for her redemption but showed her the door—she found a new live-in job on the outskirts of Geneva, and we went our separate ways. I wouldn't see her again for several years.

I had been working for the Vigiers for a few weeks, when, one day, Madame took me aside and, in confidential tones, apologized for never having paid back the grocery money she'd borrowed. Citing problems transferring funds from home, she asked if I could possibly lend them a little more money. She promised they'd pay me back in a short time, plus the wages they owed me. Ever acquiescent, I didn't think twice about sharing my dwindling resources with my employers.

Two months passed, and I was still working for and feeding my little French family. Then, leaving work one evening, I was accosted by three Swiss policemen in trench coats, who looked as if they'd stepped straight out of a 1950s B movie. They took me to the local station and questioned me for hours about M. Vigier, who was, apparently, a high-echelon embezzler in the French government. When his activities had been uncovered in Paris, he'd fled with his family to Switzerland. I was so terrified, I could hear my heart pounding, especially when they asked for my nonexistent working papers. It had never occurred to me to apply for them. It didn't help that, in my nervousness, my newly acquired French went out the window, and I could barely put a sentence together. Though I hadn't done anything wrong, I felt both stupid and guilty.

The next day, M. Vigier was taken into custody, and, with no job, no money, and no working papers, I was "invited" by the Swiss authorities to leave their country. Frantic, I took the course of last resort. I called my mother.

Her reaction was even worse than I'd feared. Mummy couldn't fathom how anyone could have been so naïve and didn't believe a word of my story, not even that I'd been working. She accused me of making a sneaky bid for more money. I guess she preferred to think her daughter was a liar than an idiot. Finally, after a severe scolding, its length mercifully curtailed by the exorbitance of international phone rates, she decided I could remain in Europe, but only under the watchful eyes of her cousin, Ulla, in Denmark. With no other options, off I went.

MADAME'S WARM CELERY ROOT SALAD WITH BLUE CHEESE VINAIGRETTE

1 cup water

$1/2$ cup white wine vinegar

2 cups dry white wine

1 teaspoon salt

Freshly ground black pepper (1 twist of the pepper mill)

1 celery root (about 2 pounds)

$3 1/2$ ounces Roquefort cheese

3 tablespoons extra-virgin olive oil

1. Place water, vinegar, wine, salt, and pepper in a saucepan, and bring to a boil.

2. While waiting for above to boil, peel celery root with a potato peeler until only white part is visible and all brown spots are gone. Using third-largest holes of a four-sided hand grater, julienne celery root into very thin strips (as you would for coleslaw).

3. Toss julienned celery root into boiling vinegar-wine liquid for 2 minutes. Drain well, saving cooking liquid (put a strainer over another saucepan, and press out liquid with a fork).

4. Arrange celery root on a serving platter. Return cooking liquid to stove, and bring to a boil. While waiting for it to boil, crumble Roquefort into a small bowl, and add oil. Stirring constantly, add $1/4$ cup of cooking liquid to Roquefort/oil mixture. Continue stirring until sauce is creamy (though Roquefort should remain a little lumpy). Spoon sauce over celery root, and serve.

Chapter 3

THE RELATIVE DISCOMFORT OF DENMARK

I arrived in Denmark near the end of April. It was gray and damp, and it seemed as if it was always raining. I was utterly miserable—humiliated by the failure of my first foray into adult life, still furious at my mother's unfounded accusations, and lonely for my friends in Switzerland. But a week later, the amazing Scandinavian spring began, the emerald-green leaves on the trees all the more vibrant against the barren bleakness of winter. The rain-soaked grass, dotted with enormous snails and mushrooms with white-spotted red caps, looked like something out of a fairy tale. Everyone was out-of-doors, planting vegetable gardens on plots of land rented from the government or taking long walks to view the seasonal foliage.

I traveled all around Denmark, meeting relatives and getting as fat as a little Danish pig. Aunts, uncles, and cousins stuffed me daily, as I drifted from smorgasbord lunch to afternoon coffee klatch to multi-course dinner.

In June, my mother, grandparents, and Uncle Brian arrived in Copenhagen for a family reunion. Karen, who was at university, stayed back in Canada, delighted to be on her own for a while. Mummy, who'd spent a year in Denmark after World War II, was thrilled to be back. She spoke fluent Danish, but took a lot of teasing about her "American" accent. Glowing with happiness, she looked especially pretty, and I was complimented when everyone said how much I looked like her. I do have her auburn hair, high cheekbones, and turned-up Scandinavian nose (Ulla said we had fox faces); unfortunately, I didn't inherit her slim figure.

Both Mummy and my grandparents seemed so much more relaxed here than in Canada. One day at the beach, they were unfazed that several women—including my ostensible guardian, Ulla—were sunbathing and swimming bare-breasted. I wondered what they would have thought if Karen and I had done the same back home at West Hawk Lake.

After a few weeks spent visiting people in and around Copenhagen, we moved north to Jutland, where both my grandparents had grown up. There I was delighted to discover six cousins, all approximately my age—three boys (Peter, Georg, and Stein) and three girls (Tove, Anne-Marie, and Johanna). Having spent their entire lives in each other's constant company, they were the most socially secure people I've ever met, as high-spirited and playful as a litter of puppies. They immediately annexed me to their cheerful group.

My grandfather's sister, Jutta, had planned a massive celebration in honor of her brother's return. Her home is in the country, just outside the town of Aarhus, and she set tables out on the lawn, overlooking fields of ripening wheat. The meal was an elaborate smorgasbord, with trays of cured and smoked fish, fresh herring in vinegar sauce, curried eggs, liver pâtés, Danish meatballs, veal and pork sausages, roast sirloin of beef, pork tenderloin in cream sauce, roast ham, cheese platters, a variety of green salads, beet salad, and at least ten kinds of homemade pickles.

There's a proper way to approach a Danish smorgasbord: You start with the fish and egg dishes; move on to pâtés and sausages, accompanied by pickles and beets; then tackle the roasts and salads; and finish up with cheese and fruit—all of it washed down with plenty of beer. Tiny glasses are filled with schnapps for an increasingly boozy and sentimental series of toasts to everyone's health, to good friends, to family, etc., etc., etc. After the table is cleared, sweets appear. Danes love soft, creamy desserts, so these always include a pudding. And, finally, coffee is served with small cakes and biscuits.

As an adult, I could now partake of the beer and schnapps at these feasts. At Jutta's, my cousins and I got so drunk, I must've blacked out later in the day. Jolted awake to find myself frolicking naked with them in the North Sea, I had no idea how I'd gotten there. My last memory was the final toast at the lunch table. Everyone was laughing—though I was a little dazed—as we dressed by the shore and walked back home.

Back at Jutta's, the grown-ups, still drinking coffee and nibbling on sweets, had moved inside to the sitting room, where they were gathered around the piano singing Danish songs. Both Mummy and Grandpa had tears in their eyes. For a moment, I felt a pang of jealousy; they were in the world of their past, one I had no part in.

Leaving Jutland, my mother, grandparents, and I embarked on a stultifying bus tour of Italy—narrated in Norwegian (of which I speak not a word)—with a group of provincial Scandinavian oldsters. Brian, who might have provided some youthful companionship, had already returned to Canada. En route to and from sights, everyone belted out rousing Nordic folk songs. Missing my cousins, and my short-lived independence in Switzerland, I endured my fellow travelers with sullen disdain. By the time we arrived in Florence, all the sights of Ravenna, Urbino, San Marino, Venice, and Rome ran together into an indistinguishable blur. Frazzled, and oblivious to my surroundings, I sat sourly sipping lemonade in the Piazza Signoria.

But the next day, my grandparents went home, and my mother and I decided to spend some more time exploring Florence. Away from the tour, we were finally able to savor an Italian city at a reasonable pace.

Mummy was predisposed to love Florence. Her favorite book was a historical novel, *The Rise and Fall of the House of Medici*, which she'd read over and over; she was the only woman I'd ever known to have a crush on Lorenzo "Il Magnifico," the Medici patron of the arts who ruled at the height of the Florentine Renaissance.

As for me, I was dazzled by the city's concentration of ancient beauty. I stood in the Brancacci Chapel off the church of Santa Maria del Carmine and stepped into the street life of the Renaissance. I was awed by austere stone palazzi, by Ghirlandaio frescoes, Della Robbia's glazed terracotta madonnas, the amazing Uffizi (room after room filled with works by everyone from Botticelli to Da Vinci), the Duomo, the charming Ponte Vecchio with its fourteenth-century stone arches, and glimpses through heavy iron gates of magnificent gardens in arched courtyards. I was struck by the handsomeness of the Tuscan people—not just the men, but the women and children, even the elderly—whose faces were identical to those in Masaccio and Masolino frescoes. My enthrallment with modern-day Florentines arose from my adoration of their fifteenth-century forbears, as depicted in paintings and sculpture. And coming from North America, where everyone huddles indoors for warmth most of the year, I was charmed by people who lived *al fresco*, dining in cafés and strolling arm in arm along the promenades overlooking the Arno.

Though Mummy had to get back to Canada, she had also fallen in love with Italy—so much so that she was willing to let me stay, and even to finance my further art education. "I'm investing in living vicariously," she explained. When she left, I enrolled in a course for foreigners at Florence's Accademia delle Belli Arti, which houses the original of Michelangelo's *David*.

Frikadeller   SERVES 4-6

DANISH MEAT BALLS

In Denmark, these meat balls are often served with red cabbage (see recipe on page 10).

$1/2$ pound ground veal

$1/2$ pound ground pork

2 tablespoons finely chopped yellow onion

2 cups milk

2 tablespoons unbleached all-purpose flour

1 jumbo egg, beaten

1 teaspoon salt

1 teaspoon white pepper

4 tablespoons unsalted butter

1. Place all ingredients except butter in a large bowl, and mix well.

2. Place butter in a skillet over medium heat. When it's sizzling, drop meat mixture—1 large dinnerware tablespoon at a time—into skillet. Fry over medium heat until dark golden-brown on one side (5 to 7 minutes). Gently turn with a spatula, and cook until other side is dark golden-brown.

DANISH PORK TENDERLOIN WITH CREAM SAUCE AND BACON

Good accompaniments for this dish are boiled new potatoes and Brussels sprouts.

4 slices bacon

2 pork tenderloins, trimmed of excess fat

Salt

Freshly ground black pepper

$1/2$ cup white wine

$1 1/2$ cups heavy cream

2 teaspoons red-currant jelly

1 tablespoon finely chopped parsley leaves

1. Fry bacon until crisp, and drain on paper towel. Crumble bacon into small bits, and set aside.

2. Pour 1 tablespoon bacon fat into a Dutch oven. Brown pork tenderloins over medium heat for 5 minutes. Turn, and brown 5 minutes on other side. Season with salt and pepper to taste.

3. Add wine, and let evaporate for 2 minutes. Add cream, stir well, cover Dutch oven, and cook for 20 minutes over low heat. Remove pork tenderloins, and keep warm.

4. Add jelly to sauce, and cook for another 2 minutes.

5. Cut pork into $1/2$-inch slices, and place on a warm serving platter. Top with sauce, distribute crumbled bacon over it, and sprinkle with parsley.

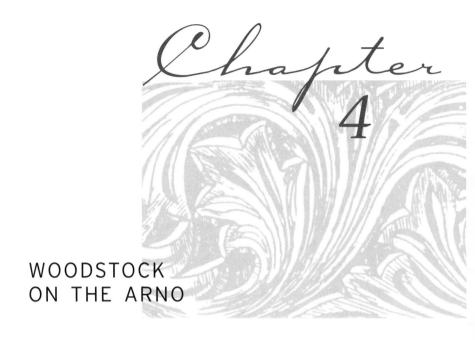

Chapter 4

WOODSTOCK ON THE ARNO

I found a tiny cell-like room in a cheap *pensione* and set about becoming an artist. I can't say my work progressed significantly from my studies at the Accademia—life as a café habitué cut into my productivity—but socially and intellectually, it was an exciting time and place to be a student. The academic world of Europe was in turmoil, and impassioned student demonstrations, ranging from marches against the Vietnam War to demands for educational reform, took place on a regular basis. Not that I ever participated. I have a lifelong terror of crowds, dating to the age of six, when I became separated from my mother in the coat section of a department store during a holiday sale. The panic I experienced that day—reaching up for her hand and finding myself alone, squeezed between winter coats amid a mob of frantic shoppers—comes back whenever I'm caught in a crowd. But I devoured Italian newspapers, studying the opposing right- and left-wing political views so that I could understand what was going on, and, incidentally, improve my Italian.

The art crowd hung out at the Café Rivoire, in the historic Piazza della Signoria, ironically, the very café at which I'd sat glumly imbibing lemonade on my first day in Florence. I must have been in very low spirits that morning not to appreciate the splendor of my surroundings. The Rivoire overlooks the fortresslike fourteenth-century Palazzo Vecchio, one-time residence of the Medici, today Florence's City Hall;

Renaissance statuary nestling in the loggia of the Uffizi; and the vast Neptune Fountain, with its prancing horses and roistering satyrs. It was in this very piazza that, in 1497, Savonarola, the ascetic monk who had ousted the Medici, ignited his notorious Bonfire of the Vanities, burning books of poetry, musical instruments, fancy clothes, and works of art that smacked of sensuality and profane decadence. A year later, the Medici returned to power, and Savonarola was taunted, tortured, and finally burned at the stake on the same site.

The Rivoire was, and still is, unlike anyone's idea of a bohemian haunt. Our counterparts abroad were staging poetry readings in the grungy smoke-filled cellars of Greenwich Village. By contrast, our hang-out was extremely elegant, with arched white-awninged windows, tables covered in crisp linen, and an enclosing border of flowering plants. Florentines, however counter-culturally minded, always opt for beauty. In this lovely piazza, we'd while away our afternoons over cups of the Rivoire's famous hot chocolate, so thick you could stand a spoon in it. Twilight would signal the switch to apéritifs of Antinori spumante brut and the decampment of our movable feast to a local trattoria for dinner.

It was at the Rivoire that I met Nancy Rica Schiff, a photography student from New York. Everyone knew her, or had seen her, an Ali McGraw look-alike—same large, soulful eyes, toothy grin, long black hair—confidently striding the streets of Florence in miniskirts and over-the-knee black patent-leather boots. Nancy was a favorite with the local art crowd, Italians and expatriates alike. To a snowbird from Winnipeg, she seemed the epitome of worldliness.

What Nancy saw in me, I don't know, but she immediately took me under her wing. I was thrilled to have an entrée into her glittering set, even though her constant refrain ("you're so innocent, Sharon") made me feel drearily provincial. But with my usual passivity, I let it pass.

One night in November, shortly after we met, Nancy invited me to a dinner party. Her apartment—two cramped rooms in a crumbling stone building—was so cold and damp, she complained it took four days for a pair of nylons to dry. And indeed, her tiny bathroom, consisting of a tub and sink (the toilet was in the hall), was strewn with a depressing array of wet laundry.

If Nancy was a whiz in the darkroom—and she was—her creativity didn't manifest itself in her closet-sized kitchen. She served us overcooked spaghetti with tasteless meatballs (no seasoning, just big orbs of beef), which we ate, huddled around the meager warmth emanating from her small gas heater.

Nancy Rica Schiff.
Courtesy of Nancy Rica Schiff

Among her guests was a young painter named Giuliano Gargani, whom everyone called Garga. A striking spectacle, with wavy black hair and brilliant blue eyes that sparkled with mischief, he wore a chamois suit over a deep-green turtleneck sweater. I noticed he bore a strong resemblance to one of the frolicking satyrs adorning the Neptune Fountain.

I was immediately attracted, but as the evening progressed, I found him increasingly *antipatico*. Focusing in on me—and my brave but rather pathetic attempts to speak Italian—Garga held forth, at length, on the impossibility of my ever mastering the language, on how the jawbone and palate of the Northern races were not genetically conducive to its beautiful tones, and on how my accent would always be stiff and unmusical. Adding to my humiliation, some of this diatribe had to be translated into English for me, and he'd sit there grinning while I took it all in. I was relieved when he turned his attention to Nancy and the disgraceful state of American cooking, ungratefully citing her dinner as a case in point. With enviable insouciance, she lobbed an oversized meatball at him.

Giuliano worked in a leather shop during the day and painted at night in his studio apartment, sometimes along with four or five other artists. Once I'd successfully merged into the Rivoire crowd, I was often part of this painting collective, and, if my broken Italian didn't meet with his approval, my work flourished under his encouragement. He admired my drawing ability and made me solemnly swear I would "never give up my art." Following these communal painting fests, he'd feed our entire crowd, effortlessly whipping up an onion omelet the size of a wagon wheel or grilling chickens with garlic, rosemary, and pancetta under the skin.

When Giuliano sets out to be charming, he's impossible to resist. His approval of my drawing—in part, perhaps, a tacit apology for his initially rude behavior to me at Nancy's dinner party—broke the ice between us, and we became friends. Now that he was no longer sniping at me, I found myself admiring him tremendously. My Italian being limited, I didn't always get his jokes, but I could tell he was a wonderful storyteller and mimic, always sending everyone into gales of laughter. He was very sweet to me, singling me out for long talks, amusing me with hilarious stories about his family, expounding on his theories about art, and serenading me with old Florentine songs.

In a way, I think he was actually "inventing" me, and, wrapped up as I was in a foreign fantasy world, I was enjoying the process. He would tell me what he thought I was thinking, and I began to believe him. And when we were with friends, he'd seemingly defer to me, ending sentences with "Isn't that right, *Nannina*?" I didn't know that *Nannina* was a common Florentine endearment. I thought he'd created it just for me. Probably, he had a hard time saying "Sharon."

It was widely known that Giuliano was madly in love with Nancy's friend, Anne, an American schoolteacher who'd recently gone back to New York. Over cocktails at the Rivoire with Giuliano, I'd heard all about Anne, about how beautiful and angelic she was, and about the special, spiritual kind of love that existed between them. Though I was, by now, attracted to him—an attraction electrified one evening when he kissed me lightly on the lips—I kept my feelings hidden, even from myself. I considered him the property of the inimitable Anne, who was coming back to Florence for the holidays. Giuliano was planning to take her to the French Riviera.

Anne arrived shortly after Christmas, and Giuliano, wildly excited, went to the airport in Rome to pick her up. Her beautiful summer tan was gone, she looked white and pasty, and she was wearing heavy winter clothes and a suede maxicoat. The maxicoat clinched matters for Giuliano; he detested it. Another man, a rational man, might have realized that outerwear comes off. This wasn't a rational man. This was Giuliano. The coat became the tangible symbol of his disenchantment.

He brought Anne to the Rivoire, introduced her to me, then left me talking to her while he sat and sulked in a corner by himself. After all I'd heard about her, I was surprised to find Anne so ordinary looking, just conventionally pretty, with the kind of deadly white skin that sometimes goes with fair hair. She was obviously uncomfortable, at a loss to understand Giuliano's sudden coldness. I told her how much I admired her maxicoat.

The next day I came to the Rivoire to find Giuliano sitting by himself, looking utterly miserable. I wondered where Anne was.

Disenchantment notwithstanding, they did go off to Nice with another couple. I spent New Year's Eve by myself, sunk in gloom. My mother had sent me a Canadian Care package for Christmas—marzipan, fruitcake, and almond cookies—and I sat in my lonely cell and ate them.

On January third, the morning of my twenty-first birthday, I got a note informing me that Mummy had wired me twenty-one long-stemmed red roses. I spent a wretched morning tracking down the florist to pick them up. Returning home, I found a second present had arrived from Canada—another fruitcake. For some reason, its advent capped my foul mood, and, distractedly opening the tin, I cut my hand badly and had to go to the hospital for a tetanus shot and stitches. I blamed my mother for everything.

The next day, Anne and Giuliano returned from the Riviera. At the Rivoire, a dispirited-looking Anne plopped herself down at my table and confided that he hadn't said one word to her the whole trip. Later, Giuliano would tell me that, in order to avoid her, he'd spent the entire train ride pacing the corridors. He felt as if he'd walked all the way to Nice and back. Anne returned to New York later that week.

On the sixth of January, the Day of Epiphany, Italian children who've been good all year get presents (usually candy), and a one-ring circus comes to town. Giuliano and I had had dinner the night before, and he'd asked if I'd like to go to this circus the following day. "I'd like to take my little girl," was the way he put it.

Sharon at twenty-one

The circus took place at the Fortezza de Basso, an ancient Medici fort. It was a freezing night, and I was inappropriately dressed in a green minidress and an equally short black coat (had I owned a maxi-coat, at this point, I probably would have thrown it out). There were very few people in the audience, and we snuggled together for warmth. Giuliano talked through the entire circus, telling me stories and, every once in awhile, kissing me softly and running his fingers through my hair, whispering to me that it looked like spun gold. When the circus was over, he asked me to go back to his studio "to warm up with a glass of wine." He didn't have to ask twice. That night we had our own epiphany; we realized we were madly in love.

Later—years later—I thought that both the circus and its setting (the fort is a visible manifestation of Medici tyranny) had aptly presaged my Felliniesque future with him. But on that magical night, when I became pregnant with our son, Andrea, I experienced only bliss.

Giuliano was thrilled to find out I was pregnant and, with zany practicality, raced off to buy a blender so we could purée fruits and vegetables for the baby's food. My own concerns were more immediate. I was terrified to tell Mummy, who justified my trepidation by hysterically convincing herself I'd been kidnapped by the Mafia and impregnated against my will. She barraged me with questions: "How do you know he's not connected to the underworld? Are you aware that in Italy a man can take custody of a child if there's a separation?" And, with rising hysteria," Do you want to have your child taken away from you?"

It was obvious that, back in Winnipeg, my plans had become the focus of family conclaves. My Uncle Lloyd wrote to tell me that it was not too late to get an abortion. I made the terrible mistake of telling Giuliano about my uncle's letter, and more than thirty years later, with operatic Italian flourish, he still rails at me occasionally: "Your family wanted to kill our firstborn!"

Via collect transatlantic telephone calls—the ruinous rates of which, once again, lessened the length, if not the intensity, of lectures from home—I tried to reassure my mother, telling her how much I loved Giuliano, what a great painter he was, and that we were going to be married. To bolster my case, I even brought the haute-cultural Renaissance atmosphere of Florence into play.

"He's a wonderful man," I assured her. "He even supports his old mother."

Grandma Gerda immediately shot back a cryptic warning via telegram: "Think twice marry man with financial burden mother."

Then Karen was sent over for two weeks to check out the situation. She was immediately taken with Florence, Italian cuisine (she's a very good cook and loves food), and my bohemian lifestyle. And Giuliano, at his most charming, easily won her over. Of course, Karen hadn't taken her *in loco parentis* duties the least bit seriously anyway. She'd simply jumped at the chance for a free vacation abroad and spent much of her time exploring Rome and Venice. She loyally returned home with a positive report.

Finally, my mother began to thaw—or at least to resign herself to the inevitable. She even sent me money for a proper wedding party, most of which we retained for living expenses.

We were married in a civil ceremony in the ornate precincts of the Palazzo Vecchio (City Hall) on June 26, 1971. I was six months pregnant, but in an empire-waist dress, I didn't show too much. It's a

Woodstock on the Arno. Nancy Rica Schiff, *first row, second from left;* Sharon, *behind Nancy;* Giuliano, *behind Sharon.*

forgiving style. I was brought up Lutheran; Giuliano, of course, was Catholic, but as a self-described Communist—and only he, hedonist to the core, would so describe himself—he wasn't religious. The whole Rivoire crowd, looking like a cross-section of Woodstock concertgoers, came to our wedding party, a joyous picnic outside an eighteenth-century farmhouse near San Casciano. Guitar-playing hippies provided the music, and everyone danced in the fields.

Giuliano and I prepared all the food: panzanella (bread and vegetable salad); big platters of prosciutto, Italian salami, and cheeses; crostini with pecorino, eggs, and basil; a giant fruit salad with zabaglione sauce; and Florentine crêpes stuffed with spinach and ricotta cheese. Champagne, thanks to Mummy's gift, flowed freely.

Shortly before the wedding, Giuliano had taken me home to meet his mother, Zoe. She was already aware of my existence. Living on his own, Giuliano still took all his laundry home to her. Ever vigilant, she'd noticed my red hair on his clothes and inquired sardonically, "Are you in love with an Irish setter?"

Despite Giuliano's frequent assertions that "my mother will just love you," I was terrified of meeting her. When she welcomed me with a big smile, I felt infinitely relieved, not only by her warm reception, but by her appearance. I had expected an old Italian widow, solemnly draped in black from head to toe. Zoe is tall, with piercing blue eyes, and her clothes are modern and stylish. It took me a long time to realize that her up-to-date appearance was deceptive. As I had feared, she was still living in the Middle Ages.

But at first, I loved her. She wasn't judgmental about my pregnancy. Both she and her daughter, Anna, had also been pregnant prior to their marriages. And, at the time, I venerated everything Italian. There are two kinds of expatriates—those who compare everything to "the way it was back home" and find it wanting (they're usually stationed somewhere for business) and those who are besotted about their chosen country and consider it superior to their native land in every respect. At twenty-one, I was entirely in the latter camp.

Giuliano's Pollo al Mattone

GRILLED CHICKEN
WITH A BRICK

1 large chicken, preferably free-range (ask your butcher to divide it in two at the breast)

2 large cloves garlic, chopped into $1/8$-inch pieces

1 tablespoon fresh rosemary, chopped into $1/8$-inch pieces

$1/4$ pound pancetta or bacon, chopped into $1/8$-inch pieces

1 teaspoon freshly ground black pepper

2 tablespoons extra-virgin olive oil

1. Place chicken, open side down, on a large cutting board, cover with plastic wrap, and pound flat with a smooth-surfaced meat mallet.

2. Thoroughly combine garlic, rosemary, pancetta, and pepper in a small bowl.

3. With the tip of a paring knife, make $1/2$-inch incisions in chicken skin to create pockets for filling—one in each leg, one in each breast, and one in each thigh. Fill them with pancetta mixture. Place chicken in a pan, drizzle with oil, and marinate in refrigerator for 24 hours.

4. Place chicken on a charcoal grill, weighing it down with a brick (if you don't have a brick handy, use any heavy weight, perhaps a cast-iron pot). Cook for 15 minutes on each side.

NOTE If you don't have a charcoal grill, cook chicken in a cast-iron skillet (with 1 tablespoon extra-virgin olive oil) on your stove over medium heat. Weigh it down—once again, assuming there's no brick around—with another heavy pan.

PECORINO CHEESE BRUSCHETTA

NOTES If you can't find pecorino cheese, use white cheddar.

You can make the cheese spread a day ahead, and keep it in the refrigerator. Take it out an hour before serving.

10 ounces soft pecorino (Italian sheep cheese)

2 jumbo eggs, boiled for 5 minutes

1 cup fresh parsley, packed

1 cup fresh basil leaves, packed

$1/2$ cup fresh mint leaves

$1/4$ teaspoon salt

$1/4$ cup extra-virgin olive oil

1 loaf Tuscan or sourdough bread

1.   Remove rind from cheese, and cut into $1/2$-inch cubes. Shell and halve eggs, and put them through a food mill, along with cheese, parsley, basil, mint, salt, and oil (you can use a food processor, but the mixture is more aesthetically pleasing when you use a food mill.).

2.   Cut bread into $1/2$-inch-thick slices, and toast on one side in broiler until golden-brown (keep an eye on them; they can burn quickly). Spread cheese mixture on side of bread that is not toasted, and serve immediately.

Crespelle alla Fiorentina

FLORENTINE CRÊPES

FOR THE FILLING:

1 pound fresh spinach

7 ounces ricotta cheese (freshly made, if available)

2 tablespoons freshly grated Parmigiano Reggiano

$1/4$ teaspoon freshly grated nutmeg

$1/2$ teaspoon salt

$1/4$ teaspoon freshly ground black pepper

1. Preheat oven to 350 degrees. Wash spinach very thoroughly, and cook for 5 minutes on medium heat (don't add water; water that clings to leaves will be ample). Drain in a colander, and squeeze out excess water.

2. Chop spinach very fine, place in a large bowl, and add remaining filling ingredients. Combine well, and set aside.

FOR THE CRÊPES:

2 tablespoons ($1/4$ stick) unsalted butter

$3/4$ cups unbleached all-purpose flour

2 jumbo eggs

$1/4$ teaspoon salt

1 cup whole milk

1. Melt butter over very low heat (don't brown it) in a small saucepan.

2. In a large bowl, mix flour and eggs together with a wire whisk. Add salt and melted butter, and continue mixing. When mixture is smooth and free of lumps, add milk, a little at a time, continuing to whisk (for best results, toss it into a blender until silky smooth). Refrigerate mixture for 30 minutes.

3. Put a 9- or 10-inch nonstick pan on the stove at high heat. Keep batter bowl near stove and a large plate close by. Spoon some batter into pan, and swirl pan to cover bottom completely with a thin layer, pouring any excess back into batter bowl. When batter becomes opaque, flip crêpe on its other side for 5 seconds, then turn out onto plate. Continue making crêpes until out of batter (it should make 8).

NOTE If you don't have a nonstick pan, melt 1 tablespoon of butter in the pan. Then, with a paper towel, wipe up most of the butter, leaving only a very thin film of it. You can fry all your crêpes without adding extra butter.

4. Place crêpes, one at a time, on a flat surface, lighter side up. Divide spinach/ricotta filling into 8 parts, and place an equal amount in center of each crêpe. Roll crêpes into log shapes.

FOR THE BÉCHAMEL SAUCE:

$1/8$ pound ($1/2$ stick) unsalted butter

$1/2$ cup unbleached all-purpose flour

$1/4$ teaspoon salt

$1/4$ teaspoon freshly grated nutmeg

2 cups whole milk

1. Melt butter over very low heat (don't brown it) in a small nonstick saucepan. Add flour, stirring continuously with a wooden spoon. Cook for a few seconds. Add salt and nutmeg. Still stirring, add milk, a little at a time. Cook for 10 minutes on medium-low heat, stirring all the while. Set aside.

FOR THE TOMATO SAUCE:

3 ripe tomatoes

2 tablespoons extra-virgin olive oil

$1/4$ teaspoon salt

1. Quarter each tomato. Heat oil in a small saucepan, add tomato pieces and salt, and cook for 5 minutes over medium heat, stirring occasionally. Pass sauce through a food mill, and set aside.

ASSEMBLING THE CRÊPES:

3 tablespoons freshly grated Parmigiano Reggiano

1. Pour half the Béchamel Sauce into an ovenproof casserole dish, and smooth it to cover surface evenly. Place crêpes on top of béchamel, and spoon Tomato Sauce over them. Drizzle remaining béchamel over crêpes, and sprinkle with Parmigiano. Bake for 15 minutes.

Chapter
5

LIFE WITH ZOE

A few months before we married, I'd moved into Giuliano's studio on the Via delle Bombarde, a dark ancient passageway of a street. The building's dingy stairway smelled of centuries of ill-washed humanity, but our cozy aerie—on the top floor of a five-story walkup—had a delicious aroma, a mingling of freshly waxed floors, oil paints, and a whiff of whatever we'd last cooked on our charcoal brazier. Our bed was covered with a big white fur spread, and sheepskin rugs were strewn on terracotta floors; Giuliano has always liked fluffy things. From the balcony, we could look out over the red-tiled roofs of Florence and see the little church of Santissimi Apostoli, which was founded in the ninth century by Charlemagne.

Our apartment was rudimentary, lacking even such basic amenities as a shower. We bathed each other in an immense stone sink in the kitchen, a cumbersome process, which seemed incredibly romantic to me. Madly in love, I basked in the reflected glow of my husband's charisma.

Marriage and my pregnancy didn't alter our lifestyle. Giuliano left for the leather shop at eight o'clock every morning. After tidying up, I spent my mornings traipsing from museum to museum and wandering the corridors of ancient chapels, crypts, and cloisters, desperate to soak up Italian culture. Surrounded by thousands of transient tourists, I enjoyed a smug feeling of superiority; I lived here.

Afternoons, I'd lie in bed and read books on the history and monuments of Florence. I set myself the task of reading something in Italian for a half-hour every day—at least a newspaper or magazine.

Most Italian men come home for a two-hour lunch, but Giuliano always went to his mother's, often with all his laundry in tow. At six o'clock in the evening, I'd stroll over to the Rivoire to meet him, and, over aperitivos, we'd tell each other about our day.

Several nights a week, we continued to host rollicking dinner and painting parties, sometimes for as many as twenty people. Around midnight, everyone starving, Giuliano would cook up big pots of pasta, saucing them with olive oil and pungent chunks of sautéed garlic. I'd fall into bed, exhausted, at one or two in the morning, but, in the living room, the sun often rose on impassioned wine-fueled conversations. Wrapped in a haze of ecstasy, I romanticized our garret existence, living through my senses, putting rational thought on hold.

Eventually, these revels began taking their toll on me. Late one night, I had such agonizing abdominal pains that I lay in bed, clutching my stomach and moaning piteously. I was certain I was going to die. Giuliano, terrified, called an ambulance to take me to the hospital, then sat stroking my head, repeating over and over, *"va tutto bene"* ("everything's all right").

Suddenly, his soothing mantra ceased, and I looked up to see six black-robed, hooded figures, their waists girded by immense wooden rosaries, silently entering our bedroom. Surrounding my bed, they swaddled me in sheets (our stairwell was too narrow for a gurney) to form a makeshift hammock, and without a word of explanation, carried me down the five flights. My pain was so intense I could barely speak. Half convinced I was hallucinating, I grimly assumed they were monks, taking me off to my last rites. Later, I learned they were from La Misericordia, a volunteer organization founded in medieval times to assist the sick and wounded. Because charity should be anonymous, its members wear hoods with eye slits.

At the hospital, I was given a sedative and fell into a deep sleep, only to be rudely awakened shortly after dawn when a nurse flung off my covers, placed a rubber sheet under me, doused my genitals with warm water from a kettle, and roughly dried them off—all without a single word of explanation and in plain view of the five other patients who shared my ward! When I tried to read the chart at the foot of my bed, she angrily snatched it out of my hands; its contents, she shrieked, were for *"il dottore"* only. By that time, I was hysterical. In paper slippers, I padded out into the hall, rang Giuliano, and told him if he didn't come get me at once, I was leaving on my own—and he'd never see me again. He came right away.

This traumatic exit from Via delle Bombarde hailed my entrance into a whole new phase of existence. Having bolted from the hospital, I was still extremely weak, and my skin had a greenish tinge. Giuliano said, "You need someone to take care of you. Let's move in with my mother."

Giuliano's mother had become a widow two years before we met. Though I was unaware of it when I married, in Italy—perhaps more so in those days than in the present—it was considered only natural that an only son should assume the burden of his widowed mother's care (daughters had to cope with their own in-laws). That we would live with Zoe eventually was an inevitability hastened by my difficult pregnancy.

Zoe came into this world in 1910, a time of terrible poverty and social unrest in Italy. Her father, Angelo Gradi, an anarchist, proudly wore the badge of his political faith, a wide black bow tie. A massive man—and brutal—he was also required to don a black wristband identifying him as a *pugno proibito* (forbidden fist)—a person of such lethal strength that he was legally barred from fighting. Angelo owned a horse and cart, with which he eked out a living transporting goods for local merchants. During World War II, when horses were commandeered for the cause, he'd simply pulled the cart, and its weighty contents, himself.

Just before the turn of the century, he'd married Serafina, a noted beauty of the Monticelli region, who bore him five daughters—something for which he never forgave her. Angelo desperately wanted a son.

One of these little girls, Rina, died at the age of thirteen in the Spanish influenza epidemic that raged through Europe in 1918. Two years later, Serafina herself succumbed to tuberculosis. Her remaining daughters were left in the hands of an uncaring, and sometimes violent, father, who made them wait for meals while he walked his six precious Pomeranians, then seized the choicest morsels for his pets, leaving the less-appetizing remains for his girls. One day, one of these pampered poms peed on Zoe's bed, provoking her pent-up rage. She stuffed the hapless animal into a flour sack and beat it with a stick. Her father never found out, though he wondered at the dog's subsequent timidity.

Soon after his wife's death, Angelo doled his daughters out to relatives. Ten-year-old Zoe was dispatched to a kindly aunt and uncle

Zoe. Courtesy of Nancy Rica Schiff

who had a farm in Santa Maria, and there she was happy for the first time in her young life. It was to be a brief respite. A year later, she was fetched home and sent, along with her sisters, to weave cloth in a windowless, fume-filled fabric mill, where the din was so deafening she developed a lifelong habit of shouting. The girls' combined wages were handed over to Angelo.

Zoe still speaks with bristling resentment about her father's cruelty and selfishness, yet always adds, with pride, how handsome he was. When I look at Angelo's faded photograph, I'm gazing into Zoe's dazzling blue eyes, and those of Giuliano.

Somehow, despite the negligence of their father, the Gradi girls arrived at womanhood, and, one by one, married. Zoe—unlike her carefully guarded contemporaries—was free to come and go unchaperoned, and fell in love with the dashing Ferdinando Gargani, a local bricklayer who'd approached her on the street. She married him in August of 1935, and three months later gave birth to a daughter, Gigliola.

Ferdinando's membership in the Communist Party met with Angelo's approval, though in many ways, he was a less than ideal suitor. Since he refused to embrace Fascism, it was impossible for him to find work. When they married, and he moved in with Zoe and her father, she was forced to become the breadwinner, supporting her husband and child with her work at the looms. Each morning, she'd take Gigliola, wrapped in a blanket, to a babysitter, then walk four kilometers to work to save tram fare. She'd come home at night to hours of housework.

In 1938, she gave birth to Giuliano, finally gaining her father's approbation. Angelo doted on his long-awaited male progeny, taking him everywhere as soon as he could walk. To this day, Giuliano speaks adoringly of his grandfather and can never understand why his mother is so bitter.

His political leanings notwithstanding, Ferdinando was drafted during World War II and was stationed in Genova during the brutal Allied bombings of that city. Ever the rebel, he was often in trouble during his service and was once tied to a stake for two days as punishment for talking back to a superior officer.

After the war, during the reconstruction of Italy, there were lots of jobs for bricklayers, though the pay was meager. Ferdinando picked up jobs here and there but never made a real living. He spent most of his time at the local headquarters of the Communist Party, appearing home for meals, then heading back to his comrades.

Living meagerly on the combined earnings of her husband and father (she'd quit the factory after Giuliano was born), eventually with three children, Zoe resigned herself to her lot, a common one in prefeminist Italy. In spite of everything, she claims to have had a happy marriage.

It never occurred to me to question moving in with Zoe, even though Giuliano referred to her as *"La Generale."* I thought he was joking. As a recent bride, I was trying my best to adapt to a new country, a new language, a new husband, and a new way of life. Ever accommodating—it's my besetting fault—I only wanted to please everyone and gain acceptance.

I leapt into this new phase of my life with the unseeing optimism of youthful inexperience. When I left Via delle Bombarde, I was a carefree young girl out to conquer the world. That girl ceased to exist

Zoe and Giuliano

the moment I stepped over the threshold into Zoe's apartment. I was now a soon-to-be mother and an extremely dubious person in the eyes of a proud and domineering mother-in-law.

Italian men are very attached to their mothers, whom they're brought up to believe are sacred and invincible. For Zoe's generation, the home was the only place a woman could wield any power. She and her contemporaries reigned supreme in arcane matriarchal realms, mystifying their housewifely activities and embellishing them with inscrutable rituals. Maternal martyrdom was their stock in trade, and the smell of burnt ashes hung in the air.

For my benefit, as Zoe mentored me in the proper care of a husband, her rites of housewifery reached new pinnacles of complexity. The week we moved in, I tagged along, fascinated, as Zoe instructed me in "the making of a salad." The process began at the market (no day-old produce languished in her refrigerator bins), where she scrutinized every tomato, cucumber, and carrot with the diligence of an agricultural-fair judge. A trip to a second shop was required to procure a worthy endive. Back home, she scrubbed the vegetables with meticulous care, placed each one in its own bowl of iced water for a specified time, chopped them into identically sized pieces, then carefully measured out the oil and vinegar for the final toss. From start to finish, it took four hours!

A great deal of her time was spent cosseting Giuliano. If he decided to take a shower, Zoe would race into the bathroom to run the water until it was sufficiently hot and set out clean towels; when he emerged, he'd find fresh underwear and clothing neatly laid out on his bed. As Giuliano's wife, I was expected to take over these obsequies, but after a few days of following Zoe's example, I decided he was old enough to find his own underpants. My passion to assimilate did have some limits.

Zoe's mystique also included the role of tribal shaman. As a healer, she had remedies, usually food-based ones, for every medical contingency. She cooked me hearty dishes she believed were strengthening to a pregnant woman, most notably an Italian pot roast served up with heaps of fresh spinach and her Florentine version of semolina gnocchi. It was all delicious, and she'd watch over me approvingly as I dutifully cleaned my plate. No matter how ill I am, my appetite never flags.

But if Zoe's rituals seemed odd to me, at first I also thought she was very sweet. I needed to be taken care of, and she thrived on having people under her control. And I thought the Gargani family's closeness was wonderful. Our relationship was also helped, initially, by my still-limited command of Italian; I didn't take in everything she said. As my health and language skills improved, our relationship became less enigmatic and more problematic.

One of our first areas of contention centered on a new washing machine, a wedding gift from Giuliano's employer at the leather shop. Zoe had always done her laundry by hand, and she distrusted the noisy gleaming intruder. When I came home from the hospital with our son, Andrea, she insisted on boiling all his dirty diapers in an immense cauldron on the stove, which she'd stand over and stir with a big stick, like a witch's brew. When I suggested that the washing machine could adequately clean his diapers, she shrieked at me excitedly in Florentine dialect, "You stupid foreigner! What do you know?"

As time went on, though, Zoe overcame her initial wariness of the machine. It was a given that she'd eventually bond with this appliance; she lives to do laundry. Once she'd mastered the machine, her attitude toward it became fiercely proprietary, and I was no longer permitted to use it at all. Running it at least once or twice every day—always in a state of tensely focused concentration, as if she were operating a dangerous power tool—she'd sit before it, watching the rotating laundry as if it were the most gripping of television dramas, poised, like an animal stalking prey, to pounce with the fabric softener at the crucial moment.

But her appropriation of the washing machine was the least of it. Zoe has no concept of privacy. Frequently, Giuliano and I were startled out of a sound sleep by a drawer or closet door slamming shut in our bedroom at six o'clock in the morning.

"I just want to put these handkerchiefs in Giuliano's dresser," she'd explain.

I would tense up every time I heard her shuffling around in slippers at the crack of dawn, but my complaints to Giuliano fell on deaf ears; brought up without boundaries, he simply didn't understand.

If she heard us making love at night, she'd invariably wake with a pulsing migraine the next morning. On a positive note, her intrusiveness added spice to our lovemaking. Because sex at home was so fraught with difficulties, Giuliano and I made love in all kinds of interesting places: on elevators; in our car, like teenagers (a cramped VW, no less); once even in a musty hunting shed filled with spider webs. Perhaps it saved us from the tedious predictability of married sex.

Shortly after Andrea's birth, poking through my dresser drawers one day, Zoe came across my birth-control pills and asked what they were for. When I explained, she told me about the homespun method she'd devised to forestall unwanted pregnancies in her own marriage. During intercourse, she'd clutch a long tailor's pin in her hand. When she felt her husband nearing orgasm, she'd ram the pin into his behind! He always withdrew immediately. I never met my father-in-law, but I remain lost in admiration for his amatory courage.

Among Zoe's many pretexts for early-morning incursions into our room—one that was to make me especially miserable—was her mania for bed making. At first, of course, as soon as I was well enough to get out of it every morning, I made the bed myself. But no sooner would I leave the room than Zoe, hovering nearby, would scurry in, pull the whole thing apart, and do it over. Though I'd been making my own bed since elementary school, complete with neatly turned nurse's corners—an accomplishment of housewifely pride in the days before fitted sheets—she considered this task beyond my competence. One dreadful morning, I heard her excitedly telling my sisters-in-law, "You should see the way she makes a bed, you should see it, you should see it!" They were laughing uproariously, and Giuliano's sister, Gigliola, added insult to injury by exhorting Zoe to be patient with me. "After all," she said, "Sharon is a *straniera*; we know what kind of homes they keep." Not only was I hopeless in their eyes, so were my family and fellow countrywomen.

Zoe brought an almost religious fervor to the task, so much so that I wondered, in light of the migraines our lovemaking induced, if her violent daily shaking out of our linens and blankets wasn't intended to divest them of any tinge of carnality. Because she didn't just make our bed. First she stripped it and hung the bedclothes out on the balcony to air—not occasionally, but every single day! Though I'd later learn this was not uncommon in Italy, as a Canadian, I found it incredible. Sheets aired in Winnipeg's forty-below weather would have made strange bedfellows. Remaking the bed, she always made sure that Giuliano's side was especially neat. And not a morning went by that she didn't comment disdainfully about what an agitated sleeper I was. More than once, she took me into her own bedroom to show me how her bed hardly looked slept in at all.

"I don't toss and turn and tumble about all night like a beached whale," she remarked, her sly simile doubly derisive, since I was pregnant.

Since Zoe almost never left the house without us, Giuliano and I were seldom alone. And It was incumbent upon us to invite her on our every excursion, the first mention of which merely comprised the opening salvo in a long, exhausting battle. Perhaps we'd decide to go for a drive or on a picnic by the river (Giuliano loved to fish, and knew all the best places). We'd always ask Zoe if she'd like to join us. Invariably, with a heart-rending sigh of resignation, she'd respond, "No, I don't feel like it. Go without me."

Though it would have been heaven to get away on our own, we'd press her to come. She'd wave us away. This would go on and on, until we were literally begging for her company. Finally, she'd relent.

Our wheedling and pleading at an end, we'd actually feel tremendously relieved at this unwanted outcome. But Zoe was only biding her time—enjoying our rejoicing while calculating, with a picador's precision, the next thrust of her lance:

"Let's go a little later," she'd say. "It's too hot now."

Or she'd be ready "as soon as I do these dishes" or "straighten up the house a little" or "change these clothes." Sometimes she insisted we all change our clothes, even baby Andrea. By the time we finally got out, our initial enthusiasm for the outing had dissipated into inertia. And, even then, we had to strap her big wicker armchair to the top of the car (often I wished we could strap her up there in it), so she could sit comfortably when we arrived.

Zoe in her traveling armchair

Only she never was comfortable. Wherever we went, it was always too hot, or too cold, or too windy. The few times we accepted her first refusal and went off without her, we paid dearly for it, returning to find her in a terrible snit and suffering from the inevitable migraine. Days of guilt-mongering glances, heavy sighs, and just-audible mutterings ("*O dio, dio, dio*") followed.

But Zoe's rigmarole notwithstanding, Giuliano and I never stopped planning outings. Once we were on the road, with or without her, the tribulations of our departure were soon eclipsed by our joy in the beauty of the Tuscan countryside. Drives to the seashore, or to lofty Alpine mountains, would wind past vineyard-covered hills, swaying fields of grain, undulating rivers, and natural hot springs.

The first thing Giuliano did upon arrival at any destination was to "discover" a restaurant and make reservations for our midday meal. That these discoveries varied dramatically was part of the adventure. In the Mugello valley, north of Florence, we celebrated our second wedding anniversary—for once, without Zoe—with a late lunch at a seafood restaurant tucked into the blue-green foothills of the dark Apennine Mountains. The place was romantically situated in a rambling farmhouse surrounded by acres of grassy meadow. We ordered platter after platter of succulent fresh grilled lobster, scampi, calamari, and pesciolini (I think we ate their entire day's supply of seafood), along with lots of spaghetti and several bottles of champagne. Afterwards, we had to lie down by the river to digest it all.

On another occasion, Giuliano was jubilant to come upon a restaurant that specialized in wild mushrooms. We ordered raw porcini salad, risotto with mushrooms, grilled mushroom caps, and veal with mushrooms. Every dish was vibrantly alive. With worms! We had to send it all back. We left this squirmy restaurant, bought some crusty Tuscan bread, salami, and sweet fresh figs, and had a picnic lunch. The whole thing had been so comical, we weren't even upset. We just kept laughing and laughing, working ourselves into a state of giddy lunacy. Giuliano had some fishing worms tied in a bag outside the car window, and Zoe and I had to restrain him from going back to the restaurant and asking if they needed extras. We laughed all the way home.

And then there was our memorable "red" meal in the mountains above Lucca, where Hannibal had marched with his troops to conquer Italy. We wandered into a tiny inn-cum-grocery store run by an ancient couple. A tattered curtain separated the kitchen from a minuscule dining area, furnished with rickety chairs and bare tables. It didn't look promising, but when Giuliano noticed that the walls were hung with portraits of Marx, Engels, and Trotsky, his eyes lit up.

For once, he put aside his quest for the culinary grail and insisted we eat there. There was no menu, and the food, as we might have predicted, was of an almost Orwellian austerity. "*Santo cielo*! There's canned meat sauce on the pasta," Zoe exclaimed in her ever-audible factory voice. But the evening was memorable, the bland food spiced by a lively political discussion (it happened to be an election day) with our hosts. After dinner, the discussion turned to reminiscences about the war. Avoiding this touchy subject (once Zoe found out my father had been a pilot during World War II, she often reminded me of how our people had bombed their people), I took Andrea for a long walk among the centuries-old chestnut trees behind the restaurant.

We'd drive home from these hard-won excursions happy and tired, everyone singing songs in the car. Even Zoe would join in, and I learned many Italian songs from her, among them "*Bandiera Rossa*" (the Communist anthem) and "*Faccetta Nera*" (Little Black Face)—a Fascist song about the Italian occupation of Ethiopia. Back home, I'd look for books to gather information, culinary and historical, about the places we'd visited. I was in love, not only with Giuliano, but all of Tuscany.

ZOE'S POT ROAST
WITH SPINACH

NOTES You can pulse the onions, celery, and carrots to $1/8$-inch pebbles in a food processor. Keep the onions separate. Do not overchop; texture is essential.

In Step 4: Save time by asking your butcher to truss the meat.

3 pounds spinach, prior to trimming

2 large cloves garlic, very finely chopped

2 tablespoons fresh rosemary leaves, very finely chopped

2 teaspoons salt

$1/4$ teaspoon freshly ground black pepper

$1/2$ cup extra-virgin olive oil

$1 1/2$ cups celery, chopped into $1/8$-inch pieces

1 cup carrots, chopped into $1/8$-inch pieces

2 cups red onions, chopped into $1/8$-inch pieces

3 pound rump roast or eye of round

$1/4$ cup extra-virgin olive oil

$1 1/2$ cups Chianti Classico

$14 1/2$-ounce can puréed Italian plum tomatoes (if unavailable, buy a can of whole plum tomatoes and purée them)

4 thin slices lemon peel (use a potato peeler)

2 cups water

$1 1/2$ teaspoons salt

Additional salt

1. Wash spinach very thoroughly. Pour about 2 inches of water into a large stockpot, and bring to a boil. Add spinach, reduce heat to medium, and cook for 5 minutes. Drain in a colander, and squeeze out excess water. Chop coarsely, and set aside.

2. Place chopped garlic and rosemary in a small bowl, and stir in 2 teaspoons salt and $1/4$ teaspoon pepper. Set aside.

3. Pour $1/2$ cup oil into a large skillet, and add celery and carrots. Turn heat to medium-high, and sauté for 5 minutes, stirring occasionally with a wooden spoon. Add onions, and sauté for another 10 minutes, continuing to stir occasionally. Turn off heat, and set skillet aside.

4. Truss roast tightly with string to keep its shape. With a sharp knife, make four cross-shaped incisions at even intervals along one side of roast, beginning about an inch from either end. Stick a finger into each incision to dig a hole. Fill each hole with a quarter of the rosemary/garlic mixture.

5. Preheat oven to 400 degrees. Heat $1/4$ cup oil in a Dutch oven. When oil is hot, place roast in pot, and brown 5 minutes on each side (though its shape is round, consider it to have four sides). Do first side on high heat, then reduce to medium.

6. Remove roast to a plate. Transfer sautéed vegetables to Dutch oven, add Chianti, stir well, and cook for 3 minutes on medium heat. Add tomatoes, lemon peel, 2 cups water, and $1\,1/2$ teaspoons salt, and stir. Return pot roast to Dutch oven. Cover, and bake for $1\,1/2$ hours.

7. Turn roast, uncover, and bake for $1/2$ hour.

8. When roast is fully cooked—just prior to serving—remove a cup of celery/carrot/onion mixture to a skillet, and sauté spinach in vegetable mix for 5 minutes, stirring frequently. Add salt to taste. Serve as a side dish with roast.

SEMOLINA DUMPLINGS

This recipe makes for a wonderful side dish with meat entrées. In Italy, however, we eat gnocchi alone as a *primo piatto* (first course), savoring its uniquely delicate taste and texture.

1 tablespoon unsalted butter, softened to room temperature

1 quart whole milk

1 teaspoon salt

1 cup coarse semolina flour

3 jumbo egg yolks, at room temperature

5 ounces freshly grated Parmigiano Reggiano

Parchment paper

2 ounces ($\frac{1}{2}$ stick) unsalted butter, softened to room temperature

1. Preheat oven to 400 degrees. Grease a large baking dish (at least 10" × 12") with 1 tablespoon butter. Set aside.

2. Pour milk into a large saucepan, and bring to a boil. Add salt, lower heat to medium, and slowly add semolina flour, stirring constantly with a wooden spoon for 7 minutes. Set aside.

3. In a large bowl, beat egg yolks with a fork until very fluffy. Add a large dollop of semolina-milk mixture; beat immediately and thoroughly to keep the eggs from congealing. Add remainder of semolina, and stir in well. Add half the Parmigiano, and mix in thoroughly.

4. Spread about 2 feet of parchment paper on your counter (alternately, you could work on any smooth surface lightly greased with peanut oil), and turn semolina dough onto it. Dip a spatula into cold water (to prevent sticking), and pat dough (which will be soft) to $\frac{3}{8}$-inch thickness. Leave dough for 30 minutes to harden a bit.

5. Fill a bowl with very cold water. Use a 2-inch round cookie cutter or glass rim to cut circles of gnocchi dough (dip cutter in cold water between each cut to prevent sticking), laying them in rows in your baking pan. You'll have to overlap a bit to fit them in.

6. When all your gnocchi are laid out, dot evenly with 2 ounces butter, and sprinkle with remaining Parmigiano. Bake for 25 minutes, or until cheese is melted and slightly golden.

Chapter 6

ANDREA

Andrea arrived two weeks early, slightly premature and a mere five-and-a-half pounds, but Giuliano and I thought he was the most beautiful thing we'd ever seen. When we brought him home, Zoe opened his little baby blankets, took one look, and said, "My God, what did the two of you make, a skinned rabbit?" I fled the room in tears. After that, of course, she doted on Andrea, and took him over entirely. If she could have squeezed milk from her breasts, I might never have gotten near him at all.

Zoe is prey to all kinds of Old World superstitions. Convinced that someone put the "evil eye" on her sister, Yolanda, who died of unknown causes at the age of eighteen, she claims to remember dolls stuck with pins and upside-down crosses being found in her sister's bed. Though I think she probably dreamt or imagined this bizarre scenario, I once suggested that, if these mystic fetishes indeed existed, someone had no doubt placed them there. She insisted that no one but family members were ever in the house and was tremendously put out when I said one of them could have done it. To this day, she believes these eerie objects arrived in her sister's bed via black magic.

Since it's one of her quaint beliefs that light-complexioned women can't produce mother's milk, she fully expected poor little Andrea to starve. To increase my flow of milk, she tried to make me eat farinata, which is plain white flour mixed with water and cooked into a gruel. Alas, even with all my youthful desire to please, I couldn't get the stuff down. It tasted like paste. It was paste. Frustrated by my intransigence in this matter, she took to weighing Andrea before and after every feeding. All in all, it's a miracle her constant harping didn't dry up my milk. Her nagging only stopped when my pediatrician—bless him—ordered Zoe to leave me alone and assured her that Andrea was, indeed, a well-nourished, beautiful, and happy baby.

Andrea wasn't underfed, but he was overdressed. Regardless of weather, even on the most sweltering summer days, she insisted on bundling him into layer upon layer of clothing: a sleeveless cotton undershirt, followed by a heavy long-sleeved woolen undershirt, a woolen sweater, and a baby dress. If I protested, she became hysterical.

Six months after Andrea was born, my mother and grandmother came for a visit. Things immediately got off to a shaky start. En route from their hotel, they'd brought a big bunch of chrysanthemums for Zoe. I was as mystified as they were when, instead of thanking them and looking for a vase, Zoe gaped at the flowers, transfixed in horror. Muttering audibly and holding the offending blossoms at arm's length, she ostentatiously flung them to the edge of the balcony. Giuliano later explained that chrysanthemums, considered funeral flowers by Florentines, are never used for decorative purposes. In Zoe's mind, my poor mother had handed her a baneful bouquet of bad luck. Her mutterings had been incantations to exorcise their evil spirit.

After that, Zoe never did warm up to Mummy and Grandma Gerda. If either of them attempted to pick Andrea up, she'd hover over them, making it patently obvious she feared they'd drop him. And right in front of them, she'd abuse my grandmother in Italian, saying things like, "Look at that woman, she's so ugly, she has no chin." She contemptuously referred to them as *signoroni* (wealthy as lords), which was far from the case. Though she's been very comfortably situated for decades, Zoe still wears her postwar poverty and suffering in the 1940s as a badge of honor. "What do you know?" she'll frequently ask me. "You've never experienced poverty and famine."

Zoe thrives on the subject of her ostensible misery and loves to bring it up in the midst of family gatherings. Once, at a festive birthday lunch I'd prepared for Giuliano, he raised his wine glass and toasted me lovingly as the reason for his great happiness in life. Our high spirits were somewhat dampened when Zoe, clinking glasses with us, grimly remarked, "I've never been happy, never in my whole life!"

I could see that Mummy was upset to see how my life centered on housework and drudgery, and, since I'd always held my own against her, amazed by my total submission to Zoe. Every morning, Mummy and Grandma's presence notwithstanding, my mother-in-law, attired in an impossibly ragged bargain-basement housedress and mended stockings, led me through her rigid domestic ritual of sheet airing, scrubbing, dusting, polishing, food shopping, and cooking. Every task was done the hard way. Floors were washed with rags on hands and knees. Only after a struggle (for once I put my foot down), did she allow me to install a shower curtain in the bathroom. She preferred to mop the entire floor every time someone took a shower.

Disdaining vacuum cleaners, Zoe daily hung the rugs (and once a week, the mattresses!) from the balcony and pounded them with a wicker beater. I must say, most Florentine housewives did the same. I woke to the sound of rug beating every morning. The first time I tried it, I was astounded at what hard work it was. These women didn't need to go to a gym to keep in shape. It was also extremely unpleasant work. My lungs filled with dust.

My mother-in-law looked askance at any of my activities that didn't directly relate to housekeeping or caring for my husband, and that included friendships with other women ("you're married, what do you need other people for," she'd ask rhetorically). She herself had few contacts or interests outside of her immediate family. Soon after Andrea was born, I set up an easel in an unused corner of the apartment to do some painting at night. I woke in the morning to find it stashed in a broom closet, my paints and brushes stowed in the back corner of the highest shelf. I put them all back out the next evening, only to find she'd risen early and returned them to the closet. I politely suggested to her that it made no sense to put away all my painting things every day and haul them out again every evening.

"I can't stand all this clutter of your things around," she exclaimed impatiently, waving me away.

It became a game between us, the supplies going in and out, in and out on a daily basis. One morning, I woke to find she'd thrown out all the half-squeezed paint tubes I'd left out.

"Zoe," I moaned, "those tubes still contained plenty of expensive oil paint."

"*Madonna mia*, how am I to know about such things? If you don't want me touching your things, why do you leave them around?" After that, I gave up and put my supplies away every night.

Why didn't I confront her? My family was very soft-spoken, not given to emotional scenes, or even, frankly, to introspection. And I had never met an adult before who would viciously abuse people to their faces, make fun of them, and call them names. I had no defenses against such behavior. I was so terrified of my mother-in-law's explosive temper, especially since Giuliano never backed me up in disputes, that I almost always gave in. Italian men take no interest in household matters. If Zoe and I fought, he called us hens. When I'd complain to him about her domineering ways, he'd soothe me and ask me to be patient with his mother, because she was old (in fact, she was only in her early sixties) and set in her ways. He'd remind me how hard her life had been and how lonely she was since her husband died.

"She's so happy to be part of a family now, Nannina," he'd say. "We have so much, and she has so little; we must be good to her."

In spite of the fact that all the "being good to her" devolved solely on me, I'd actually feel guilty after these little talks, and I made it my mission to try to make everyone happy. But sometimes, at night, I'd look at myself in the mirror and ask myself what kind of insane life I was living.

Though she didn't say anything, I could sense my mother's discomfort with Zoe's hold over me. During her stay, Giuliano came down with a slight cold, and Zoe insisted he sleep in her bed to avoid infecting the baby. When I meekly suggested that this seemed a bit drastic, Zoe hit the roof, and my mother's presence didn't prevent her from giving vent to the full violence of her rage. I was less upset about the incident itself than the humiliation of its taking place in front of my mother. I desperately wanted to put up a good front and for her to approve of the life I'd chosen.

I knew Mummy was aching to have a private talk with me, but Zoe never left us alone for a minute. Perhaps it never occurred to her that I might want to spend time alone with my mother. More likely, it did, and she didn't like the idea. One day, making the excuse of taking me shopping for clothes, Mummy snuck me out to a fancy restaurant for lunch. We literally dashed from the apartment before Zoe, still in her tattered houserags, could think of a way to include herself in our outing.

I was looking forward to a conversation about something other than housework, but I wasn't pleased when, no sooner had we ordered our meal, Mummy launched into a critique of my life. At first, I clammed up and accused her of interfering, but soon, my pent-up resentment came pouring out, and my mother heard a very different tale from the one I'd been telling in rosy letters home.

"Sharon," she exhorted me, "you're living like a woman in the nineteenth century. You've got to stand up for yourself." When we got back home that day, I must've had a guilty look. Zoe fixed me with a stony gaze and went straight to bed, claiming a migraine. She didn't say another word to my mother for the rest of her stay.

I did take Mummy's advice to heart (I fully knew she was right) and tried to convince Giuliano that we should move to our own apartment. He listened patiently, but he just didn't understand what the problem was. Finally, we did find a larger apartment, and I hoped (hope being the last refuge of emotional cowards) that Zoe would take the hint and decide to stay put. I once heard someone say, "live in hope, die in despair," and it's always stuck with me. Zoe not only moved in with us but also snagged the biggest of the bedrooms and insisted on choosing all our new furniture. And in spite of the fact that our new apartment was nicer in every way than our previous one, with central heating and a lift, among other amenities, she complained constantly. From the kitchen window, she'd gaze out at the flickering votive lights in the cemetery of Soffiano, sighing piteously,

"I'm so miserable here, like a plant that's been moved. I'll soon be in the grave, and you'll be rid of me."

But though I was increasingly in conflict with Zoe, the one place we bonded was in the kitchen. She had never really enjoyed cooking and was only too happy to pass on the responsibility. I soon discovered that a potato peeler was an exotic object to her, and that she'd never heard of a can opener. She opened cans of tomatoes by forcing the point of a big tailor's scissors through the top and banging it in with her hand. We had much to learn from each other.

Many Italian foods were new to me, especially in the realm of produce. I had never seen an artichoke in Winnipeg, let alone tried to cook one, but I'd enjoyed them many times at Florentine trattorias. They were delicious, simply poached and drizzled with extra-virgin olive oil. One day, Nancy and I bought some artichokes at the greengrocer's and tried to prepare them at her apartment. We dumped them into a kettle of boiling water and waited to see what would happen. As the minutes went by, the water turned blacker and blacker, but the artichokes, when prodded with a fork, seemed totally uncooked. An hour later, when we finally retrieved them from the pot, the outsides were blackened and tough as shoe leather, the insides a disgusting liquefied greenish mush. Zoe howled with laughter when I told her of our debacle with the artichokes. She taught me to trim them properly and put them in water acidulated with lemon juice, which prevents the blackening. And she showed me several ways to cook them.

With uncharacteristic patience, she guided me through the basics of traditional Florentine cuisine, teaching me a number of delicious recipes I still prepare regularly. I learned that most Florentine sauces are thickened with a mixture of vegetables sautéed in oil. Zoe taught me how to do this, at the same time introducing me to a utensil found in every Italian household, the *mezzaluna*. This half-moon-shaped (hence the name) blade with handles is used to cut the *odori* (odorous vegetables)—usually a mixture of carrots, celery, and onions—on a wood cutting board. When sautéing the vegetables, Zoe insisted—and right she was—the heat must not be too high, lest they burn, nor too low, lest they seem poached. She also taught me how not to burn garlic when sautéing it: add the garlic to the oil in the pan off the heat, then start heating the oil.

Many of the roasts and braised meats in Florentine recipes are cooked on the stove. That's because, until fairly recently, cooking in ovens was a privilege of the wealthy, who had large kitchens. Zoe, who had acquired a stove with an oven only in the mid-1960s, had never used it! Unlike the washing machine, its function was not sufficiently seductive to override her instinctive distrust. However, her small roast beef, cooked in a pot, was simply delicious, as were many of her stove-top creations.

She also introduced me to a few basic soups, but she liked them runny—perhaps a taste arising from childhood poverty. When I'd prepare them with more substance, she'd add hot water to her own portion.

Zoe's recipes are excellent, but her repertoire is limited. She isn't really into food and eats what I'd call an actual meal only at lunch. Dinner for her is often a bowl of caffelatte with bread dunked in it, or a bowl of chicken broth with pasta in the shape of rice (she claims real rice makes her choke). My heartier appetite and culinary curiosity soon led me to further explorations of Italian cuisine.

Carciofi Ripieni

STUFFED ARTICHOKES

NOTE When preparing artichokes, it's best not to use iron cookware, which turns them brown.

1 medium-sized lemon

8 medium-sized artichokes
(make sure they're firm; the firmer the better)

4 slices, $1/2$-inch-thick, day-old Tuscan or sourdough bread

1 cup whole milk

2 cloves garlic, finely chopped

1 tablespoon finely chopped fresh parsley leaves

2 jumbo eggs

$3/4$ cup freshly grated Parmigiano Reggiano

2 teaspoons salt

Freshly ground black pepper

2 ripe tomatoes

$1/2$ cup extra-virgin olive oil

8 fresh basil leaves

$1 1/2$ cups water

1. Preheat oven to 350 degrees. Grate entire peel of lemon for zest, and set it aside in a small dish. Fill a large bowl with 2 quarts of water, and squeeze juice of lemon into it.

2. Remove outer leaves of artichokes, approximately 3 layers, until inner leaves appear pale in color. (Foliage removed is about half the weight of the artichokes.) Peel stems, and cut them off artichokes at the base, so each artichoke is flat on the bottom. Put stems in lemon water. Slice top off each artichoke, and discard. The remaining artichokes will measure about 2 inches. Place them in lemon water for 5 minutes.

3. Take an artichoke, and, holding it in both hands, gently pry open its leaves with your thumbs. If it has a hairy part inside (the choke), gently remove it with the point of a paring knife. Place artichoke back in lemon water, and repeat process with others.

4. Remove crusts from bread. Cut each slice in half, and place in a medium-sized bowl. Pour milk on top. Set aside.

ANDREA

⋄ 57 ⋄

5. Place garlic, parsley, eggs, Parmigiano, 1 teaspoon of the salt, and pepper (about four turns of the pepper mill) in a bowl. Mix well with a fork.

6. Take half the bread in your hands, and squeeze out milk. Add to bowl with eggs and cheese. Repeat with other half of bread. Using a spoon, mix ingredients well.

7. Divide bread/egg/cheese mixture into 8 equal portions. Place an artichoke on a flat surface. Holding it with one hand, use the fingers of the other to gently push in filling in the center and between the leaves. Repeat with remaining artichokes. Set aside.

8. Remove core and seeds of tomatoes, chop into $1/2$-inch cubes, and place in a 9" × 12" nonstick baking pan. Add olive oil and lemon zest. Take artichoke stems out of lemon water, cut crosswise into very thin slices, and place in baking pan. Add basil leaves, and sprinkle with second teaspoon of salt. Place artichokes in baking pan between tomatoes and stems. Add 1 $1/2$ cups water.

9. Bake for 45 minutes, or until middle of artichoke feels tender when poked with a fork. Place artichokes on a serving platter, and top with sauce from pan.

SERVES 4

STOVETOP ROAST BEEF

Accompanied by mashed potatoes and sautéed spinach, this stovetop-cooked roast is my son Alessandro's favorite meal.

4 large cloves garlic, very finely chopped

2 teaspoons salt

$1/4$ teaspoon freshly ground black pepper

1 tablespoon unsalted butter, at room temperature

2 pound rump roast

$1/4$ cup extra-virgin olive oil

$1/2$ cup beef broth

1. Place garlic, salt, pepper, and butter in a small bowl, and combine well.

2. Truss roast tightly with string to keep its shape. With a sharp knife, make four cross-shaped incisions at even intervals along one side of roast, beginning about an inch from either end. Stick a finger into each incision to dig a hole. Fill each hole with a quarter of garlic mixture.

3. Heat oil in a Dutch oven. When oil is hot, place rump roast in pot, and brown 5 minutes on each side (though it's round, consider roast to have four sides). Do first side on high heat, then reduce to medium.

4. Add broth, and turn roast over, cooking 2 minutes on each side.

5. Slice thin (meat will be rare), and serve with pan juices.

Penne Strascicate

ZOE'S QUILL-SHAPED PASTA "DRAGGED" WITH MEAT SAUCE

NOTE You can pulse the onions, celery, and carrots to $\frac{1}{8}$-inch pebbles in food processor. Keep the onions separate. Do not overchop; texture is essential.

$\frac{1}{2}$ cup extra-virgin olive oil

$1\frac{1}{2}$ cups celery, chopped into $\frac{1}{8}$-inch pieces

1 cup carrots, chopped into $\frac{1}{8}$-inch pieces

2 cups red onions, chopped into $\frac{1}{8}$-inch pieces

$\frac{1}{4}$ pound ground beef

1 cup beef broth

1 cup puréed Italian plum tomatoes (if unavailable, buy a can of plum tomatoes and purée them)

1 tablespoon kosher salt

1 pound penne

1 cup freshly grated Parmigiano Reggiano

1. Pour oil into a large skillet, and add celery and carrots. Turn heat to medium-high, and sauté for 5 minutes, stirring occasionally with a wooden spoon. Add onions, and sauté for another 10 minutes, continuing to stir occasionally.

2. Add beef, and sauté with vegetables for 10 minutes.

3. Add broth and cook for 15 minutes. On another burner, put up 3 quarts of water to boil in a large stockpot.

4. Add tomatoes to beef and vegetables, and cook for 15 minutes.

5. When water in stockpot is boiling, add kosher salt, and cook penne for $\frac{1}{2}$ the time indicated on the package. Drain penne (saving some of the water in a separate bowl), and add to the sauce. Stir over low heat for 10 minutes. If the sauce seems too dry, add a few tablespoons of the pasta water. Remove from heat, add Parmigiano, stir in well, and serve.

ZOE'S CHICKEN BREAST
WITH VEGETABLES

2 tablespoons extra-virgin olive oil

2 large boneless chicken breasts, cut into 1-inch cubes

Salt

Pepper

3 large carrots, peeled and thinly sliced

1 small yellow onion, thinly sliced

2 stalks celery, thinly sliced

1 cup diced fresh tomatoes

2 cups canned chicken broth

2 tablespoons finely chopped fresh basil

1 bay leaf

1. Heat oil in a large Dutch oven over medium heat. Sprinkle chicken pieces with salt and pepper. Add chicken to pot, and sauté until light brown, about 5 minutes per side. Transfer chicken to a large bowl.

2. Add sliced carrots, onion, and celery to Dutch oven. Cook 8 minutes, stirring occasionally.

3. Add tomatoes, and cook for 2 minutes. Add chicken broth, increase heat, and bring to a boil.

4. Return chicken pieces to Dutch oven. Add 1 tablespoon basil and bay leaf. Reduce heat, cover, and simmer until chicken and vegetables are cooked through, turning chicken occasionally, about 30 minutes.

5. Serve chicken garnished with remaining tablespoon of basil.

Chapter 7

HOW GIULIANO SAVED OUR MARRIAGE

After we married, Giuliano continued to support his painting by working in one of Florence's upscale leather emporia. One day he came home with the exciting news that he'd sold a handbag to Britain's Princess Margaret. For the occasion of her visit, they'd closed the shop to other customers, and his boss, Enzo, had instructed the staff to stand silently in the back. Only he, the proprietor, was to address Her Royal Highness.

The princess arrived with a large entourage. Seated in a velvet armchair, she was shown bag after bag but found none to her liking. Giuliano, unobserved, slipped into the storeroom, grabbed a certain bag, and, to the horror of Enzo and the royal entourage, marched straight up to the princess, grinning ear to ear, purse in hand. Without so much as a bow or a Ma'am, much less a "Your Highness," he blurted out, "This is the Grace Kelly model, designed especially for her. Isn't it lovely?" Wordlessly, not even looking at Giuliano, the princess waved her hand to an assistant, who rushed to pay for the purchase. Enzo was furious, but Giuliano, who claimed to have observed the hint of a smile on the royal face, was thrilled. He went on and on about her—"such bright blue eyes, *Nannina* . . . so petite . . . so much prettier than she looks in photographs . . . ." It amused me to think that even a British princess was susceptible to an Italian man who's putting himself out to be charming.

Working at the leather shop for years, Giuliano had become adept at flirtation. As a bachelor, he'd delighted in one of the job's fringe benefits—a steady supply of carefree young American girls on the lookout for more than a new handbag. He'd have brief romantic flings with them, unhampered by the specter of commitment. Then they'd go back home, and he could move on to fresh conquests.

Of course, I'd assumed our marriage had put an end to Giuliano's ambassadorial role as a Latin lover. With youthful naiveté, I never doubted his fidelity; he was so loving and affectionate to me. So I was shocked, and hurt, when he confessed one night that he was finding it difficult to break the habit of coming on to women customers . . . not to mention resisting their own bold advances to him. The fine line between salesmanship and seduction had been bridged too often. He decided that, to remain faithful to me, he'd have to leave the leather shop. Or perhaps this affecting presentation was merely a ploy to gain my sympathy and support for a new venture he had in mind.

As a child, Giuliano had apprenticed in a butcher shop on the Via della Spada. He'd recently heard that his old *padrone*, Signor Dini—the "meat maestro"—was finally retiring at the age of seventy-five. The place was up for sale, and he'd decided we should buy it.

I wasn't enthusiastic. Cold slabs of raw beef played no role in my romanticized life view, and, secretly, I harbored the elitist feeling that butchering was beneath me. But when Giuliano wants something, expense is no object, rational argument no obstacle. Scraping together our meager savings—and borrowing a truly terrifying amount of money that would enslave us in years of debt—we took the plunge.

We ran it, like all Florentine shops, as a family business. I created quite a stir, with my flaming red hair, biking around town delivering pork chops and sausage links. Giuliano said I was Florence's most beautiful delivery boy. I loved this part of the job, which not only gave me a sense of freedom, but, in winter, got me out of the freezing shop and into the well-heated homes of customers. As I sat behind the counter operating the cash register—a frozen Madonna in a marble niche—my fingers would turn blue and my feet would go numb. Zoe and Giuliano, both impervious to the shop's icy ambience, railed at me: "How can you be so cold? You're a Canadian."

"I didn't grow up in an igloo," I retorted. "We had central heating."

My first day on the job, I took an order for two hundred grams of beef liver from the cook of an octogenarian duchessa. I wrapped it up and biked it over to her palazzo. As a democratically reared Canadian, it never occurred to me to use the service entrance. I marched right up to the front door and rang the bell, which was answered by a very grand, white-gloved majordomo. Haughtily, he extended a silver tray in expectation of a visitor's calling card. I plopped the liver—a little bloody packet—onto it instead and fled without a word. I knew, from his horrified expression, that I'd committed a major gaffe.

Most of my customers, though, were more approachable. They were fascinated to see a young Canadian girl delivering meat and usually invited me in for an espresso or a glass of vin santo. And one Christmas Eve, as I was coming from the market with a whole calf's head in my bicycle basket, its ears flapping as I pedaled along, a group of Japanese tourists, enchanted by the spectacle, stopped me and snapped dozens of photographs.

One thing going for us was Giuliano's extensive knowledge of his trade. Beginning at age ten, he'd spent most of his childhood in this very shop, working seven days a week, twelve hours a day for more than a dozen years. The stories of his apprenticeship make a convincing argument against child labor, which was then common in Europe.

He began working shortly after World War II, when money was scarce, and strapped housewives were desperate to feed their families. People were so hungry, women would beg for the opportunity to launder the butcher's aprons in exchange for soup bones—not even meat, just soup bones! And any purveyor of food was insured an active sex life. Young Giuliano often saw local women disappear into the refrigerator room with Signor Dini, where they swapped sexual favors for meat to put on their family's table.

One of these women was a Signora Sofia, who, perhaps in an excess of sexual excitement, would grab and squeeze Giuliano's little balls every time she came into the shop. Finally, he decided to put a stop to this somewhat painful fondling ritual. On the morning of Sofia's next regular shopping day, he blew up a piece of beef lung and wrapped it in the middle with an esophagus to simulate big meaty testicles and a penis. He stuffed this contrivance into his trousers (he was so young, he was still wearing short pants). When Sofia came in and grabbed him she shrieked. After that, she left him alone, and his prank became a legend on the Via della Spada.

All things considered, it wasn't surprising that Signor Dini's wife, Viola, suffered from any number of vague maladies. She had been to several doctors, but none of them could figure out what was wrong with her. Their consensus was that she was subject to "nerves." Her inchoate afflictions may have been a bid for attention from a husband whose sexual needs were so amply met on the job. If so, when doctors failed to diagnose her problem, she upped the ante. She began to claim that her illnesses were due to a curse laid on her by her mother-in-law, a stern matriarch who disapproved of her son's marriage.

Signor Dini confided his marital problems—possibly with a few sins of omission—to his priest, who advised an exorcism. He arranged for Viola to be taken to Sant'Andrea in Cercina, a lovely eleventh-century Romanesque church in the Florentine hills, where the parish priest, Don Pio, had the reputation of being able to drive out demons. The exorcism was conveniently scheduled for a Wednesday, when butcher shops are traditionally closed in Italy; it's the day shop owners make excursions to the countryside to purchase cattle. Signor Dini had always taken Giuliano along for company on these beef-buying expeditions. In the same spirit—without even a thought to the appropriateness of subjecting a child to such a horrifying spectacle—he took him along to witness his wife's exorcism.

Sant'Andrea is entered via a loggia adorned with ancient frescoes; known as La Sala Dei Quaranta (the Room of the Forty), it's a memorial to a Renaissance confraternity—a charitable organization much like the Misericordia, which had come to my rescue at our Via delle Bombarde apartment. Signora Dini's agitation became intense the moment they entered this room, and she had to be literally dragged into the church. At the sight of the beautiful Della Robbia *Madonna and Child* that graces the altar, she exploded with rage and began wildly thrashing about like someone having an epileptic fit. As several people held her down, face to the floor to keep her from hurting herself, she spewed green bile and other strange things, including, Giuliano swears, braids of hair. Don Pio, attired in special liturgic vestments, sprinkled her with holy water and repeatedly chanted a prayer to drive out her demons:

> Behold the cross of the Lord,
> Flee to the other side,
> Ye hateful seed of Satan.

At this point, she began to speak in a deep masculine voice, completely unlike her own, and, astoundingly, in Latin. It sounded like an echo from the grave.

Signora Dini was barely educated. Even her Italian vocabulary was limited; certainly, she wasn't fluent in Latin. As she began to calm down, Don Pio began a dialogue with the demon—the unearthly voice—asking it why it was in her body and begging it to depart and relieve the poor woman's suffering. The demon explained that it was the spirit of one departed, doomed to travel through other bodies by way of punishment for a cruel and sinful life. It went on to confess a chilling litany of crimes—extortion, murder, and sexual profligacy—all this out of the mouth of a woman who'd probably never so much as stolen an onion.

Don Pio blessed Signora Dini, blessed the departed spirit so that it could find peace, and repeatedly commanded the demon, in the name of Jesus Christ, to leave her body.

But try as he might, the priest was never able to drive out Signora Dini's tortured demon. Viola would calm down immediately following the ritual, but her symptoms always returned. Exorcisms at least twice a month—always following the same pattern and always failing—went on for the rest of her life (she was over eighty when she died) and became an integral part of Giuliano's childhood. Perhaps that's why, though Giuliano scoffs at Zoe for her belief in spells and curses, he's not totally immune himself. In times of crisis, he'll pace from room to room frenziedly reciting the exorcism prayer in Latin and flinging salt over his shoulder.

Still, however rigorous and corrupting life was for working children, there were some benefits. They did learn a trade and learn it well. Giuliano is a master butcher.

And after all, it was dire necessity that drove him, and so many other young people, into the work force. Unremitting hunger was a constant fact of my husband's formative years. At home, there was never anything in the pantry for breakfast. If he was lucky, his mornings would include meat deliveries to nearby *pensiones*, where he could scrounge leftovers from the wondrous breakfasts of rich American and British tourists—coffee with hot milk, brioches, and croissants. Complementing these rare treats, he'd sneak little pieces of raw meat from the shop, wolfing them down when Signor Dini was otherwise occupied. This furtive practice generated three separate incidents of tapeworm.

The first time a customer gave him a tip, Giuliano was ecstatic. Because his small salary was paid directly to Zoe, he'd never had so much as a lira of his own before. As soon as he could get away from the shop, he raced out and bought a big, crusty two-pound farmer's loaf, a hundred grams (about a quarter-pound) of butter, and a similar amount of anchovies. Grabbing a knife from the butcher shop, he took his feast to the curb outside, cut the enormous loaf in two, larded it with the entire quarter-pound of butter, and filled it with anchovies, creating a sandwich so huge he couldn't wrap his little mouth around it. He had to sit on it and bounce up and down to flatten it out. Then he devoured it all in one glorious sitting.

Most of our clientele, remembering Giuliano from the old days, welcomed him back with great warmth. In the 1970s, before the advent of big supermarkets in Florence, the local butcher shop was more than just a meat store. It was a gathering place, much like an old-fashioned American cracker-barrel, where customers lingered for hours chatting and gossiping. Giuliano presided over the assemblage from atop a pedestal fronted by a high, old-fashioned marble counter.

Butchering, to him, was an art, the marble-walled shop a gallery in which he presented his wares with aesthetic flourish. Cubed meat was displayed on long skewers interspersed with bay leaves and pieces of bread; rump roasts were butterflied into heart shapes; and, at Easter, the walls were adorned with lambs, hung by their ankles on stainless-steel bars and entwined with garlands of red carnations.

Much respected, Giuliano knew the best methods for preparing all the kinds of meat he sold, which he could cut to the most exacting specifications of any customer. He was revered among the local chefs and food *conoscitori* (experts), but less-knowledgeable customers sometimes resented his adamant integrity. One such was a woman who came in for ground meat for polpettone (meat loaf) and asked for lean beef. He told her that fattier meat would make the polpettone juicier, but she thought he was trying to take advantage of her. A heated argument ensued, and she stalked angrily out of the shop. No matter. Giuliano would rather sell no meat at all than the wrong meat.

Spiedini di Filetto di Suino, Alloro, e Piccone

PORK AND SQUAB SKEWERED WITH BREAD AND BAY LEAF

NOTE For this recipe, you'll need eight 12-inch skewers, available at culinary supply stores.

$1/4$ cup extra-virgin olive oil

$1/2$ cup dry white wine

2 cloves garlic, very finely chopped

2 teaspoons salt

$1/2$ teaspoon freshly ground black pepper

1 pound pork fillets

2 squabs, about 1 pound each (or 4 quail, divided in half)

1 thin baguette

16 large fresh bay leaves

1. Pour oil and wine into a medium bowl, and add garlic, salt, and pepper. Refrigerate marinade until ready to use.

2. Divide pork fillets into cubes approximately $1 1/2$ to 2 inches (you'll need 8 pieces).

3. Remove necks, feet, and wings from squabs, and discard. Divide remainder of each squab into four pieces (once again, giving you 8 pieces). Place pork and squab in marinade, and refrigerate for 3 hours or longer.

4. Preheat oven to 350 degrees. Slice baguette into 16 pieces, $3/4$-inch thick. Remove meat from refrigerator, retaining marinade for basting. Take two skewers, and, placing them parallel to each other, about an inch apart, double skewer a slice of pork, a bay leaf, a slice of bread, a piece of squab, another bay leaf, and another slice of bread. Repeat this sequence twice. Do the same on remaining pairs of skewers.

5. Place skewers over a baking pan no wider than 11 inches (so that skewers can rest on the edges). Bake for 20 minutes. Baste with marinade, and bake 20 minutes more.

Garga's Polpettone
con Salsa Vigliacca

ITALIAN MEAT LOAF
WITH SCOUNDREL SAUCE

In Italy, the culinary *raison d'être* for a polpettone is to use up left-over cold cuts. If you can't buy the small amounts used in this recipe, reverse the process by buying more and using the remainder for sandwiches. Like other meat loaf recipes, Garga's is great with mashed potatoes.

2 ounces day-old Tuscan or sourdough bread, crusts removed

1 cup whole milk

$1/2$ pound ground beef (slightly fatty)

$1/2$ pound ground veal

1 clove garlic, finely chopped

1 tablespoon fresh parsley leaves, finely chopped

2 ounces prosciutto crudo (raw, cured ham)

2 ounces cooked ham

1 ounce freshly grated Parmigiano Reggiano

1 teaspoon salt

2 jumbo eggs

1 twist freshly ground black pepper

1. Preheat oven to 350 degrees. Place bread in a small bowl, and pour milk over it. Set aside.

2. In a large mixing bowl, thoroughly combine beef, veal, garlic, and parsley. Set aside.

3. Chop prosciutto and cooked ham into $1/4$-inch pieces. Add—along with Parmigiano, salt, eggs, and pepper—to beef and veal, and mix thoroughly.

4. Squeeze milk from bread, and, crumbling it with your fingers, mix thoroughly into meat mixture.

5. Place meat mixture in a 5" × 9" loaf pan, creating a rise in the middle. Bake for 45 minutes. Serve with Salsa Vigliacca, which you can prepare while meat loaf is baking.

SALSA VIGLIACCA:

$1/4$ cup extra-virgin olive oil

2 garlic cloves, very finely chopped

$1 1/2$ pounds ripe tomatoes, halved, with seeds removed

$1/2$ teaspoon cracked red pepper

1 teaspoon salt

1. Pour oil into a large skillet. Add garlic, turn heat to medium-high, and sauté until golden. Remove pan from heat. Squeeze tomato halves with your hands into oil and garlic, add cracked red pepper and salt, cover pan, and cook on high heat for 5 minutes.

2. Uncover, and mash tomatoes with a fork. Cook uncovered on high heat for 5 minutes, stirring occasionally.

Chapter 8

APRÈS LE DÉLUGE, LE DÎNER: THE DROWNED CHICKEN PARTY

Italian food shops, especially butchers, enjoyed great working hours in those days. From June through September, except on Fridays, we were open mornings only. The rest of the year, we closed early Wednesdays and Thursdays.

By 1976, the butcher shop was flourishing. For weekend getaways, we rented a small nineteenth-century farmhouse, ten kilometers outside Florence in the nearby village of Roveta, known for its natural springs. We spent every weekend there and many afternoons as well. Our "country house," set on a few hilltop acres, overlooked a pine forest, rolling hills of vineyards, orchards, and fields of wildflowers.

Each season had its special beauty. To the north, a road led to the town of Ginestra, which means "broom" in Italian. Every spring its hills were covered with broom in bloom—lovely yellow flowers with an intoxicating scent. Spring's pink-blossomed peach trees, by summer, were heavy with ripe fruit. Fall colors reminded me of home. And in winter, fields of grain sprouted brilliant green, especially vibrant against a misty background of leafless trees and gray skies.

Our house was built during the days of sharecropping, an agricultural system in place from the end of the eighteenth century until after World War II. We were intrigued to hear (I can't lie; Giuliano was thrilled to hear) that the previous tenants had been members of the infamous *Brigate Rosse* (Red Brigade), the Marxist–Leninist terrorist group whose stated goal was a "concentrated strike against the heart of the State . . . ." The brigade started out sabotaging factory equipment and went on to kidnap and murder Prime Minister Aldo Moro. Another notorious case was their abduction of J. Paul Getty III, whose ear they cut off before releasing him for ransom. But whatever evil doings may have been planned there prior to our tenancy, our little house emitted no vibes of past violence. It was very rustic, which is to say, almost devoid of comfort, but its weathered beamed ceilings and massive stone fireplace were charming. We had very little furniture—just a bed and dresser in each of the two bedrooms and a long cypress table in the kitchen with a dozen straw-seated chairs—all of which had seen better days.

Andrea had a teepee, which my grandfather had sent him from Canada, and he spent many a rapturous hour running naked around the farm, brandishing his tomahawk and bellowing savage war whoops. On our little plot of land, Giuliano and I started growing vegetables, and we bought twenty young chickens to raise.

One night in Roveta, we were awakened at three o'clock in the morning by a violent thunderstorm. Rain came pouring through the roof, and we ran around frantically setting up buckets to catch the drips.

Zoe, who almost never stayed overnight—she usually came out for the day and dinner, then insisted we drive her home and ourselves back to Roveta—had this, of all times, chosen to remain.

Terrified by the great rumblings of thunder and flashes of lightning, she came scurrying into our bedroom and squashed in next to Giuliano, pushing me to the far edge. Andrea, sensing a decline in the social order, insisted on coming in as well. It was all too much for me. I abandoned the bed and curled up alone on Andrea's tiny cot.

It was an uncomfortable night, and, with one thing and another, we didn't think about our flock until the next morning. In the bright sunshine, I walked into the garden to be confronted by a pathetic pile of drowned chickens. To get away from the rain, they'd all climbed on top of each other. The few survivors, at the apex, were wet and muddy. Those below had been smothered and looked as if they'd fallen asleep. So much for survival of the fittest: the last to join the pile had lived, while the first to seek a dry, warm haven had died.

We couldn't let these chickens, which were about the size of Cornish game hens, perish in vain. Patiently, we plucked them, marinated them in oil, garlic, and rosemary, and invited friends and neighbors over for a grilled-chicken feast (the poor drowned darlings were very tender), supplemented by dishes using tomatoes, beans, eggplants, and fresh herbs from our garden. People brought cakes and biscotti, and we had a festive banquet that lasted from two in the afternoon to midnight. Wine flowed like the rain the night before.

It was our first country house dinner party. After that, like Giuliano's studio on Via delle Bombarde, the Roveta farmhouse became a gathering place for our artist friends and the scene of frequent dinners under the pines. We were becoming adept at feeding large numbers of people, and, unconsciously, I think we were moving towards the idea of having a restaurant.

It was a happy time. I told Giuliano I thought we should have another child, and he enthusiastically agreed. Soon I was pregnant with Alessandro.

Pollettini Grigliati con
Rosmarino e Limone

GRILLED BABY CHICKENS
WITH ROSEMARY AND LEMON

4 poussins (baby chickens), 1 pound each
(if unavailable, use Rock Cornish game hens)

1 cup extra-virgin olive oil

2 tablespoons rosemary, finely chopped

4 cloves garlic, very finely chopped

2 teaspoons cracked red pepper

Zest of 2 lemons

Juice of 2 lemons

Salt

1. Wash and dry chickens. Cut them in half, and pound flat with a smooth-surfaced meat mallet.

2. In a large casserole, mix oil, rosemary, garlic, cracked red pepper, lemon zest, and lemon juice. Place chicken, skin side down, in marinade, and let rest for at least 2 hours.

3. Place chicken on a charcoal grill, and cook (over hot coals, not on a blazing fire) for 15 minutes on one side, brushing frequently with remaining marinade. Salt to taste, turn over, salt other side, and grill for another 15 minutes, still brushing frequently with marinade.

Fagiolini Verdi in Umido

STEWED GREEN BEANS

$1/4$ cup extra-virgin olive oil

$1/4$ pound celery (use only the whiter part, closer to the core), cut into $1/4$-inch slices

2 medium-sized carrots, cut into $1/4$-inch slices

1 small yellow onion (3 $1/2$ ounces), cut into $1/4$-inch slices

1 pound green beans (whole, with ends trimmed off)

3 ripe tomatoes (each cut into 8 wedges)

1 cup water

$1/4$ cup chopped fresh basil leaves

1 teaspoon chopped fresh thyme leaves

Salt

1. Pour oil into a stockpot, and add celery, carrots, and onion. Cook over medium heat, for 5 minutes, stirring occasionally.

2. Add green beans, tomatoes, water, basil, and thyme. Cook over medium-low heat for 15 minutes, or until carrots are tender. Salt to taste.

SUMMER EGGPLANT PARMIGIANA

NOTE This recipe should be made only in summer, when fresh, ripe tomatoes are available.

2 large eggplants

6 ripe tomatoes, cut into $1/2$-inch slices

$3/4$ cup extra-virgin olive oil

12 fresh basil leaves

$1/2$ pound fresh mozzarella, chopped into $1/2$-inch cubes

Salt

1 cup freshly grated Parmigiano Reggiano

1. Preheat oven to 350 degrees. Halve eggplants lengthways, and cut into $1/2$-inch slices (still lengthways). Place slices on a stovetop grill, and cook over medium heat for 4 minutes on each side. (Alternatively, you could grill the eggplant on an outdoor barbecue).

2. Divide eggplant and tomato slices into 3 even piles. Drizzle 3 tablespoons of the oil into a shallow 8" × 10" baking dish, and place $1/3$ of the eggplant slices on it. The next layer will be $1/3$ of the tomato slices, then 4 basil leaves, topped with half the mozzarella.

3. Lightly salt, drizzle with 3 tablespoons oil, and repeat.

4. The final layer should be eggplant, topped with remaining tomato and basil leaves. Drizzle with remaining oil, evenly distribute Parmigiano on top, and bake for 50 minutes or until well browned and bubbly.

Chapter 9

ROCKS AHEAD /
CHICKENS REDUX

Our life in Roveta was idyllic, but back in town, Giuliano and I were having problems. Like his father and grandfather before him, he'd gotten into the habit of going out at night to play cards. His fellow gamblers ran the gamut from rich businessmen and food wholesalers to professional thieves, black market jewel dealers, and Mafiosi. The games took place in illegal gambling dens called *bische*. Ever the bad boy, Giuliano couldn't resist the allure of an illicit activity in low company. He was especially thrilled one night when the police raided his *bisca*, hacking through the door with hatchets, throwing out all the card players, and arresting the owners.

When this card-playing mania first took hold, Giuliano would be out a few nights a week. Soon it was every night, and all night. He'd stay out gambling until four in the morning, making a brief appearance at home for a quick nap before heading off to the Central Meat Market at dawn. I was miserable, stuck at home night after night with Zoe, staring at the tube. There were only two TV stations, both state-run and specializing in noisy variety shows, which I've always hated. Zoe loved them; she'd watch, scandalized, clicking her tongue censoriously and muttering, *"che schifo"* (how sickening), not about, but actually to, the scantily clad female singers. Throughout her evening programs, she interacted with the television set as if it were a live person in the room, directing a stream of commentary (usually abusive) towards the screen. If I left her to read or paint, she'd accuse me of avoiding her, or call me every five minutes to see something she considered extremely amusing.

When I'd wake in the middle of the night to find Giuliano's place next to me empty, I'd be overcome with anxiety. I think I knew, deep down, that something terrible was happening. But when I complained to him about these nightly meanderings, he'd be so charming, he'd always talk me around. Coming in near dawn to find me waiting up for him, he'd cuddle me and tell me how much he loved me. Sometimes he had an expensive-looking brooch or bracelet for me. I've never really cared about jewelry—certainly, I'd never asked for it—but I clung to these gifts as proof of my husband's love.

"That's what Italian men do," Zoe rebuked me, when I appealed to her for help. And indeed, to her, ours was a typical marriage. I began to feel trapped, wondering if my whole life had been a terrible mistake. But I was blissfully unaware of the magnitude of real troubles looming on my horizon.

In 1978, the day before New Year's Eve, shortly after Alessandro was born, I bumped into Giuliano's friend, Sergio, at the Rivoire. He offered me a lift home, and en route, uttered the ominous words, "Sharon, I think there's something you should know."

Immediately my mind leapt to another woman. I thought he was going to tell me Giuliano was having an affair. For a while now, I'd noticed he wasn't eating regular meals or sleeping very well. He looked awful. I knew something was wrong, but whenever I asked, he'd clam up and insist everything was fine. If I persisted, he'd accuse me of nagging and become uncharacteristically nasty. Once, he hadn't come home until six in the morning, and some afternoons, when I'd call him at the butcher shop, no one would answer the phone. When I'd ask him about it, he'd say he'd been out for coffee.

"Garga's in big trouble," Sergio told me. "You have to do something about it. He's been gambling at cards and has gotten himself heavily into debt. Talk to him."

Sergio refused to give me any more details, but when Giuliano came home that night, I confronted him. At first, he denied there was a problem, but, little by little, the truth came out. It took several weeks before I got him to admit the staggering amount of money he'd lost. We were in debt to the tune of more than 200 million lire (about $320,000)! On top of money he'd actually lost, he owed fortunes to his meat suppliers, though, as he pointed out with maddening pride, he always paid his gambling debts. The presents he'd been giving me, it seems, he'd won from his fellow gamblers who'd put up their unfortunate wives' jewelry as stakes. Recently, he'd been gambling afternoons as well as at night, hence the unanswered phone when I called.

Giuliano attempted to console me by pointing out that "at least it wasn't another woman."

"Giuliano," I answered, "there are many forms of betrayal." I gave him an ultimatum: "Stop gambling, or I'll leave you."

With a new baby and a seven-year old, I felt paralyzed with fear and resentment. How could a man do this to his family? But I shoved down my feelings. The ramifications, should I choose to leave my marriage, were immense. The thought of going back to Canada with two little children in tow, of admitting failure, of throwing myself on my mother's mercy, was too crushing. My pride wouldn't allow it.

I shelved my rage and panic in some compartment of my brain where I tend to stow life's unpleasant realities and switched into "fixing" mode, spending hours calculating how we could ever get out of debt. It helped that Giuliano was so appreciative of my ability to confront trouble with a positive attitude.

To wean himself from cards, and make some much-needed extra money, Giuliano now threw himself into agricultural pursuits at the Roveta country house. He bought 250 chickens and fed them on leftovers from the butcher shop. On this meat regimen—poultry is usually raised on grains and seeds—they grew terrifyingly fierce and aggressive. I still have a scar where our vicious rooster, *Il Gallo*, pecked a hole in my leg. Giuliano was the only one who could dominate him.

Every day, after we closed the butcher shop, we'd drive out to feed the chickens. Giuliano did the slaughtering, and we all—even Zoe—plucked, cleaned, and eviscerated them. It was a smelly and disgusting job. Back in town, though, our customers loved these farm-raised carnivores. They were big—one chicken could amply serve six people—and they tasted great.

We also grew tomatoes, beans, cucumbers, artichokes, eggplants, zucchini, lettuces, and peppers on our "farm." And, nearby, there were ancient fig and apricot trees. With an abundance of fruit free for the picking, I immersed myself in recipes for Italian pastries, and, to my family's delight, created new desserts daily. In addition, I was constantly canning tomatoes and making jams, pickles, and preserves of every kind. Of course, with this agricultural project, my workload increased exponentially. But physical labor took our minds off our problems. And it wasn't all drudgery. With little Alessandro in a Snugli, we'd take family hikes in the adjoining forests, go wild-berry picking, and search for mushrooms. And we still had friends coming out all the time for big country dinners that centered on the *spécialité de la maison:* grilled chicken. We'd buy prosciutto and sausages from a local pig farm, cook up big pots of savory mushroom soup, and bake pies with the fresh fruit we'd picked.

After a while, though, we realized that no matter how hard we worked at farming, we weren't making much money. With creditors pressing us, it was time to face the inevitable: to pay Giuliano's gambling debts, we'd have to sell the butcher shop.

Andrea, *left*, and Alessandro at Roveta country house

PORCINI MUSHROOM SOUP

5 pounds very ripe tomatoes

2 tablespoons extra-virgin olive oil

3 cloves garlic

1 tablespoon thyme leaves

$^1/_2$ cup fresh basil leaves

$^1/_2$ cup fresh mint leaves

1 pound porcini mushrooms

Salt

2 cups heavy cream

3 slices Tuscan or sourdough bread ($^1/_2$-inch thick)

Sprigs of mint

NOTE It's fine to use frozen porcini mushrooms for this recipe. They may even be better, because they're sure to be packed fresh.

1. Cut tomatoes in half, and put into a large stockpot with oil, garlic, thyme, basil, and mint leaves. Cover and cook over medium heat for 20 minutes.

2. While tomatoes are cooking, carefully wash porcini, removing any dirt or sand that may be attached. Slice mushrooms, lengthways, into $^3/_8$-inch strips. Set aside.

3. Put tomato-herb mixture through a food mill, and transfer back to pot. Add mushrooms, and salt to taste. Cook another 10 minutes on medium heat. Add cream and warm through. Taste, and add more salt if necessary. Toast bread.

4. To serve, place half a slice of toast in each bowl, and ladle soup over it. Garnish with sprigs of mint.

COUNTRY HOUSE
APRICOT TART

The basics of this tart—its flaky, feather-light crust and pastry-cream filling—can be adapted to dozens of different dessert pies. Try, for instance, substituting berries (perhaps alternating with kiwi slices) or peaches for the apricots.

NOTE If you use berries, skip the jam glaze; instead, dust with powdered sugar just prior to serving.

FOR THE PASTRY:

$\frac{1}{4}$ pound (1 stick) unsalted butter, melted

$\frac{1}{4}$ cup confectioner's sugar

$1\frac{1}{4}$ cups unbleached all-purpose flour, sifted

$\frac{1}{4}$ teaspoon salt

1. Preheat oven to 350 degrees. Using a fork (or your hands), thoroughly combine above ingredients in a bowl to form a pastry dough.

2. Using your fingers, crumble dough evenly into bottom and up sides (crust should go 2 inches up sides) of a 10-inch springform pan, pressing it down well. Make sure your crust comes to a nice right angle where bottom and sides of pan meet; there should be no bunched-up crust forming a curve. Prick crust at 1-inch intervals, bottom and sides, with the tines of a fork. Bake for 15 minutes, or until crust turns the tiniest bit golden. Do not overbake, or it will taste dry. Let cool for 10 minutes, during which time you can prepare pastry-cream filling.

FOR THE PASTRY CREAM:

2 jumbo eggs

$^3/_4$ cup sugar

3 tablespoons unbleached all-purpose flour

1 pint half-and-half

Zest of 1 lemon, finely grated

1. With an electric mixer, beat eggs and sugar in a large bowl until thick and foamy. Add flour, a little at a time, and mix in well.

2. In a medium saucepan, bring half-and-half to a boil.

3. Slowly add boiling half-and-half to egg/sugar/flour mixture, stirring constantly with a wooden spoon as you pour. Transfer mixture back into saucepan, and, on low heat, continue stirring until it has a pudding-like texture (at least 10 minutes).

4. Stir in lemon zest. Let cool for 10 minutes, stirring occasionally so that it doesn't form a skin.

FOR THE TOPPING:

6 fresh apricots (buy 1 or 2 extra in case you get a bad one)

2 tablespoons apricot jam

1. Pour pastry cream into piecrust, slowly over the back of a cooking spoon (to prevent damaging the crust). Wash apricots well, carefully cut them in half, and remove pits. Arrange apricot halves in concentric circles atop pastry cream. (An alternate plan is to cut the apricots into eighths and arrange them in concentric circles.)

2. Place apricot jam in a small saucepan, and cook on very, very low heat for 2 minutes, stirring constantly, until it becomes liquidy. With a pastry brush, gently and carefully brush jam onto tops of apricots, creating a glaze. Try not to drip jam on pastry cream layer. Open springform pan just before serving. Serve at room temperature. If you need to refrigerate leftover pie, take it out at least two hours before serving again.

Chapter 10

OUR FIRST TRATTORIA: HOSTS SERVING HOSTS

An elderly customer at the butcher shop, Signor Ottavio, was the proprietor of a tiny trattoria, where he served up inexpensive fare to an impecunious clientele. Knowing our plight, when he decided to retire in 1979, he suggested we buy his little hole-in-the-wall and open a restaurant. We've both always loved to cook, and the idea appealed to us.

The problem was coming up with the money to launch this exciting new venture. How, one might ask, could anyone in our situation manage to secure a loan? Our current debt was to meat wholesalers, most of whom had known Giuliano as a boy. Their patience about getting paid was nothing short of saintly. Since we had no outstanding loans (our debts were unofficial, in the form of scribbled IOUs) we had no trouble borrowing money from the bank. Plunging ourselves still further into debt, we opened our first Trattoria Garga.

I was extremely nervous about the risks we were taking, but Giuliano waved away my fears with a bit of ancient Roman wisdom: *Meglio un giorno da leone, che cento da pecora* (better one day as a lion than a hundred as a sheep). Later, I learned that this bold adage was the motto of Mussolini. But whatever apprehensions we had about this new enterprise were quickly submerged in our excitement and ambition.

Signor Ottavio's eatery had been a bare-bones establishment, with only stools for seating. We put in burgundy wall-to-wall carpeting, created upholstered banquettes, had silk lampshades made to order, set tables with embroidered cloths, and purchased good silverware and crystal wine glasses.

To make our menu more interesting, we gave our listings exotic names. A veal scaloppina with black olives was called, for no discernible reason, Scaloppina alla Selvaggia (wild cutlet). And we worked hard at perfecting exotic signature dishes. Inspired by a book about Renaissance cooking—from which we learned that communion wafers had once been used in place of pasta for dumplings—we created a ravioli dish called Ostie del Cardinale (cardinal's hosts). Not only was it original, it seemed daringly sacrilegious. Giuliano would buy oversized communion wafers from a church supply shop in the Piazza del Duomo, which we'd stuff with sweetbreads and truffles and drizzle with sage butter. The wafers became soft when moistened and made lovely translucent raviolis, so thin you could see the succulent fillings inside. They were so popular, Giuliano was soon purchasing vast quantities of these transubstantial treats. One day, a saleswoman at the shop commented, "Goodness, Father, you must have a big parish. You certainly have a fine turnout for mass every day." He didn't have the heart to disillusion her.

I baked old-fashioned Florentine desserts, such as a cream pastry topped with toasted pine nuts and sugar, an apple cake—Zoe's favorite—that is the *ne plus ultra* of its genre, and a ricotta and pastry cream cheesecake. Though, as a tribute to the previous owners, we kept Signora Ottavia's minestrone soup on the menu, we gloried in serving exotica such as lamb intestines sautéed with rosemary, stuffed spleen, and bull's balls sautéed in lemon butter, the latter listed on our menu as Palle alla Medici (balls are a Medici symbol). I felt we were really sophisticated and recherché, and often thought, "if they could only see me back in Winnipeg . . . ." As for Giuliano, he was loving getting back to his roots.

To the trattoria's old rough-and-tumble customers, the place had become forbiddingly elegant, and they drifted away. But we soon attracted a new and loyal clientele. We learned as we went along. The first time I purchased peppercorns for the restaurant, I ordered five kilos. They would have lasted us for years, but after a while, I threw most of them out. Spices have to be fresh.

More costly was the magnificent debacle of our first New Year's Eve. Today, we're fully booked with reservations every night, but back then things were less formal, and most of our customers were walk-ins. Assuming large numbers of people would turn up, and eager to put our best foot forward, we prepared a massive holiday banquet. One might say we went overboard.

For appetizers, we offered the finest Iranian caviar and cuts of smoked salmon, raw oysters, Arancini di Riso (deep-fried onion-scented rice balls filled with wild porcini mushrooms), and three different kinds of crostini—little toasts brushed with olive oil and topped with chicken liver pâté, smoked scamorza cheese, or fresh salmon in a creamy dill sauce. These were followed by *primi piatti* of Florentine crêpes; spaghetti with morsels of fresh sautéed lobster in a garlicky tomato-cognac flambé sauce; and buttery, oniony risotto embellished with fresh white truffles from Alba. *Secondi* included Canard à l'Orange (the recipe Caterina de' Medici introduced to France); eels—a traditional Florentine New Year's dish—skinned alive (Giuliano did it), chopped in small pieces, and sautéed with garlic, parsley, and chili peppers; fat beef fillets sautéed in sage-scented olive oil; succulent Norwegian salmon in lemon-butter sauce; and rabbit stuffed with prosciutto and pistachios. A similar number of desserts ran the gamut from crème caramel to sponge cake crowned with wine-poached peaches and champagne-nuanced zabaione.

Our first two customers arrived at 7:30 and by 9 P.M. had finished and paid their bill. Then we waited. And waited. And waited. At 10:30, we realized no one else was going to show up. Alas, we weren't yet significant enough for people to think of us for a big night like New Year's Eve.

We sent home the help, lit the candles, set out a table with all the food we'd prepared, dined lavishly, and got roaring drunk on the best French champagne. Then we turned on the radio and danced, toasted in 1980, and made love on one of the tables.

MRS. OTTAVIO'S MINESTRONE SOUP

1 leek

4 small carrots

4 celery stalks

1 medium onion

4 small Yukon gold potatoes

$^2/_3$ cup extra-virgin olive oil, plus extra for drizzling

4 small zucchini

3 small vine-ripened tomatoes (off-season, used canned Italian plum tomatoes)

5 cabbage leaves

1 bunch Swiss chard (leaves only)

3 cups chicken stock (use vegetable broth if you're a vegetarian)

1 can, 15.5 ounces, cannellini (white kidney beans)

1 tablespoon finely chopped fresh parsley leaves

8 fresh basil leaves

$^1/_4$ pound ditalini pasta

Salt

Freshly ground black pepper

Parmigiano Reggiano

1. Remove tough outer leaves and root of leek, retaining only very light green part that separates easily into layers. Peel and trim carrots. Wash and trim celery stalks. Chop these vegetables into $^1/_8$-inch pieces (it's okay to use a food processor, but don't over-chop; you want some texture), and place in a bowl. Chop onion equally fine, and place in a separate bowl. Peel potatoes, dice into $^1/_2$-inch cubes, and set aside in a third bowl.

2. Pour $^2/_3$ cup olive oil into a large stockpot. Add leek, carrots, and celery, and sauté over medium-high heat for 5 minutes, stirring occasionally with a wooden spoon. Add onions, and sauté for another 10 minutes, continuing to stir occasionally. Add potatoes to stockpot, and lower heat to medium.

3. Wash, but do not dry, zucchini, tomatoes, cabbage leaves, and Swiss chard. Slice zucchini into $1/2$-inch pieces, quarter tomatoes, and tear cabbage and chard leaves into approximately 2-inch pieces. Add to stockpot, and stir well. Cover, and continue cooking over medium heat for 10 minutes, stirring occasionally.

4. Add chicken stock, beans, parsley, and basil, and turn heat to high. When soup comes to a boil, add pasta, and cook until tender. Add salt and pepper to taste. Ladle soup into bowls, and drizzle a little olive oil into each serving (Florentines say you should drizzle just enough to make a small *c*). Serve with freshly grated Parmigiano.

RICE "ORANGES"

1. Put 2 quarts of water up to boil in a large pot. While waiting for it to boil, prepare Béchamel Sauce.

   FOR THE BÉCHAMEL SAUCE:

   $1/8$ pound ($1/2$ stick) unsalted butter

   $1/2$ cup unbleached all-purpose flour

   $1/4$ teaspoon salt

   $1/4$ teaspoon freshly grated nutmeg

   2 cups whole milk

1. Melt butter over very low heat (don't brown it) in a small nonstick saucepan. Add flour, stirring continuously with a wooden spoon. Cook for a few seconds. Add salt and nutmeg. Still stirring, add milk, a little at a time. Cook for 10 minutes on medium-low heat, stirring all the while. Set aside.

NOTE You're going to end up with a little more sauce than you need, but it's impossible to prepare it in a smaller amount.

   FOR THE RICE "ORANGES":

   3 cups Arborio rice

   2 jumbo egg yolks, beaten

   $1/4$ pound cooked ham, chopped into $1/4$-inch pieces

   1 cup freshly grated Parmigiano Reggiano

   $1/2$ teaspoon salt

   $1/4$ teaspoon freshly ground black pepper

   $1/4$ pound fresh mozzarella, cut into $1/4$-inch cubes

   Breadcrumbs

   Peanut oil

1. Pour rice into boiling water, and cook on low heat for 18 minutes. Drain well, place in a large bowl, and let cool slightly.

2. Add egg yolks, ham, Parmigiano, salt, and pepper. Mix well.

3. Make balls the size of small oranges (hence, the recipe name) out of rice mixture. Place a teaspoon of béchamel and a few cubes of mozzarella in the center of each "orange," and reconstruct their spherical shapes.

4. Roll rice balls in breadcrumbs, and place on a plate covered with waxed paper. Refrigerate for at least 2 hours.

5. Deep-fry rice balls in oil on medium heat, turning gently a few times, until they're an even golden color.

Filetto di Manzo alla Salvia   SERVES 4

SAGE-SCENTED BEEF FILLETS

$^1/_4$ cup extra-virgin olive oil

12 cloves garlic

4 beef fillets or New York strip steaks ($^1/_2$-pound each)

12 fresh sage leaves

Salt

Freshly ground black pepper

1. Pour oil into a large, heavy skillet. Add whole garlic cloves, turn heat to medium-high, and sauté for 2 minutes.

2. Arrange fillets in skillet, and place 3 sage leaves atop each. Cook over medium heat for 5 minutes (3 minutes for rare).

3. Slide sage leaves off fillets, salt fillets to taste, and turn. Salt other side of fillets, and replace sage leaves on top of them. Also turn garlic cloves to brown evenly. Continue cooking on medium heat for another 3 to 5 minutes.

4. Serve each fillet topped with 3 sage leaves and 3 cloves garlic. Drizzle with pan juices from skillet, and season to taste with pepper. Serve with Patate Novelle Saltate (Fried New Potatoes). See recipe on page 293.

Torta di Mele alla Fiorentina

APPLE CAKE, FLORENTINE STYLE

This is Zoe's favorite dessert. She's very nice to me whenever I bake it.

1 lemon, at room temperature

5 large Golden Delicious apples

$1/2$ cup (1 stick) unsalted butter, softened

1 cup sugar

3 jumbo eggs

1 cup unbleached all-purpose flour, sifted

1 teaspoon baking powder

$1/4$ teaspoon salt

3 tablespoons pine nuts

6 tablespoons dark raisins

Unsalted butter for greasing pan (at room temperature)

1 tablespoon sugar for dusting pan

1. Preheat oven to 350 degrees. Finely grate entire lemon peel for zest, and set aside in a small dish. Halve lemon horizontally, remove pits, and squeeze juice into a large bowl.

2. Peel apples, cut in half lengthways, and remove cores. Cut halves, still lengthways, into paper-thin slices. Place apple slices in bowl with lemon juice, mix well (lemon juice keeps the apples from turning brown), and set aside.

3. In another large bowl, using an electric mixer, cream $1/2$ cup butter with cup of sugar. Add one egg at a time, mixing after each addition. Add flour, baking powder, and salt, and beat for 3 minutes with an electric mixer. Add lemon zest, pine nuts, and raisins; using a wooden spoon, mix in well.

4. Grease a 10- or 11-inch springform pan with butter, and dust lightly with sugar. Pour batter into pan, and level with a rubber spatula. Top with sliced apples, pressing gently, leaving a $1/2$-inch border of batter from circumference of pan. Don't bother arranging apples aesthetically; the batter is going to rise up and pretty much cover them. Bake for 45 minutes, or until a baking pin inserted into the center comes out clean.

Chapter 11

YOU TALKIN' TO ME?

In 1981, we celebrated Andrea's first communion with a dinner for twenty friends and relatives at the trattoria, which was closed on Sundays. To give ourselves a break, we decided not to do the cooking. The meal's centerpiece was a galantine of chicken that Giuliano, somewhat to my surprise, purchased from a local *pizzicheria* run by two beefy brothers, Fabrizio and Rinaldo Ugolini.

The Ugolinis were the self-proclaimed culinary connoisseurs of the neighborhood, jealously guarding their gastronomic turf against all contenders. Their shop was stocked with a mouthwatering array of exotic cheeses, prosciuttos, salamis, smoked meats, and charcuterie—all of it of the highest quality. They never tired of singing their own praises, carrying on as they proffered savory samples to waiting customers: "Ah yes, *la signora* has made an excellent choice, certainly much better than where you've been shopping up to now [histrionic wink]. Didn't you know that only the Ugolinis carry first-rate merchandise in Florence . . . ."

Bawdy remarks and double entendres were another specialty of the brothers. God forbid a young housewife should be foolish enough to request some spicy sausage. They'd barrage her with salacious banter until she rushed out of the shop, cheeks blazing, the Ugolinis' hearty guffaws echoing in her reddened ears.

We never questioned their exalted status, but, shortly after we opened, Giuliano and I heard through the grapevine that the Ugolinis doubted our ability to produce first-rate fare at Trattoria Garga. "After all," Fabrizio had sneered to one of our customers (who, of course, immediately told us), "Giuliano's just a butcher, and *she* is a foreigner."

Soon after, they came in for dinner, during which they dissected every course with thinly disguised disdain, though they left nothing uneaten. Then, slowly rising from their seats like a pair of elephants departing a watering hole, they lumbered out, barely squeezing through our tiny corridor. Passing me at the door, Rinaldo muttered, "*Può andare*" (it'll do).

Two weeks after Andrea's party, Giuliano stopped by the Ugolinis' shop for some prosciutto. Like royalty, my husband never carries money or pays a bill at point of purchase. When Giuliano asked for the prosciutto, Fabrizio snidely remarked, "When are you paying me for the galantine?" Giuliano took umbrage, Fabrizio brandished a carving knife, and angry words were exchanged: "You got a problem? No, you got a problem?" Abandoning waiting customers, Fabrizio and Rinaldo invited Giuliano to take it outside. As they advanced menacingly towards him, Giuliano—with no hope of victory against this brawny duo—bravely charged them, slipped on a manhole cover and badly gashed his head. The Ugolinis, laughing uproariously, left him there bleeding profusely, returned to their store, and resumed slicing salami. Giuliano, dazed, picked himself up and stumbled to a nearby hospital, where he required seven stitches. I only found out what happened because the local streetwalker rushed over to tell me.

Injured or not, he still had to work at the restaurant that evening, not only through dinner but well into the night. We were preparing for our first big catering job the next day, a wedding. Returning home at four in the morning, tiptoeing in pitch darkness for fear of waking Zoe, Giuliano didn't see that Andrea had left his new racing bicycle in the hallway. He went flying over it and crashed heavily to the floor, fracturing his toe and further bruising his already battered body. Zoe was, of course, awakened.

With only a few hours of sleep, we rushed to the wedding early the next morning—groceries, pots, pans, and cooking utensils piled onto my lap and strapped to the roof of our little Fiat. The "young couple" (she was thirty-four, he forty-five) had been engaged for fourteen years! The groom's domineering mother, whose tyrannical interference in her son's life put even Zoe's in the shade, had until then successfully opposed the marriage. We had to be crazy to take on a catering job. The restaurant was open six days a week for lunch and dinner, we had almost no staff, and we were raising two little children. But the bride and groom were loyal customers. They'd begged us to do it, and Giuliano and I could never resist a challenge.

The party was held at the bride's family estate, a sprawling fifteenth-century villa with at least twenty rooms. Poor Giuliano, bruised and bandaged, limped forlornly into the rustic kitchen—an enormous stone-walled room with a walk-in fireplace, a wood-burning stove against one wall, a marble sink against another, and a big wooden table in the center. We were introduced to three farm wives who worked on the estate; they would be doing the serving and washing up.

As I began unpacking our supplies, I was horrified to realize I'd forgotten the sauce for our featured entrée, herbed lemon chicken. I raced into the villa's adjoining fields to forage for wild herbs to improvise a new sauce. I'll never know to this day exactly what herbs I found; they were green, aromatic, and evidently comestible. At least the sheep seemed to be grazing on them with no ill effects.

It was a magnificent day. The wedding ceremony was held in a small chapel, from which the bride and groom emerged into a sunlit garden. As soon as they were congratulated by all the guests, it was time to eat. Everything went smoothly. Trays of our signature Insalata del Garga, were passed around, along with Crostini Piccanti and plates of prosciutto with melon. The guests raved about our homemade tagliatelle with sausage and ricotta, and the uniquely herbed sauce for the chicken was delicious.

We worked for hours without any time for a break. Later, desperate to pee, I set out in search of facilities. Wandering through a labyrinth of rooms—including a chapel where a wooden statue of Christ was laid out in a coffin (in the dark, I momentarily panicked, convinced I'd encountered a corpse)—I was unable to locate the loo. Finally, I couldn't wait any longer. Again, I hurried outside to the fields and peed behind a hedge, narrowly escaping detection by guests who'd come out for a garden stroll.

Traumatized with exhaustion, Giuliano and I swore we'd never take another catering job. The couple, Emanuele and Caterina Vittorini, moved in with his mother. Their marriage broke up after six months.

Crostini Piccanti

LITTLE TOASTS WITH SPICY GARLIC AND TOMATO SAUCE

$1/4$ cup extra-virgin olive oil

2 garlic cloves, very finely chopped

$1\,1/2$ pounds ripe tomatoes

$1/4$ teaspoon cracked red pepper

$1/2$ teaspoon salt

4 large slices ($1/2$-inch thick) Tuscan or sourdough bread

2 tablespoons fresh parsley leaves, very finely chopped

1. Pour oil into a skillet, add garlic, turn heat to medium, and sauté until golden.

2. Squeeze tomatoes with your hands into oil and garlic. Add cracked red pepper, and cook on high heat, covered, for 5 minutes.

3, Uncover, mash tomatoes with a fork, add salt, and continue cooking on high heat for another 5 minutes.

4. Cut bread slices in half, and toast on both sides. Place toasted bread on a serving dish (or individual plates), spoon sauce on top, and sprinkle with parsley.

FETTUCCINE, SHEPHERD'S STYLE

NOTE If preparing fresh tagliatelle (see Pasta Fresca recipe, for 4, on page 228), do that first. When dough is rolled out thin, dust well with flour, roll into a very loose log, and cut into $1/4$-inch strips. Unravel strips, and place on a linen cloth that is sprinkled with flour.

$1/2$ cup extra-virgin olive oil

5 $1/2$ ounces spicy Neapolitan sausage or pepperoni, cut into $1/8$-inch slices

1 tablespoon kosher salt

14 ounces fettuccine

16 large fresh basil leaves

3 $1/2$ ounces aged ricotta, sliced into flakes

1. Fill a large stockpot with 3 quarts of water, and bring to a boil. While waiting for water to boil, heat oil to sizzling in a large skillet, add sausage slices, and remove immediately from heat. Set aside.

2. When water is boiling, add kosher salt, toss in fettuccine, and cook until *al dente*. Lightly drain, add pasta to skillet with oil and sausage, and toss with tongs.

3. Transfer to a warm serving dish, and garnish with basil leaves and ricotta flakes.

Petto di Pollo alle Erbe e Limone SERVES 4

BONELESS CHICKEN BREASTS
WITH FRESH HERBS AND LEMON

4 boneless chicken-breast fillets ($^1/_4$ pound each)

Flour for dredging

$^1/_4$ pound (1 stick) unsalted butter

Salt

1 teaspoon fresh thyme leaves, very finely chopped

$^1/_2$ teaspoon fresh sage leaves, very finely chopped

$^1/_2$ teaspoon fresh rosemary leaves, very finely chopped

$^1/_2$ teaspoon fennel seeds, very finely chopped

Juice of 2 lemons

1 tablespoon fresh parsley leaves, very finely chopped

Lemons for garnish

1. Wash chicken fillets, pat dry, and dredge in flour.

2. Melt half of the butter in a heavy skillet, and brown chicken on high heat, 5 minutes on each side. Move chicken around pan with a fork while cooking.

3. Salt fillets, and add thyme, sage, rosemary, and fennel. Brown another 2 minutes, and add lemon juice. Turn off heat, and add remaining butter, stirring for 1 minute. Sprinkle parsley on chicken, and serve on plates garnished with lemon slices.

Chapter 12

VIA DELLE BOMBARDE REDUX

By 1982, Trattoria Garga had a loyal clientele, and though we were still heavily in debt, business was good. We were gaining confidence as restaurateurs, and I was learning to stand up to the chauvinistic arrogance of Florentines, who openly doubted the culinary competence of a Canadian. Ever sensitive to criticism, I devoted many hours to boning up on Florentine cuisine, reading everything I could get my hands on. My diligence was rewarded one night when a particularly arrogant customer tried to trip me up with the challenge: "If you know so much, prepare me a *cibreo*." Having recently come across this obscure, and rather hideous-sounding, fricassee in my studies, I was able to snap right back: "I will, if you can get me a rooster's cockscomb, testicles, and liver!"

As I feverishly studied indigenous recipes, Giuliano continued to search the city's markets for exotic new foods. His delight was to create recipes—and ingredient combinations—unknown, at the time, in Florentine restaurants. He started buying smoked mozzarella to serve atop toast drizzled with anchovy sauce; nuanced our zucchini salad with truffle oil (when noted Berkeley chef Alice Waters came in for lunch one day, he gave her a bottle of it to try); grilled red Trevisan lettuce and topped it with ground walnut sauce; and capped grilled squid with porcini mushrooms. Instead of cooking the traditional black cabbage in soup, he sautéed it crisp with garlic and oil over a very high flame and served it mixed with spaghetti. And on a fishing trip, he discovered bottarga (cured grey mullet roe) and began grating it on fresh white cannelloni beans and raw fish carpaccio.

Culinary inventiveness revived the creative spirit in Giuliano. As of old, he began inviting fellow artists in for painting parties that began when the restaurant closed at 11:30. We'd clear off the tables and paint till 4 A.M., with arias blaring and wine flowing; one night I absentmindedly drank my paint water. We had lots of art supplies on hand, which we shared with everyone. I did mostly portraits or still-life paintings in tempera on large sheets of drawing paper, but Giuliano and many of the others simply appropriated the trattoria's white linen

Sharon creating a mural at Trattoria Garga

tablecloths for canvases. They were supplied by a service and picked up in sacks once a week. Luckily, the company never counted them.

I tended to be dissatisfied with everything I did, often tearing up my creations. Giuliano, on the other hand, would hang up and exclaim over every piece of work he produced, eventually framing thirty of his tablecloth paintings and displaying them at a local gallery. In a precise hand, they depicted a variety of scenes—fields of flowers populated by tiny figures underneath the trees; a little boy in a striped T-shirt holding a big fish; tiny people, once again, climbing towards a hilltop cathedral. Later, he went through a period of painting big, happy figures in strong primary colors, which I especially loved. They gave me such a joyful feeling.

These were exciting times. After years stuck at home with Zoe, it was great being out among people again. Though we were working very hard, the business was engaging . . . and I was painting again. Zoe, however, never ceased complaining. When I'd dress up at night to work as hostess at the trattoria, she'd act as if I was tarting up for a night on the town. We'd never told her about Giuliano's gambling debts, which still dominated our lives. One day, after a harrowing morning at the bank, trying in vain to borrow desperately needed

Sharon, Giuliano, and some restaurant staff in front of Trattoria Garga (painting is Giuliano's)

funds, I was beside myself with exhaustion and anxiety. When she began carping at me, I blurted out the truth.

"How you exaggerate," she retorted accusingly. "My husband played cards every night, too, just like Giuliano. He never lost any money."

I had sense enough not to argue that that had no bearing on our situation, or to suggest that he'd probably lost plenty (no use defaming the dead), but I continued to assure her that Giuliano had indeed lost a fortune.

"If that was true," she insisted, "he certainly would have told his own mother." And that was the end of it. She'd hear no more.

Zoe never mentioned the subject again, nor—as far as I know—confronted Giuliano about it. I think she knew I was telling the truth but didn't want to think about it or acknowledge, even to herself, that it had happened. For a few weeks, she ceased her daily litany of complaints and stopped insinuating I was going to work just for the fun of it. But things soon returned to normal. It's hard to break the habit of a lifetime.

At about this time, I made a trip back to Canada with the boys to visit my mother, who was struggling with emphysema. I was very touched when my old traveling companion, Andrea, heard from her parents that I was in town and came to see me, making a special trip from Toronto. The last time I'd seen her was in Florence, where she had come to visit shortly after my son, Andrea, was born. As with my mother and grandmother, Zoe had made it difficult for me to spend time alone with Andrea and done nothing to make her feel welcome.

"Why do you have to have friends visit?" she'd asked me. "Aren't you happy enough with your husband?"

Though thrilled to see Andrea, I'd been torn between pleasing my family and entertaining her. Though she didn't say anything, I could tell she was critical of my whole situation. We'd parted on strained terms. I knew I'd been judged and found wanting, and I felt guilty that I hadn't managed to be more hospitable.

Now, years later in Winnipeg, we were able to laugh about the harsh judgments and insecurity of our youth. The estrangement I had built up in my mind melted away, and we chatted happily about our husbands and children. It was tremendously consoling to have an old friend accompany me to the hospital to see Mummy. We talked about the time she'd visited in Florence and agreed it had been a misunderstanding with faults on both sides. Not realizing the pressures I'd been under, she'd found me distant and thought I didn't really want her company.

It made me realize how easily we can become alienated from friends, and how little it often takes to repair a rift. If I hadn't seen her again, we both might have gone through life with bad feelings towards each other.

Mummy died a year later. She had often talked about spending her old age in Tuscany. Sadly, she had waited too long to realize that dream. Though I returned to Winnipeg the last month of her life, this time leaving the boys with Giuliano and Zoe, I've always felt guilty that Karen—though she never complained—had to cope with Mummy's long illness alone (as well as with our aging grandmother), guilty that I hadn't done more to help Mummy emigrate to Italy earlier, guilty and sad that she had missed so much of my adult life and barely knew her grandchildren. Familial guilt is the unavoidable lot of expatriates.

Calamaro Grigliato con
Cappella di Fungo Porcino

GRILLED SQUID TOPPED WITH PORCINI MUSHROOM CAP

$1/4$ cup extra-virgin olive oil

Juice of 1 lemon

1 clove garlic, very finely chopped

1 teaspoon salt

I pound squid (cleaned)

Extra-virgin olive oil

4 porcini mushroom caps, 4 inches in diameter
(portobello mushrooms can also be used)

1 tablespoon finely chopped fresh parsley

1. In a small bowl, mix $1/4$ cup oil, lemon juice, garlic, and salt. Set aside.

2. Cut squid bodies open (leaving tentacles attached) to make flat pieces. Holding your knife almost parallel to your work surface (at a 30-degree angle), score inner side of flattened squid in a cross-hatch pattern (do not cut all the way through). Pat squid dry.

3. Lightly coat grill pan with oil. Place pan over moderately high heat until oil is hot but not smoking. Grill squid (in batches if necessary), crosshatched sides down first, turning once, until just cooked through (about 2 minutes; squid will curl up as it cooks). Transfer grilled squid to a cutting board, and cover to keep warm.

4. Brush mushroom caps lightly with oil. Once again, place lightly oiled grill pan over moderately high heat until oil is hot but not smoking. Grill mushroom caps for 2 minutes on each side.

5. Place squid on a warm serving platter, drizzle with a bit of the oil/lemon juice mixture, top with mushroom caps, and drizzle with remaining mixture. Sprinkle with parsley.

SPAGHETTINI WITH BLACK CABBAGE

NOTE Black cabbage is also called elephant kale or California kale.

12 large black cabbage leaves
2 cloves garlic
$1/2$ cup extra-virgin olive oil
$1/4$ teaspoon cracked red pepper
1 tablespoon kosher salt
$3/4$ pound spaghettini
Salt

1. Put up 3 quarts of water to boil in a large stockpot. Wash cabbage, and remove central stalk. Dry well. Rip each leaf into 2 or 3 pieces.

2. Slice garlic cloves into $1/8$-inch pieces. Pour oil into a large skillet, toss in garlic, and sauté on medium heat until golden.

3. Add cabbage leaves to skillet, turn heat to high, and sauté for 3 to 4 minutes, until crisp. Add cracked red pepper, and stir. Immediately remove skillet from heat.

4. When water is boiling, add 1 tablespoon kosher salt, and cook spaghettini until *al dente*. Drain pasta well, transfer to skillet with cabbage, toss with tongs, and salt to taste. Sauté for 1 minute over high heat.

Spaghettini alla Bottarga di Muggine

SERVES 4

SPAGHETTINI WITH MULLET ROE

3 $\frac{1}{2}$ ounces Sardinian bottarga (it comes in a stick form)

$\frac{1}{2}$ cup extra-virgin olive oil

1 tablespoon kosher salt

$\frac{3}{4}$ pound spaghettini

8 fresh basil leaves

1. Put up 3 quarts of water to boil in a large stockpot. Grate bottarga with a box grater on the medium-fine side.

2. Pour oil into a large skillet, and add $\frac{1}{2}$ the bottarga. Add $\frac{1}{4}$ cup of the boiling water to skillet. Stir well, and cook over medium heat for 1 minute.

3. Add kosher salt to boiling water in stockpot, and cook spaghettini until *al dente*. Drain pasta well, transfer to skillet with bottarga, toss with tongs, and sauté for 1 minute over high heat.

4. Place in a warm serving dish, and top with remaining grated bottarga and basil leaves.

Chapter **13**

HEAVEN HELP US

One day in 1983, a Health Department inspector visited the restaurant and gave us some bad news: To stay open, we had to do major renovations—to the tune of ten million lire (about $16,000). Once again, we needed to borrow money. Signor Edoardo del Ponte, a distinguished elderly gentleman who'd known Giuliano as a boy, owned a small private bank. He'd been a loyal customer, first at the butcher shop (when I'd delivered meat to their house, his lovely wife, Liliana, had always invited me in for coffee) and, later, at Trattoria Garga.

I don't think anyone likes asking for money. Giuliano assured me it would be better if I approached Signor del Ponte for the loan. Gathering my courage, I made my way to his bank, where he ushered me into a plush office. We made some small talk, mainly about Winnipeg, where he'd once done some business with the Grain Board. Then I explained our situation. Edoardo asked how much money I needed, had me sign a few papers, and picked up the phone. In a flash, his assistant came into the office with an envelope containing the full amount in cash. The whole transaction had lasted about fifteen minutes. Escorting me out of his office, Signor del Ponte looked me directly in the eyes and said, "What a lucky man little Giuliano turned out to be." I'll never forget his kindness.

We hired contractors, who said they'd need two weeks to complete the work... two weeks during which the restaurant would have to be closed.

To occupy himself during this stressful time—and keep an eye on the progress of the renovation—Giuliano began chiseling away at a plaster wall, revealing beautiful ancient brickwork in an arched pattern. Two months later, he was long done with this project, the workmen were still on the job, and the restaurant remained closed. Fraught with anxiety, we were both sleeping badly. Creditors were hounding us, and we were down to our last 50,000 lire (about $30).

On a glorious sunny day shortly before Easter, trying to forget our troubles, we took a long walk through the Boboli Gardens. We sat down on the grass, and I unpacked a picnic lunch of bread, mortadella, and cheese. But this meager fare only served to whet Giuliano's appetite.

"You know what we're going to do, *Nannina*," he said. "Let's blow our last 50,000 lire on a steak dinner."

We walked to a restaurant just outside the fortification walls above San Niccolò (though it's in town, this area is countryside) and ordered up a feast—angelhair pasta with wild porcini mushrooms, a thick grilled Florentine steak big enough for four, stewed artichokes, and panna cotta with fresh berries—and we went through two bottles of Chianti Classico. Clinking wine glasses, Giuliano said, "*Qualche santo ci sarà*" (there will be help from heaven).

After lunch, Giuliano visited his cousin, Valentino, who owned a leather factory in Ponte a Greve and was doing very well. Hearing about our plight, he surprised us by offering Giuliano a sizable loan. The next day, the contractors finished the renovations.

After the contractors left, it took a few days to clean up, after which business immediately flourished. While the work was being done, we had completely changed our décor. Up came the burgundy carpeting, revealing 1920s-style tile floors. We'd done away with the embroidered tablecloths and crystal glassware, and silk lampshades had been replaced with white glass and brass. Customers loved our new minimalist look.

Carciofi al Tegame

STEWED ARTICHOKES

4 artichokes (make sure they're firm; the firmer the better)

Juice of $\frac{1}{2}$ lemon

$\frac{1}{2}$ cup extra-virgin olive oil

2 cloves garlic, finely chopped

$\frac{1}{4}$ teaspoon cracked red pepper

4 ripe tomatoes, cut into wedges (off-season, substitute a cup of canned Italian plum tomatoes)

1 tablespoon finely chopped fresh parsley leaves

1. Prepare artichokes by stripping off tough outer leaves. Slice off tops, where leaves are darker in color, and trim off bitter outer part of stems with a paring knife; discard these parts.

2. Cut artichokes in half, lengthways. If any of them has a hairy part inside (the choke), gently remove it with the point of a paring knife. Slice artichokes vertically into $\frac{1}{2}$-inch wedges, making sure you include some of the heart in each wedge (otherwise your wedges will separate into leaves). Immediately put wedges into a bowl of cold water mixed with lemon juice. Set aside.

3. Pour oil into a large saucepan (not an iron one, which will turn artichokes brown), add garlic, and sauté on medium heat until golden. Drain artichokes, and add to pan. Sprinkle evenly with cracked red pepper, cover saucepan, and cook on medium heat for 10 minutes.

4. Add tomatoes, and cook for another 10 minutes. Sprinkle with parsley, and serve.

PANNA COTTA WITH STRAWBERRY SAUCE

4 teaspoons unflavored gelatin

1/8 cup cold water

1 quart heavy cream

1 teaspoon pure vanilla extract

1/2 cup sugar

1. Place gelatin in a small bowl with 1/8 cup cold water, mix well, and set aside.

2. Pour cream into a heavy saucepan. Add vanilla and sugar, and turn heat to medium-high, stirring frequently with a wooden spoon. When cream comes to a boil, remove it from heat, and stir in gelatin.

3. Pour equal amounts of mixture into 8 to 10 custard cups or ramekins (depending on their size), and refrigerate for at least 2 hours. While custard is chilling, make strawberry sauce.

FOR THE STRAWBERRY SAUCE:

1 pound strawberries, halved

1/2 cup sugar

Finely grated zest and juice of 1 lemon

1. Put strawberries into a saucepan, mix in sugar, lemon zest, and lemon juice. Stirring with a wooden spoon, bring to a boil over medium heat; then, still stirring, lower heat, and simmer for 5 minutes.

2. Pass sauce through a sieve, using back of a spoon to press out all juice (about 1/2 cup of pulp will remain). Discard pulp, and refrigerate sauce.

TO SERVE:

1. Fill a bowl with an inch of hot water. Take one custard cup at a time, run a small knife around edge, set cup in hot water to further loosen it, then turn out custard onto an individual serving plate. Spoon strawberry sauce over each, and serve.

Chapter 14

PUTTO AMONG THE PIGEONS

By the mid-eighties, we were getting good press and continuing to develop exciting new dishes. Bobby, a customer from California, got Giuliano excited about avocados, which, imported from Israel, had recently been introduced in Italy. We added them to our signature salad and used them to embellish our veal in cognac-cream sauce. We'd been written up in *Travel & Leisure*, customers had begun coming in with various guidebooks in hand that had recommended us, and we'd hosted a dinner for the opening of Polimoda, a design school affiliated with the Fashion Institute of New York (American ambassador Maxwell Rabb was the guest of honor). Everyone crowded into our tiny eatery, while Italian policemen and C.I.A. agents stood vigil outside.

On winter Sundays, Giuliano began a ritual of taking Andrea and Alessandro on afternoon walks culminating at the Café Rivoire. On arrival, he'd give the boys money to buy corn to feed the pigeons, order an apéritivo, and sit reading his paper. It was Alessandro's fervent dream to actually catch one of these birds.

One Sunday, Giuliano, chatting with friends at the café, heard a commotion nearby. People were screaming in horror. Parting the crowd, Alessandro, who looked like a little blond *putto* (cherub) in his camel's hair coat, entered the Rivoire drenched head to toe in blood. Giuliano's heart sank, but Alessandro was exultant. "*Babbo*," he yelled

Alessandro (*putto* among the pigeons) in the Piazza della Signoria

excitedly, "I caught one!" Against all odds, he'd picked the poor bird up by both feet and, in his excitement, inadvertently pulled it in half. Everyone was appalled, but our heartless boys found the whole thing hilarious.

Well, after all, Giuliano was a butcher, and his sons were well acquainted with the visceral side of life. If he opened a chicken when the boys were around, he'd display its glistening innards to them and patiently explain how the state of these organs indicated the freshness of the fowl. And they were often on hand when he'd halve an entire lamb with a few precise blows of his knife. As a special treat for them, he'd remove the tiny sweetbreads, and sauté them quickly in butter and lemon.

Both boys, by this time, were showing a lot of interest in the restaurant. Andrea, coming in daily from school for lunch, would don an apron and help clear tables. A mini-Garga, he'd imitate his father, mingling with customers and telling them knock-knock jokes. Little Alessandro, age four, was allowed to come for lunch every Saturday. Mysteriously, the pigeon population outside the restaurant seemed to increase dramatically whenever he was on the premises. We soon discovered he was luring them by strewing fistfuls of our expensive pinoli (pine nuts) on the sidewalk!

Alessandro, Sharon, and Andrea. Courtesy of Nancy Rica Schiff

Insalata del Garga

TRATTORIA GARGA
SIGNATURE SALAD

4 small bunches arugula

4 small ripe tomatoes

4 stalks hearts of palm (available in cans, packed in water)

2 medium avocados

Juice of 1 lemon

Salt

$1/4$ cup extra-virgin olive oil

$1/4$ pound fresh Parmigiano Reggiano

1 ounce pine nuts

NOTE As you prepare items in Step 1, keep them separate.

1. Wash and dry arugula, and tear into small pieces. Cut tomatoes into approximately $1/2$-inch cubes. Slice hearts of palm crosswise into $1/2$-inch rounds. Slice avocados into $1/4$-inch wedges, and place in a small bowl; add lemon juice.

2. Arrange arugula on a large serving platter. Top with tomatoes, leaving a border of arugula. Layer next with hearts of palm, then avocado wedges. Salt to taste, and drizzle with oil.

3. With a sharp paring knife, slice Parmigiano into paper-thin shavings. Distribute Parmigiano shavings and pine nuts on top of salad.

NOTE Obviously, if you prefer, you can create individual portions.

Scaloppine di Vitella all'Avocado

VEAL CUTLET WITH AVOCADO AND TRUFFLE CREAM

4 pieces boneless veal loin, 4 $^1/_2$ ounces each

4 tablespoons ($^1/_2$ stick) unsalted butter

Salt

2 tablespoons (1 ounce) cognac or brandy

1 cup heavy cream

1 teaspoon white truffle oil

1 large ripe avocado, halved lengthways and carefully pitted and peeled (try to keep it intact)

1. Place veal slices on a flat surface, sprinkle very lightly with water, cover with plastic wrap, and pound to $^1/_4$-inch thickness with a smooth-surfaced meat mallet.

2. On high heat, melt butter in a large, heavy skillet, and sauté veal for 3 minutes. Salt to taste, turn, and sauté 3 minutes on other side, once again salting to taste.

3. Remove skillet from heat, carefully add cognac, return skillet to heat, and ignite with a kitchen match to flambé. Cook until flame subsides.

4. Once again, remove skillet from heat, add cream and oil, return skillet to high heat, and cook for 2 more minutes.

5. Cut avocado into neat $^1/_4$-inch slices. Place a slice of veal on each plate, arrange avocado slices on top, and spoon sauce over each serving.

Animelle di Vitella
al Burro e Limone

VEAL SWEETBREADS
WITH LEMON AND BUTTER

2 veal sweetbreads (from the heart)

Flour for dredging

$\frac{1}{2}$ stick unsalted butter

Salt

Juice of 2 lemons

1 tablespoon parsley, very finely chopped

1. Clean sweetbreads by carefully pulling off all tough and fibrous skin.

2. Place sweetbreads in a dish of cold water for 10 minutes or more. Remove from water, dry carefully, and slice into $\frac{1}{2}$-inch cubes

3. Dredge cubes in flour, dusting off excess.

4. Melt butter in a large skillet. Turn heat to high. When butter turns a nutty brown color, add sweetbreads.

5. Sauté sweetbreads over high heat for 8 to 10 minutes, turning constantly until they're nicely browned on all sides. Salt to taste.

6. Add lemon juice, and sauté for 1 minute. Place in a serving dish, sprinkle with parsley, and serve immediately.

Fegato di Vitella alla Salvia SERVES 4

CALF'S LIVER WITH SAGE

4 slices calf's liver, $1/_2$-inch thick

Flour for dredging

$1/_2$ cup extra-virgin olive oil

4 whole cloves garlic, with jackets on

Salt

Freshly ground black pepper

8 large sage leaves

1. Dredge liver in flour, dusting off excess.

2. Pour oil into a large skillet, and heat until smoking. Add liver to pan, and turn down heat to medium. Add garlic cloves. Cook liver for 5 minutes on one side, and season with salt and pepper.

3. Turn over, season other side with salt and pepper, and place 2 sage leaves and a clove of garlic on each slice of liver. Cook for 4 minutes. Leave sage leaves and garlic in pan; remove liver, and cover to keep warm.

4. Sauté sage leaves and garlic for 1 minute more. Garnish each slice of liver with 2 sage leaves and a garlic clove, and pour pan juices over them.

Chapter 15

THE YEAR OF
THE SUNFLOWER

By 1987, after eight years as restaurateurs, we were a resounding success, popular with the designers, models, and fashion-magazine editors who flock to Florence for its biannual fashion shows. Alessandro Pucci (son of designer Emilio) and his sister, Laudomia, became regulars and close friends. One night they turned up with Paloma Picasso, who, from then on, has dined with us whenever she's in town. And they introduced us to Donna Karan, who has also continued to frequent Trattoria Garga—on one visit bringing Barbra Streisand!

But glitterati notwithstanding, with only twenty-five tables, we still weren't making enough money. When we heard that a neighboring art gallery, housed in a fourteenth-century palazzo, was going out of business, we made a deal to rent the space. Once again, we spent a fortune we didn't have renovating. Along with talented artist friends, we adorned every square inch of the walls with incredible frescoes, from a lovely floral still life painted by Princess Fiona Corsini to Giuliano's portrait of himself as Don Quixote.

As if there wasn't enough work running one restaurant while remodeling another, Giuliano chose this time to plant a block-long garden along the embankment of the Arno. *Il Giardino del Garga,*" which has since generated dozens of articles in local magazines and newspapers, solidified Giuliano's reputation as Florence's reigning eccentric. Bare-chested, his loins draped in a toga fashioned from a white table-

Giuliano, in tablecloth toga, tending his Arno garden

cloth, he'd march through town every afternoon, stopping en route to his Arno garden to down an apéritivo at the posh Harry's Bar. Alessandro, walking home with school friends one day, spied his father in this bizarre get-up and crossed the street to avoid him.

Sometimes, Harry's would lower a martini in a basket down to Giuliano as he worked away tilling soil and planting seeds. Giuliano would drink it down and return the basket filled with fresh mint for their juleps along with his empty glass.

The garden was glorious. Giuliano planted hundreds of brilliant yellow sunflowers, as well as roses, oleanders, weeping willows, and geraniums. And he's kept it up every year since, despite winter floods and the disapprobation of city authorities, who repeatedly levy fines and cut down his plantings with chain saws. Spring through fall, one can see him daily at dusk, standing on the Carraia Bridge admiring the fruits of his labor by the light of the setting sun.

The new Trattoria Garga opened in September 1988 and immediately began doing a bang-up business. We had tripled our seating capacity and created a glassed-in exhibition kitchen fronting a cozy warren of candlelit dining rooms under vaulted ceilings. After operating for so long in cramped quarters, we felt like we were working in a football field. For the first time ever, we had a real staff, with four actual

Giuliano walking in
Arno garden

waiters and three sous-chefs working alongside Giuliano. And there
was an actual coatroom, replacing our old rickety stand that frequently
toppled over. I had become very adept at leaping across the room to
catch it before it fell on customers. Giuliano bought a beautiful antique marble well from a local dealer and placed it in the central dining area.

As our renown grew, more and more celebrities—many of them
in Florence for fashion events—found their way to our door, among
others, Matt Dillon, Robin Williams, Harrison Ford, Billy Joel, Bette
Midler, Steve Martin, Mel Brooks and Anne Bancroft, even Oprah. One
evening, an hour before opening time, two policemen came in to check
the restaurant for security. When we inquired why they were doing this,
they looked puzzled. "Didn't you know that the Queen of Denmark
[Margrethe II], and her husband [Prince Henrik], are dining here
tonight?" asked one. We didn't; the reservation had been in the name of

Interior of Trattoria Garga, with antique well

a regular customer. As soon as the last diner had gone that evening, I rushed to the phone to tell my grandmother. I knew she'd be thrilled. How I wished Mummy was alive to share in the excitement.

Andrea, who loves food and wine and has a great flair for cooking, now begged us to take him straight into the business after high school. But we insisted he go to college first. Then, on Andrea's eighteenth birthday, while washing dishes, I broke a ceramic tray and cut two tendons in my left hand, requiring a cast for three months. With me out of commission, Andrea pressed his case, and we finally gave in.

Giuliano's love affair with the Arno continued. In 1990, he mounted a major show of river-themed paintings, and both he and Alessandro spent many leisurely hours gardening on the banks and fishing from our rowboat. I'd send them off in the morning with a big picnic basket filled with panzanella (bread salad), cold frittata, and watermelon.

One afternoon, they proudly presented me with an immense carp that had, miraculously, survived the ten-minute drive home. Reluctant to cook anything drawn from the muddy waters of the Arno, I filled our bathtub with water and tossed him in; he took up the entire tub. Our cat, Foufie, considering himself directly concerned in any household proceeding involving fish, had followed me into the bathroom. Shooing him out with some difficulty, I shut the door on the problem.

I was alerted that Zoe had returned from shopping by a shrill screech emanating from the bathroom. Racing to explain, I found her wearily shaking her head, muttering, "Madonnina Santa" (Holy Mother of God)! Now what have they brought home for me to take care of?"

The next morning, my fish was still alive, if a little sluggish. I stuffed him into a big plastic garbage bag and hailed a taxi to the banks of the Arno. In the rear-view mirror, I could see the driver glancing suspiciously at my squirming bundle. What must he have thought when he saw me empty it into the river? I stood watching on the embankment for ten minutes. The carp lay on his side, then suddenly came alive and slithered off. I felt great. I had saved a life.

Spaghettini all'Astice

THIN SPAGHETTI WITH LOBSTER

This is designer Donna Karan's favorite Garga creation; she orders it whenever she comes in.

NOTE Purchase lobsters as close to cooking time as possible, and ask your fishmonger to divide them in half, lengthways.

2 cloves garlic, finely chopped

2 tablespoons extra-virgin olive oil

1 1/2 pounds ripe tomatoes, cut in quarters

1/4 teaspoon cracked red pepper

Salt

2 lobsters (1 pound each)

2 tablespoons extra-virgin olive oil

1/4 cup cognac

1 tablespoon kosher salt

14 ounces spaghettini

2 tablespoons chopped fresh parsley leaves

1. In a large, heavy skillet, on high heat, sauté garlic in 2 tablespoons oil until golden.

2. Add tomatoes, cover, and cook for 2 minutes on high heat. Uncover, and squash tomatoes with a fork. Cook uncovered for another 3 minutes, still on high heat. Add cracked red pepper, salt to taste, turn off heat, and set aside.

3. Leaving shells whole, remove tail meat from lobsters, and chop into 3/4-inch pieces. With a meat hammer, crack claws, leaving lobster meat in shells. Put up 3 quarts of water to boil in a large stockpot.

4. In a second large skillet, on high heat, sauté lobster and shells in 2 tablespoons oil for 3 minutes. Remove skillet from heat, carefully add cognac, and return to heat. Ignite very carefully with a kitchen match to flambé. When flame dies down, add tomato sauce from other skillet, and cook for another 3 minutes. Remove shells, and keep them warm in a covered bowl.

5. When water comes to a boil, add 1 tablespoon kosher salt, and cook spaghettini until *al dente*. Drain lightly, transfer to skillet with sauce, and sauté over high heat for 1 minute, moving everything around with tongs to combine ingredients. Serve immediately on warmed plates, topped with lobster shells (aesthetically arranged) and sprinkled with chopped parsley.

Panzanella

TUSCAN BREAD SALAD

This salad has been enjoyed for centuries in Tuscany. Renaissance painter Agnolo Bronzino even wrote a poem in praise of it, from which I quote:

> *Un' insalata de cipolla trita,*
> *Colla porcellanetta e citriuoli,*
> *Vince ogni alio piacer di questa vita,*
> *Considerate un po' s'aggiungessi bâssilico e ruchetta . . .*

A salad with chopped onion,
With wild herbs and cucumbers,
Wins over any other pleasure in this life,
And just think if you added a little basil and arugula . . .

4 slices day-old Tuscan bread
(if unavailable, use a hard-crusted peasant bread)

3 ripe, firm tomatoes, diced into $1/2$-inch cubes

1 cucumber, diced into $1/2$-inch cubes

1 red onion, cut into $1/4$-inch slices

$1/8$ cup red wine vinegar

$3/8$ cup extra-virgin olive oil

Salt

Freshly ground black pepper

12 fresh basil leaves

1. Place bread in a large bowl of very cold water, and let rest for 15 minutes.

2. Take a little bread at a time in your hands, and gently squeeze out excess moisture (bread should appear fluffy). Repeat until all bread is squeezed.

3. Transfer bread to a salad bowl, and add tomatoes, cucumber, and onion. Dress salad with vinegar and oil, adding salt and pepper to taste (an old Florentine saying advises: Salt as someone wise, vinegar as someone parsimonious, and oil as someone crazy). Garnish with basil leaves torn by hand.

Frittata di Fiori e Zucchine

ZUCCHINI AND ZUCCHINI BLOSSOM OMELETTE

16 zucchini blossoms

5 jumbo eggs

$1/4$ cup extra-virgin olive oil

1 small yellow onion, finely chopped

8 small zucchini, sliced into $1/8$-inch coins

$1/2$ teaspoon salt

$1/4$ teaspoon freshly ground black pepper

12 fresh basil leaves

1. Preheat oven to 350 degrees. Remove prickly green leaves from base of each zucchini blossom, and, with your fingers, squash base of flower to flatten it.

2. Beat eggs with a fork until yolks and whites are barely combined. Set aside.

3. Pour oil into an 11-inch cast-iron frying pan. Add onion, and top with zucchini blossoms and zucchini. Cover with a lid, and cook over medium heat for 10 minutes.

4. Remove lid, add salt and pepper, stir well, and cook for another 5 minutes. Pour beaten eggs over zucchini, and cook for 5 minutes over medium heat, lifting cooked edges with a spatula as eggs cook in order to let uncooked egg run under.

5. Place pan in oven for 5 minutes. Remove frittata to a warm serving dish, and garnish with basil leaves.

Chapter 16

GIULIANO FALLS DOWN, ANDREA STEPS UP

La Casa Piu Pazza del Mondo

THE CRAZIEST HOME IN THE WORLD

BY ALESSANDRO GARGANI

This is the story of a family in the author's imagination. Many strange things happen in this family. Dring! Dring! The alarm clock goes off, and another infernal day begins. The daughter-in-law stumbles into the kitchen sleepy-eyed. "Good lord," she mutters. "I have to ring the grocery store. It's seven o' clock." The mother-in-law goes into the grandchildren's room, opens the window wide, and rips off their blankets. Just think, the temperature is 4° this morning! The little boy is furious and begs the mother-in-law to shut the window. The mother-in-law takes off her slipper, and, waving it menacingly, advises the boy to respect the old shoe. The little boy is tired of all this commotion and yells at her to be quiet.

The daughter-in-law comes into the bedroom to try and make him get dressed and go to school. He makes enough lame excuses about not feeling well to convince her to let him stay home. The old cat (the most slipper-beaten cat in the universe) walks into the room. The cat is sleepy, too, and jumps into bed with the little boy.

The mother-in-law goes into the closet and gets her heaviest slipper (the one with cleats and old cat bones stuck to it). She hits the cat with it. Now a normal cat would have had a broken back from such a blow, but not Foufie. He's used to it. He isn't too hurt and only screeches once.

The little boy asks the mother-in-law how she would like it if someone were to do the same thing to her. She replies, "Shut up you big billy goat!" and goes into the kitchen to take it out on the daughter-in-law. The little boy shouts after her: "When that poor old cat dies, I'm going to get a German shepherd, and I want to see if you'll smack THAT."

Eleven-year-old Alessandro's little school composition—which, incidentally, told his teacher considerably more than I wanted her to know about our home life—planted a seed in Giuliano's mind. He became obsessed with the idea of getting a German shepherd puppy. Rallying the troops, he kept asking excitedly, "does everybody want a dog?" The boys, of course, were wildly enthusiastic.

I knew who would end up caring for that dog, but I didn't take the matter seriously enough to register a real protest. Giuliano often spins out fantasies that don't develop. For a while, he'd talked about nothing but moving to South America and opening a restaurant in Bogotá! So I was actually surprised one evening when he marched into our bedroom with a little bulge in his jacket and disingenuously exclaimed, "Look what I got for you!"

Enter Nilde (short for the Wagnerian queen, Brunhilde). Zoe, adamantly antidog, threatened to move into the Monte Domini (a state-run home for aged paupers). Of course, she didn't. And, of course, as predicted, caring for Nilde soon became my responsibility. On the up side: Recognizing an enemy in Zoe, Nilde growled ferociously whenever she tried to enter our bedroom; after almost two decades of marriage, we'd finally managed some privacy. The down side: Nilde gets equally ferocious if Giuliano and I kiss, let alone make love.

Since Zoe refused to have the dog around during the day, Nilde was now my constant companion, accompanying me even to work. One day, I asked Giuliano to stay with the dog for a few hours while I went to see the accountant.

Giuliano loves to roughhouse. He often provokes Nilde and the boys into wild bouts of wrestling, during which Zoe provides a kind of Greek chorus to the pandemonium, screaming, "What is this, a gypsy encampment?" When this is going on, I usually hide in the bathroom to get some quiet.

Left alone with Nilde, Giuliano took her for a walk to his beloved Arno, where he initiated a rowdy game of fetch. With Nilde chasing a stick, they raced up and down the steep cement walls of the embankment, which were slippery from a recent rainstorm. In her excitement, Nilde dashed between Giuliano's legs, sending him reeling down the slope.

It was a gray November day, and no one was walking by the river. Giuliano, in agony, lay immobile and unseen for an hour, thirty feet below street level. Then, by the grace of God, his old friend Marco, driving along the bridge, heard a dog barking wildly and saw someone lying below. He stopped to investigate.

With immense difficulty, Marco somehow managed to get Giuliano up the slope, settle him and Nilde into the car, and drive them to the emergency room. Giuliano's leg was broken in three places. He was put in a cast up to his hip and told to stay in bed for a month.

Andrea stepped into the kitchen in his father's place and managed extremely well. A beautiful adolescent, delicate-looking with blond hair and dreamy blue eyes, Andrea reminds me of Tadzio, from *Death in Venice*. But though he looks fragile, he's no creampuff. With youthful arrogance (like all adolescents, he thought he knew everything), he reveled in being the boss, barking imperious orders at our staff, which did not go over well with them and required a lot of tactful soothing from me. But the customers loved him; they called him "Garghino" (little Garga).

Giuliano felt useless and unneeded for the first time in his life, and, despite our assurances that he was still "the maestro," he became very depressed.

Andrea has always idolized his father, following him around like a faithful puppy and drinking in his every word. Until recently, he'd even sat on Giuliano's lap. Now, he'd not only taken over Giuliano's kitchen, he'd fallen in love with a Swedish textile student named Martina. His father was no longer the center of his life. Usurped by the foreigner, "Tina," whom he irrationally hated, Giuliano was devastated. I remonstrated with him that it was the mother who was supposed to be jealous of girlfriends, but to no avail.

Zoe was thrilled to have Giuliano home. She doted on her incapacitated son, even braving Nilde, who, like Cerberus guarding the underworld, growled savagely whenever she approached her son's room. Scurrying back and forth with bedpans, Zoe would check in on him every ten minutes. If he dozed off, she'd shake his shoulder to inquire, "*Nano, Nano*, are you sleeping?" Needless to say, her unrelenting attentions only increased his irascibility.

To cheer him up, I cooked one of his favorite dishes, which required deboning a capon; stuffing it with veal, sweetbreads, and truffles; and artfully reconstructing it prior to roasting. Enthroned in his wheelchair, Giuliano lifted a gloomy forkful, then launched into a diatribe of criticism, berating my lack of finesse in serving the bird a bit too early, so that the stuffing was slightly less firm than perfection would require. I fantasized about cooking him a risotto with ground glass.

At last, Giuliano's cast came off, and he was able to get around on crutches. Life returned to normal . . . or at least what passed for normal in the Gargani household. But Andrea, eager to assert his independence, moved in with Tina.

Polpettini in Guazzetto

BABY OCTOPUS IN TOMATO BROTH

Andrea loves anything from the sea. This dish frequently appears on our menu when he's in the kitchen.

1 pound cleaned baby octopus

$^3/_4$ pound ripe tomatoes
(or, off-season, the same amount of canned tomatoes)

$^1/_2$ cup extra-virgin olive oil

2 cloves garlic, very finely chopped

2 tablespoons parsley, very finely chopped

$^1/_2$ teaspoon cracked red pepper

$^1/_2$ cup dry white wine

Salt

1. Wash octopus and pat dry.

2. Plunge tomatoes into boiling water, remove from heat, and let sit for 5 minutes. Drain, and under cold running water, remove skins and seeds. Dice into $^1/_2$-inch pieces, and set aside.

3. Place oil, garlic, 1 tablespoon of the parsley, and cracked red pepper in a Dutch oven. Cook over medium heat for 2 minutes.

4. Add octopus and, stirring often, continue to cook on medium heat for 5 minutes.

5. Add wine, and let evaporate for 2 minutes. Add tomatoes, salt to taste, and cook over low heat for 1 hour. Serve sprinkled with the remaining parsley.

Cappone Farcito con
Animelle e Tartufo

ROAST CAPON STUFFED WITH SWEETBREADS AND TRUFFLES

1 deboned capon (about 4 pounds)

$1/4$ pound unsalted butter

10 ounces sweetbreads (from the heart), blanched and cut into $1/8$ inch pieces

1 bay leaf

1 teaspoon cinnamon

10 ounces ground veal

8 ounces finely chopped prosciutto

2 eggs, beaten

$1/2$ cup grated Parmigiano Reggiano

1 small black truffle, diced

$1/4$ cup heavy cream

2 tablespoons brandy

Salt

Parchment paper

1. Preheat oven to 350 degrees. Wash capon, and dry well.

2. Place butter in a large skillet, and melt over medium heat. Add sweetbreads, bay leaf, and cinnamon. Sauté for 5 minutes over high heat, and remove bay leaf.

3. Add veal and prosciutto, and sauté for another 5 minutes, stirring occasionally with a wooden spoon to break up meat. Place mixture in a large bowl, and add eggs, Parmigiano, truffle, heavy cream, brandy, and 1 teaspoon salt. Mix well.

4. Spoon filling into capon, recomposing the shape of the bird. Sew up extremities with butcher's twine (or use skewers) to keep the filling from oozing out.

5. Place capon in a large roasting pan. Rub skin with 2 teaspoons salt, and cover bird with parchment paper. Bake for 2 hours.

6. Remove from pan to carving board and let rest for 20 minutes before serving.

Chapter 17

ARM
WRESTLING

For several years now, editors from *GQ* magazine, including its food editor Alan Richman, had been patronizing Trattoria Garga during Florence fashion shows. In December of 1992, a *GQ* representative asked us to host a special dinner for them in the new year and told us to be sure to look at the January 1993 edition of the magazine. The minute it came out (I'd been haunting the newsstands) I grabbed a copy. It was the issue in which *GQ* announced their Golden Dish awards, worldwide in scope, for the ten best entrées of 1992. The first recipe to appear was our Taglierini del Magnifico, a citrus-scented pasta in cognac-cream sauce! On the evening of the dinner, we were presented with the "golden dish" and received heartwarming congratulations from the *GQ* staff.

The new year also brought us a glowing review in *Gourmet* ("Large oval platters of il magnifico pasta . . . or piquant vigliacca [tomato-sauced tagliatelle] keep sophisticated diners twirling their forks"), with a special bouquet to me ("Mrs. Gargani's cheesecake and chocolate torta both win raves from dessert fans").

Even Japanese magazines had discovered us. For some reason they all wrote up the same dish, spaghetti with artichokes.

Our struggles to succeed were behind us. For Giuliano, this precipitated a midlife crisis. Life was no longer a challenge to him, and he was almost maniacally restless. In addition to putting in long hours at the restaurant, he engaged in a frenzy of painting, worked daily to the point of exhaustion in his Arno garden, and stayed out until all hours carousing with pals.

Because Giuliano was a master butcher, he'd always taken charge of the meat at the trattoria. Whole cows and sheep would arrive at our door, and Giuliano would quarter them by hand, then hoist the sections on his shoulder and carry them to the refrigerator. His swordsmanlike style of butchering was impressive; he seemed to be dueling with, rather than dissecting, the animals.

But butchering is taxing physical work, and a lifetime of it had left him with a shoulder injury that was exacerbated by his reckless pace of living. At last, he required surgery for ripped tendons and muscles in his shoulder cap.

Released from the hospital, he was once again ordered to stop working, this time for two months. One day, during this ostensible

Giuliano (arm in sling) with Zoe at Trattoria Garga

healing period, his doctor and friend, Carlo Bufalini, walked into the restaurant and was appalled to discover Giuliano hacking away at lamb chops in the kitchen. "Garga," he cautioned, "I'm not God. I fixed your arm, but you have to cooperate."

Giuliano behaved for about a week. Then, beside himself with restlessness, he snuck down to his Arno garden with a scythe and spade to cut the grass and turn over the soil for spring planting. While at it, he came upon two big smooth rocks, each of them weighing hundreds of pounds, which he fancied for sculpture. He lugged them back to the trattoria and began chipping away at them so frenziedly with a builder's hammer and chisel that I feared he was going to lose a finger. He carved out two stone heads that looked like Easter Island idols. A customer of ours, who collects Giuliano's work, wanted to buy them, but I fancied them as household gods and kept them for our apartment.

Giuliano sculpting rocks from the Arno

Taglierini del Magnifico

THIN FETTUCCINE WITH CITRUS ZEST

The inspiration for this pasta came from a simple citrus cake eaten during Carneval—the season between Epiphany and Ash Wednesday. During the Renaissance, citrus fruits were a status symbol in Florence: the climate being too cold to grow oranges and lemons outdoors in winter, a greenhouse or *limonaia* (an *orangerie* in France) was required. Naturally only the wealthy had such accommodations. We named the pasta "Magnifico" after Lorenzo il Magnifico.

NOTE If preparing fresh taglierini (see Pasta Fresca recipe, for 4, on page 228), do that first. When dough is rolled out thin, dust well with flour, roll into a very loose log, and cut into $1/8$-inch strips. Unravel strips, and place on a linen cloth that is sprinkled with flour.

1 cup heavy cream

1 cup half-and-half

Zest of 1 lemon

Zest of 1 orange

1 ounce cognac

$1/2$ cup fresh mint leaves

Salt

1 tablespoon kosher salt

10 ounces thin fettuccine

1 cup roughly grated fresh Parmigiano Reggiano

1. Fill a large stockpot with 3 quarts of water, and bring to a boil. While waiting for water to boil, pour cream and half-and-half into a skillet with lemon and orange zest. Cook over medium heat, stirring frequently with a wooden spoon, until cream lightly coats sides of pan (2 to 4 minutes after it comes to a boil).

2. Add cognac and mint leaves, and cook another 2 minutes. Season with salt to taste, and set aside.

3. When water is boiling, add 1 tablespoon kosher salt, and cook fettuccine until *al dente*. Lightly drain, transfer to cream mixture, and sauté for 1 minute, moving everything around with tongs to combine ingredients. Add Parmigiano, stir well, and serve.

Spaghettini al Carciofo Crudo

THIN SPAGHETTI
WITH RAW ARTICHOKES

4 large artichokes (make sure they're firm; the firmer the better)

$\frac{1}{2}$ cup extra-virgin olive oil

2 cloves garlic, sliced into $\frac{1}{8}$-inch pieces

1 tablespoon kosher salt

$\frac{3}{4}$ pound spaghettini

$\frac{1}{4}$ teaspoon cracked red pepper

Salt

2 tablespoons finely chopped fresh parsley leaves

1. Fill a large stockpot with 3 quarts of water, and bring to a boil.

2. Prepare artichokes by stripping off tough outer leaves. Slice off tops (where leaves are darker in color), and trim off bitter outer part of stem with a paring knife; discard these parts. Cut each artichoke in half lengthways (if any of them has a hairy part inside [the choke], gently remove it with the point of a paring knife). Cut halves, still lengthways, into $\frac{1}{8}$-inch strips.

3. Pour oil into a large skillet (not an iron one, which will turn artichokes brown), toss in garlic, cook on high heat for 1 minute, and add artichoke strips, removing skillet from heat immediately after. Set aside.

4. When water comes to a boil, add 1 tablespoon kosher salt, and cook spaghettini until *al dente*. Lightly drain pasta, and add to artichoke mixture in skillet. Add cracked red pepper, and salt to taste. Sauté for 1 minute over high heat, moving everything around with tongs to combine ingredients. Sprinkle with parsley.

Torta al Cioccolato

CHOCOLATE TART

FOR THE CRUST:

NOTE It's easy to crush the cookies in a food processor.

$\frac{1}{4}$ cup ($\frac{1}{2}$ stick) unsalted butter
2 $\frac{1}{2}$ cups finely crushed whole wheat digestive biscuits
(if unavailable use Petit Beurre cookies)
1 tablespoon sugar

1. Preheat oven to 350 degrees. Melt butter over very low heat (don't brown it) in a small saucepan. Add crushed cookies and sugar, and mix thoroughly with a spoon.
2. Line bottom and sides of a 9 $\frac{1}{2}$-inch tart pan with this mixture, using your fingers to press it down evenly. Bake for 10 minutes, or until crust is set and lightly golden. Set aside until completely cool.

FOR THE FILLING:

NOTE Use the finest quality chocolate you can find.

1 pound bittersweet chocolate, chopped
2 cups heavy cream
3 jumbo egg yolks

1. Over medium-low heat, melt chocolate in the top of a double boiler, stirring constantly. Remove from heat, and set aside.
2. Cook cream in a saucepan over medium heat until bubbles form around inside edge (just short of boiling). Remove from heat.
3. In a small bowl, beat egg yolks with a wire whisk until smooth. Gradually, whisk about $\frac{1}{4}$ cup of hot cream into yolks, then stir egg-cream mixture back into pot of hot cream.
4. Gradually add egg-cream mixture to melted chocolate, stirring until well combined and smooth.
5. Pour chocolate filling into piecrust—carefully, over the back of a spoon—and set aside until cool (about 30 minutes). Then refrigerate until chocolate is completely set (about 3 hours).

Chapter 18

DINNER
WITH NANCY

That December, our good friend, Nancy Schiff, came over from the States to celebrate Giuliano's birthday, which happens to be on the fourteenth, the same day as her own. I had serious misgivings, when, on the morning of the party, she arrived at our house with three large shopping bags containing the ingredients for our dinner. "You've been working too hard," she said. "I'm going to do the cooking." Shooing me out of the house, she swore her culinary skills had improved.

Nancy's menu was spaghetti with ricotta cheese, roast chicken, and mashed potatoes. As requested, I left her alone for the day, though I worried about how she'd manage in a strange kitchen, especially with Zoe breathing down her neck. But when I got home, everything seemed to be under control. Nancy and Zoe were in the kitchen together and seemed quite chummy. Later Nancy told me they'd discussed the weather for at least an hour. Though it was sunny, Zoe was sure it was going to turn for the worse—she could feel it in her bones. The subject of her bones segued into a recital of all the accidents and operations she'd had in her life—from the time, in 1945, when a stone cornice fell off a window and hit her on the head as she was nursing baby Anna to a more recent hip replacement. With each story, the appropriate scars had been displayed.

With my arrival, Zoe went off to her bedroom to do some dusting, and Nancy, still refusing my help, banished me to the living room.

Giuliano, already seated at the table with the boys, whispered to me, "*Speriamo bene*" (let's hope for the best).

I was relaxing with a glass of wine in the living room, when I received a frantic summons from the kitchen. The pasta and ricotta had somehow formed a mass the size and shape of a basketball, with about the same consistency. Zoe, following in my footsteps, took one disdainful glance, muttered "*Queste americane!*" and informed us she wasn't hungry.

Undaunted, Nancy *sliced* the pasta and portioned it out. After a few brave bites, she fetched a garbage pail and passed it around. In a sad little ceremony, one by one we dumped the contents of our plates. Then we all burst out laughing. Giuliano gave Nancy a big hug and consoled her, saying, "It's good to know you haven't changed."

In the commotion, Nancy had completely forgotten about the chicken. She rushed to the oven and pulled the door open, to be greeted by a cloud of black smoke. I removed the charred skin from the chicken, and, with the mashed potatoes and a few other ingredients, made croquettes. The dinner was saved, and a cheesecake from the restaurant, with birthday candles, ended a happy celebration among friends. Zoe, steadfast in her martyrdom, ate nothing.

REHABILITATED CHICKEN CROQUETTES

1 pound cooked chicken, finely chopped

1 $1/2$ cups mashed potatoes

2 jumbo eggs

1 clove garlic, very finely chopped

1 tablespoon fresh parsley leaves, finely chopped

1 tablespoon dried porcini mushrooms (previously soaked), finely chopped

3 tablespoons grated Parmigiano Reggiano

$1/4$ cup whole milk

$1/2$ teaspoon freshly grated nutmeg

$1/2$ teaspoon salt

$1/4$ teaspoon freshly ground black pepper

Flour for dredging

Peanut oil

1. Place chicken, mashed potatoes, eggs, garlic, parsley, mushrooms, and grated Parmigiano in a large bowl. Mix well.

2. Add milk, nutmeg, salt, and pepper. Mix well.

3. Form croquettes approximately 3" × 1". Pour flour into a shallow dish, and dredge croquettes.

4. Heat oil in a large skillet, and fry croquettes over medium heat until brown on both sides, turning over once or twice.

CHEESECAKE DELLA SHARON

At Trattoria Garga, customers tell us almost every night that they've never had a better cheesecake.

FOR THE CRUST:

NOTE It's easy to crush the cookies in a food processor.

$1/4$ pound (1 stick) unsalted butter, at room temperature

$1 1/2$ cups crushed whole wheat cookies (digestive biscuits); if unavailable, use Petit Beurre cookies

2 tablespoons sugar

1. Preheat oven to 350 degrees.

2. Melt butter over very low heat (don't brown it) in a small saucepan. Add crushed cookies and 2 tablespoons sugar. Mix thoroughly with a fork.

3. Using your fingers, line bottom and sides of an 11-inch springform pan with this mixture, pressing it down well. (Crust on sides of pan should go up most of the way; leave about $1/2$-inch space from top of pan.) Make sure your crust comes to a nice right angle where bottom and sides of pan meet; there should be no bunched-up crust, forming a curve. Bake for 10 minutes.

FOR THE FILLING:

1 pound 6 ounces Philadelphia or Breakstone cream cheese

$1 1/4$ cups mascarpone cheese

$1 3/4$ cups sugar

5 jumbo eggs

1. While crust is baking, using an electric mixer at slow speed, blend cream cheese and mascarpone in a large bowl. Add $1 3/4$ cups sugar, and continue to mix until batter is smooth. Lower mixer speed to very slow, and add eggs, 1 at a time, mixing just enough to combine after each addition.

2.　Remove crust from oven, pour in filling slowly over the back of a cooking spoon (to prevent damaging the crust), and bake for up to 45 minutes, checking at 35. Remove from oven before filling begins to puff up.

FOR THE TOPPING:

2 cups plain whole-milk yogurt (do not use low-fat or nonfat varieties)

2 tablespoons sugar

$\frac{1}{2}$ teaspoon pure vanilla extract

1.　Combine yogurt with 2 tablespoons sugar and vanilla in a bowl. Mix well. After cheesecake is out of the oven for 5 minutes, pour on topping—once again, slowly, over the back of a spoon. The cheesecake must rest at least 2 hours in a cool place (room temperature, but away from the stove); do not refrigerate. Open springform pan just before serving.

NOTE　If you need to refrigerate leftover cake, take it out a few hours before serving; it's best at room temperature.

Chapter 19

GOING UNDERGROUND

Rebounding from convalescence, Giuliano now threw his inexhaustible energies into a new project. With the idea of creating a proper wine cellar, he hired some workmen and began excavating the foundations of our restaurant, which date to the beginning of the twelfth century. Medieval palaces, built to be autonomous fortresses, were equipped with interior wells so that inhabitants wouldn't go without water in times of siege. By the sixteenth century, these wells had long been in disuse, and during plagues, anything touched by sick people was thrown down their shafts. Many of these ancient Florentine founts (known as *butti*, from *buttare*—to throw) have been explored, and valuable ceramics have been unearthed. When the workmen uncovered a beautiful round well on our premises, Giuliano was convinced it harbored museum-worthy treasures that would leave our family wealthy for generations to come.

The exploration of an old well, long run dry, is a rather dangerous affair, but nothing fazes my intrepid husband. With a rope around his waist, lest fumes should overcome him, he dropped some twenty feet into the abyss. Alas, though he brought up hundreds of ceramic fragments, testimony of daily life in the past, there was to be no major find. With the help of a professional archaeologist, we were able to reconstruct one beautiful painted terra-cotta dish from the late 1400s. I keep it on my desk.

Andrea and Giuliano

The workmen also sandblasted the foundation's interior, revealing rosy-hued brickwork and a beautiful vaulted ceiling. Since, over the centuries, the ground level had risen considerably, we dug down three feet to lower the floor (it seemed as if a ton of dirt was hauled away), which made our now-loftier ceiling look even grander. Everyone was thrilled, except Zoe, who viewed our discoveries with scorn:

"Those filthy old bricks," she exclaimed, when Giuliano proudly took her on a tour of the site. "I can't understand why the two of you don't find some clean place in the suburbs."

When our wine cellar was complete, Giuliano put Andrea, always a wine enthusiast, in charge of it. They've been playing a game of wine one-upmanship ever since. They're the only two people I know who can have a passionate argument while not actually disagreeing about anything. I once observed the following exchange, initiated by Giuliano:

"Come here a minute, Andrea, I want to tell you about . . . "

"Okay, but hurry up. I've got an appointment."

"Shut up and let me finish. *Porca Madonna* (filthy Madonna)! I can never get a word in edgewise in this family."

"It's only you that does all the talking."

"Yes, but nobody ever does any of the listening."

"C'mon, *babbo*," said Andrea impatiently, "what do you want to say."

"Never mind. I'm not going to say anything, since you're in such a rush."

"Well, I had something I wanted to mention to you."

"Don't try to change the subject."

"If you would just listen, *babbo* . . . "

"If you would just listen to me . . . "

"I was looking at Frescobaldi's new wine brochure and . . . "

"Hah! I know exactly what you're going to say."

"Let me at least finish," Andrea pleaded.

"No, I want to talk to you about the wine . . . "

"*Babbo, babbo*, I only wanted to say . . . "

"*Porco Giuda!* (filthy Judas)," screamed Giuliano. "If I can't talk to my own son, who can I talk to?"

Andrea, also screaming, rushed his words to get in an entire sentence:

"I just wanted to say that Marchese Frescobaldi's new wine is on the market now."

"As usual, you're a bit late," exclaimed Giuliano triumphantly. "That's what I was going to say to you! I made an appointment with their salesman for tomorrow, and I wanted you to come along with me."

"*Pappino*, so did I. That's the appointment I was going to now!"

Vino Cotto

WINE SAUCE

This sauce is delicious drizzled on Torta di Mele alla Fiorentina (Apple Cake, Florentine Style; see page 91) or on aged, sharp cheese.

1 $\frac{1}{4}$ cups dry red wine

1 $\frac{1}{2}$ cups sugar

Juice of 3 lemons

1. Place the wine and sugar in a small saucepan, and bring to a boil. Turn heat to low, and cook for 30 minutes.
2. Filter lemon juice through a sieve to remove pulp, and add to wine syrup. Cook for another 15 minutes.

Mostarda Toscana al Vin Santo

TUSCAN MUSTARD
WITH VIN SANTO

This homemade mustard is an excellent condiment for roasted meats. In an attractive jar, it also makes a lovely gift.

4 $\frac{1}{2}$ pounds white grapes

2 pounds baking apples (rennettes if available)

2 large pears

1 cup vin santo

2 tablespoons vin santo

$\frac{1}{4}$ cup dry mustard

4 $\frac{1}{2}$ ounces candied lemon peel, diced

4 jars, 8 ounces

2 tablespoons cinnamon

1. Crush grapes in a large bowl, cover, and refrigerate for 2 days.
2. Squeeze juice through a cheesecloth into a bowl, and set aside. Discard pulp.
3. Peel, core, and slice apples and pears very thin. Place in a large nonstick saucepan, and add 1 cup vin santo. Cook over medium heat for 5 minutes or until wine is absorbed.
4. Add apple/pear mixture to grape juice, and cook over low heat until mixture has a jamlike consistency (about 30 minutes). Let cool completely.
5. In a small saucepan heat 2 tablespoons vin santo, and mix in dry mustard. Add to jam. Stir in candied lemon peel.
6. Pour into small jars, and sprinkle top of each with the cinnamon.

Chapter 20

RENEWAL

In these last years—what with business anxieties and Giuliano's illnesses and accidents—our love life had been sadly lacking. Missing this closeness, we were both growing irritable. Giuliano and I had never had any success in the marital arena with getting things out in the open. With my Scandinavian Protestant upbringing, I am, by nature and nurture, emotionally reserved, and that tendency had been reinforced by Giuliano's wild irrationality when challenged. Italians revel in making a scene, but I dread it. Zoe's constant presence, and her total lack of inhibition in joining in our arguments, always on her son's side, was a further deterrent. And, like most men, Giuliano was only too content not to engage in marital confrontations. After all, he's the one who would have been confronted.

One night, after a grueling day at work, Giuliano suggested we stay after hours. We opened a bottle of champagne and sat talking about everything except our strained relationship. We even did a drawing together with colored pens on a linen table napkin—shades of our old tablecloth art.

When we got home, Giuliano put Nilde in the bathroom, and we started to make love. At a crucial moment, our bedroom door flew open, and Zoe, a phantom in white—hair, nightgown, eyes wildly glacial—stood over us, demanding: "What's all this confusion in here?" I replied that perhaps her memory could assist her.

The whole scene was so comical, Giuliano and I couldn't even get angry. After she left, we snuggled up with each other and giggled under the covers, like children caught doing something naughty. The spell that had been hovering over us was broken.

Soon afterward, my friends Daniela and Luciano invited me to spend some time at their beach house on the tiny island of Elba. I realized that I hadn't had a proper vacation in two decades. For one thing, it's very expensive for mom-and-pop restaurant owners to close up shop and go away together. And for another, Giuliano, who grew up without the concept of vacations, hates going anywhere—especially to the seaside. He doesn't like being out of his element and is far too hyperactive to bask in the sunshine.

Over the years—ever since we'd opened the butcher shop—I'd been slowly regaining the independence I'd so lightly relinquished when we moved in with Zoe. Now I decided to go off to Elba on my own.

There's a point on Elba from which you can see Corsica, Napoleon's native land. People say that when exiled there, he used to stand and gaze wistfully at his homeland. But unlike Napoleon, I love Elba. A jewel in the Mediterranean Sea, its mountainous terrain forms a backdrop to pristine beaches. The air is delicately perfumed by roses, and the hills are covered with wild rosemary, sage, thyme, and fennel. In this lovely setting, Daniela and I went sailing (Luciano works as a skipper on tourist-leased sailboats), sunbathed nude in the privacy of rock coves, read novels, and, of course, cooked. Daniela, who has a wonderful feeling for food, taught me many incredible seafood recipes, including a lasagne with seafood ragout that I still prepare frequently. Every evening, we'd invite friends in for dinner parties in her garden.

Meanwhile, back home, *"Il Giardino del Garga,"* Giuliano's Arno garden, more beautiful than ever, was getting a lot of notice in the newspapers. This attracted the attention of local authorities, who took him to court and sentenced him to two weeks in jail or a fine of 500,000 lire (about $265). Giuliano paid the fine, but he's never stopped gardening, and the battle with the city still rages on today.

I returned to Florence refreshed and happy at the end of August. But with things going smoothly at home, and at the restaurant, Giuliano, once again, required a challenge. Across the street from Trattoria Garga is a magnificent sixteenth-century palazzo with a charming Renaissance courtyard. Originally owned by a banking family named Spinelli, who conducted their business out of doors under the loggia (Renaissance merchants knew better than to shut themselves up in stuffy offices all day), it currently housed an art-restoration school. One day the proprietor, who had more space than he needed, approached Giuliano with the idea of renting out the ground floor (which has a massive fireplace) and five rooms on the mezzanine. Giuliano was immediately galvanized. We could renovate again. We could have our own art gallery, start a cooking school ("that you could run," he enthused), open up a wine bar.

I protested mildly, but it's useless to stand between Giuliano and a dream. In 1997, we signed a six-year lease.

Lasagne al Sugo di Pesce

LASAGNE WITH
FISH RAGOUT

NOTE If preparing fresh lasagne noodles (see Pasta Fresca recipe, for 6 to 8, on page 228), do that first. Cut dough into a dozen 3" × 5" rectangles, and place them on a linen cloth that is sprinkled with flour. If using prepared lasagne noodles, begin at Step 1, below.

FOR THE FISH SAUCE:

1 big yellow onion, chopped very fine

$1/4$ cup extra-virgin olive oil

1 clove garlic, finely chopped

1 cup octopus meat

1 cup calamari (squid)

1 cup dry white wine

14 $1/2$-ounce can puréed Italian plum tomatoes (if unavailable, buy a can of whole plum tomatoes and purée them)

$1/4$ teaspoon cracked red pepper

2 teaspoons salt

8 ounces shrimp in shells (remove heads)

1 tablespoon chopped fresh parsley leaves

1 tablespoon lemon zest

1. In a large skillet, sauté onion in oil on medium heat until translucent but not brown. Add garlic, and sauté 5 minutes more. Remove skillet from heat.

2. Slice octopus in very thin pieces. Chop calamari into $1/4$-inch pieces. Add octopus and calamari to skillet. Cook for 20 minutes on medium heat, stirring occasionally and adding $1/4$ cup of the wine every 3 minutes, until used up.

3. Add tomatoes, cracked red pepper, and salt. Stir, and cook over medium heat for another 20 minutes. During this time, devein and shell shrimp, setting 6 aside for garnish.

4. Remove sauce from heat, and add shrimp (except for 6 you're saving for garnish). Stir in chopped parsley and lemon zest. Set aside. Before you make the roux, put up 3 quarts of water to boil in a large stockpot, and preheat oven to 350 degrees.

FOR THE FISH ROUX:

2 tablespoons unsalted butter

$1/2$ cup unbleached all-purpose flour

2 cups fish broth (or 1 fish bouillon cube dissolved
in 2 cups boiling water)

1. In a large saucepan, melt butter over medium heat. Add flour, stir-
    ring with a wooden spoon for 4 minutes. Remove saucepan from
    heat, and continue stirring. Add fish broth, $1/2$ cup at a time, stir-
    ring continuously. Return saucepan to heat, and bring to a boil.
    Cook for 5 minutes.

ASSEMBLING THE LASAGNE:

12 lasagne noodles, 3" × 5"

1 tablespoon kosher salt

1 tablespoon peanut oil

1. When water comes to a boil, add kosher salt and oil. Then add
    lasagne noodles, 3 at a time. Cook for 1 minute, and carefully re-
    move with a slotted spoon. Drain on a damp cloth. Repeat until all
    12 are cooked.

2. Pour $1/4$ of the fish roux into the bottom of a 9" × 11" baking dish,
    and spread evenly. Arrange a row of 4 lasagne noodles on top to
    cover (they'll overlap). Ladle $1/3$ of the fish sauce on noodles, and
    drizzle with $1/4$ of the fish roux. Add two more layers of noodles,
    fish sauce, and drizzled roux, finishing up with a layer of lasagne
    noodles, drizzled with remaining fish roux. Arrange 6 raw shrimp
    you've set aside on top, each shrimp corresponding to a portion.
    Bake for 20 minutes.

Chapter 21

ALESSANDRO DEFENDS HIS COUNTRY

In Italy, military service is obligatory for all young men. Andrea, born in the baby boom year of 1971, was called up in 1990, but as there was a surfeit of boys his age, some were exempted by lottery. Andrea was thrilled, and greatly relieved, to find himself among the exonerated. From a delicate boy, he'd developed into an elegant young man with highly refined tastes. The idea of pigging it in a dreary barracks, of being crammed in with a bunch of crude strangers and at the mercy of sadistic superior officers, revolted him. Worse yet was the thought of what he might have to eat.

When Alessandro was nineteen, he in turn was called up. As robust and outgoing as Andrea is introverted and Camille-like (he only looks frail; he's actually healthy as a horse), Alessandro thought serving in the military would be a great lark. During his physical, he purposely hid a roster of old soccer injuries that would surely have disqualified him. His knees are shot.

Alessandro was accepted into the air force. Zoe immediately got into gear, sending our housekeeper out to buy him a week's supply of new underwear—including itchy long-sleeved woolen undershirts, which Alessandro detests. She hovered over his suitcase, making sure everything was neatly packed in individual plastic bags and sneaking in the woolens to which Alessandro had issued a *nolle prosequi*. Her coddling annoyed him no end.

A week later, at three in the morning, I went with Giuliano, Andrea, and two chefs from the restaurant, Elio and Lorenzo, to see him off at the train station in Campo di Marte. Stories I'd seen on television about the "*nonni*" (senior officers, literally "grandfathers") brutalizing new recruits raced through my mind, and I was filled with trepidation. I can't imagine how mothers can bear sending their sons off in actual wartime. But Alessandro was in high spirits, horsing around with his fellow recruits and smoking cigarettes. Giuliano, who'd also served in the air force, was bursting with pride to have a son following his example, his unrestrained enthusiasm somewhat putting Andrea's nose out of joint. Accustomed to being the star of the family, he was a little jealous that Alessandro was getting so much attention. I, too, felt a little left out of things in what was clearly a male ritual. And I think the middle-of-the-night departure added an ominous note.

When the train pulled out of the station, Giuliano reached for my hand and squeezed it. He put his arm around me as we walked back to our car, talking about how it seemed only yesterday Alessandro was a cherubic toddler with golden ringlets.

If Giuliano and I have lived a life of Darwinian struggle, our children have grown up in a loving cocoon. An hour after his arrival in boot camp, Alessandro, slightly hysterical, his voice trembling, was on the phone to us. Stripped of his identity and barked at by officers, he begged, "*Mammina, babbo*, get me out of here!"

We made it clear to him that there would be dire consequences for all of us if we tried to kidnap him from the Italian state. I tried to calm him down and promised we'd come pick him up in Viterbo (the town where his boot camp was located) at the end of his forty days of basic training. I told him the time would fly.

Soon after, in the rigors of training, Alessandro's knee problems became manifest, and he was exempted from exercise, shooting practice, and marching. With nothing to do all day, he was bored to distraction.

Given leave for Easter, he came home for the holiday, looking ever so handsome in his blue aviation uniform. I have a photograph of my own father in his air force uniform, and I was startled to see how much Alessandro resembled him. He told us that an epidemic of German measles had hit his barracks, and half his buddies were in military hospital.

Easter Sunday we observed a religious tradition, Gargani-style. You're supposed to take eggs to morning mass, where the priest blesses them for the holiday meal. Zoe had created a shortcut to this holy rite: She simply placed the eggs in front of the TV and tuned in to Pope John Paul II's benediction from Rome.

We sat down twenty-five for a dinner of cured ham from Assisi (with the blessed Easter eggs, hard-boiled), followed by fresh pasta wrapped around asparagus and topped with melted teleggio cheese. Our main course, naturally, was lamb, with a side dish of incredibly tender sweet spring peas. Alas, poor Alessandro was not among the assembled. He was in bed with a high fever and a terrible rash: German measles.

Upon recovery, he was transferred to a base in Florence, where his commanding general was a customer of ours. When word got out that Garga's son was in service there, he was at once made sous-chef in the officer's mess, where dinners and banquets were served on numerous occasions to NATO commanders. Alessandro likes to believe that the Garga tradition of cooking helped seal many a pact. Whatever the case, once again in the familiar environs of a kitchen, he contentedly finished out his tour of duty.

Alessandro and Elio Cotza, partner and chef, in Trattoria Garga kitchen

Guancialino di
Asparagi al Taleggio

PASTA PILLOWS STUFFED WITH ASPARAGUS AND TALEGGIO CHEESE

FOR THE PASTA:

$3/4$ cup finely ground hard-grain semolina flour
(use Rob's Red Mill or Antoine's Pasta Flour)

1 jumbo egg

1 teaspoon extra-virgin olive oil

$1/2$ teaspoon salt

Extra semolina flour for flouring dough-rolling surface

1. On a flat surface, pour out flour in a mound, and make a crater in its center. Place egg (unbeaten), oil, and salt in center of crater, and work mixture, kneading with the flats of your hands, until your dough is smooth and elastic.

2. Divide dough into four equal parts. Place one piece of dough at a time on a well-floured surface, sprinkle more flour on top, and roll very thin (you should be able to see your skin through it). Repeat with remaining dough. Cut dough into 3" × 5" rectangles, place them (not overlapping) on a cloth sprinkled with flour, and set aside.

FOR THE PILLOWS:

10 ounces Taleggio cheese (if unavailable, use Brie)

$1/4$ cup heavy cream

16 spears asparagus

Unsalted butter for greasing baking dishes

1 tablespoon kosher salt

1. Preheat oven to 400 degrees, and put up 3 quarts of water to boil. While waiting for oven to heat, and water to boil, melt cheese and cream in top of a double boiler. Remove tough parts of asparagus spears, and, in a separate pot (not the one with 3 quarts water), cook until just tender.

2. Butter 4 individual-portion (approximately 4" × 7") ovenproof dishes.

3. Add kosher salt to boiling water, and, one at a time, blanch pasta rectangles for 30 seconds. Remove with a slotted spoon, and lay flat on a damp cloth. Lay a pasta sheet in each buttered dish, topped by 4 asparagus spears (cut spears to fit if necessary).

4. Pour half the cheese sauce into a bowl. Spoon approximately $1/4$ of it over asparagus in each dish, and fold pasta flaps over spears, creating little pasta pillows. Top each pillow with $1/4$ of remaining sauce. Bake for 15 minutes, or until golden-brown. Let rest 5 minutes before serving.

Agnello Disossato Farcito
di Menta e Aglio

ROLLED LEG OF LAMB
WITH MINT AND GARLIC

2 pound leg of spring lamb, after deboning
(ask your butcher to trim and debone the meat)

4 cloves garlic, very finely chopped

1 cup fresh mint leaves, very finely chopped

Salt

Fresh-ground black pepper

$\frac{1}{8}$ cup cognac

2 cups dry white wine

1. Preheat oven to 450 degrees. Place lamb on a flat surface. With a long, sharp knife, make 4 diagonal 3-inch cuts where the meat is thickest. Lay meat out flat, sprinkle very lightly with water, cover with a sheet of plastic wrap, and pound to an even flatness with a smooth-surfaced meat mallet.

2. Thoroughly combine garlic and mint leaves, and spread on top of lamb. Sprinkle with salt and pepper.

3. Roll the lamb, tuck in ends, and secure roll lengthways with string. Now tie roll horizontally, around the center, and again halfway to either end. Place in a roasting pan, and bake for 10 minutes.

4. Remove roast from oven, and pour off all fat. Lower oven temperature to 350 degrees, add cognac, and bake for another 10 minutes.

5. Add 1 cup wine, and bake 20 minutes.

6. Add remaining wine, and bake 20 minutes more.

7. Transfer lamb to a platter, remove string, and slice into medallions. Serve topped with pan juices.

FRESH PEAS, FLORENTINE STYLE

1 small clove spring garlic (if unavailable, use a shallot)

2 1/2 pounds unshelled fresh peas (or 1 pound shelled)

1 tablespoon fresh Italian parsley leaves (whole)

1/4 cup extra-virgin olive oil

1 tablespoon sugar

Salt

1. Slice garlic into 1/8-inch pieces. Place shelled peas in a medium-sized pot with garlic, parsley, and oil. Add enough water to barely cover peas. Cook on low heat, uncovered, for 10 minutes. Add sugar, then salt to taste. Peas will still have their broth and should be served soupy.

Chapter 22

MAGRITTINGS–
LA CUCINA DEL GARGA

In August of 1997, we started the cooking school in our newly renovated palazzo. Giuliano and I, along with a few friends, decorated the interior with paintings and murals, one of the latter depicting ancient masks from the Roman theater. Inspired by our most nonculinary friend, Nancy, creator of the dread spaghetti basketball, we named the school Magrittings. That year, Nancy had designed a Christmas card featuring a photograph of herself dressed—after the famous painting by surrealist René Magritte—in a bowler hat with a shiny red Christmas tree ornament in front of her face. The card read "Magrittings!"

We advertised cooking classes in our menus, and, amazingly, many people signed up. On the evening of my first class, the palazzo's beautiful wrought-iron gates were lit on either side by flaming torches, and the archways of the loggia were illuminated by dozens of large candles flickering in terra-cotta pots.

Giuliano positioned himself at the entrance, effusively greeting each student as he or she arrived. Then he led them up the three steps to the vaulted entrance room where he officially introduced them to me. He'd lit a roaring fire in the hearth, and we all gathered around it and sipped fizzy prosecco.

As a rule, I'm a hopeless chatterbox, but suddenly, with the class arriving, I had terrible stage fright. Though I'd been cooking for so

Sharon in official cooking-school attire. Courtesy of Nancy Rica Schiff

many years, as I led my first group of students upstairs to our gleaming new kitchen, I suddenly felt unsure of my abilities. It's one thing to cook in your own kitchen, another to explain everything you're doing in front of an audience. What if someone asked a question I couldn't answer? Humiliation loomed.

I took a deep breath and started talking. I'm used to my family, with whom it's a struggle to get a word in edgewise or make myself heard. These people listened in rapt, almost religious, silence. I was elated.

Our menu for the evening was tagliatelle pasta with garlic and porcini mushrooms (everyone was fascinated that this dish is spiced with nepitella, otherwise known as catnip) and veal with baby artichokes in white wine sauce. In honor of Nancy's influence in naming the cooking school, for dessert we prepared Apple Tart alla Nancy—a recipe I'd created for her years ago.

I had set out all the ingredients in advance on a nineteenth-century oak sideboard—in baskets and ceramic bowls, and on faïence platters—and a profusion of fresh herbs was arranged in bouquets. Someone commented that it looked like a still-life setting for an art class. As eggs were cracked and beaten, pasta dough kneaded, veal pounded, herbs ripped off their stems, and Granny Smith apples sliced, everyone began getting acquainted, and the class took on a party atmosphere. In addition to our meal, we prepared a few snacks to nibble on while cooking—deep-fried zucchini blossoms and fettunta (toasted Tuscan bread rubbed with raw garlic and doused with green extra-virgin olive oil)—these antipasti accompanied by a glass of Tocai Friulano, a bold dry white wine with an almond aftertaste.

Finally the meal was complete, and we sat down at our beautiful old oak table, which was draped in white linen, candlelit, and elegantly set with fine silver and china. With its stone walls and rough-hewn beamed ceilings, a sixteenth-century Florentine palazzo has no lack of ambience; our dinner party looked like a scene out of *La Dolce Vita*.

Everyone dug into the tagliatelle, exclaiming over the distinct flavor of homemade pasta, which is complemented, not eclipsed, by its sauce. Pouring a 1997 Chianti Classico, we toasted ourselves, the chefs. It was the first of many convivial cooking-school dinners at Magrittings.

The work complete, Giuliano made his entrance, accompanied by maestro Nando, a doddering octogenarian violinist, who, in his prime, played all the major concert halls of Europe. Nando's hands shook badly as he performed a Vivaldi concerto, but in spite of all the sour notes he hit, everyone was charmed. Several glasses of wine, the food, the surroundings, all combined to make everything appear wondrous. Then, with dramatic flourish, Giuliano ceremoniously tasted a single strand of the tagliatelle. We held our collective breath until he nodded his approval, lifting his wineglass to toast the "chefs" with a one-word accolade: *Bravi!* Master of ceremonies, he welcomed everyone to his city, wished them joy for the rest of the evening, and made his excuses: "*Il dovere mi chiama* (duty calls); I must get back to my kitchen." Only I knew that he was headed back to the courtyard, where his pals and another glass of wine awaited him.

"Isn't he amazing?" exclaimed the students.

In 1998, we began hosting art shows at Magrittings. One of these presented the works of Onofrio Pepi, a Florentine sculptor, for which we turned our Renaissance courtyard into a sculpture garden. Visitors arrived at dusk, and, after a spectacular sunset, we lit the courtyard with torches. Inside, Pepi's creations were seen by the light of hundreds of candles. It was a magical evening. We purchased Pepi's life-size sculpture of me—a smooth, rounded bronze figure—to grace the entrance to Magrittings.

Giuliano and friends in Magrittings courtyard

FETTUCCINE WITH PORCINI MUSHROOMS

If preparing fresh tagliatelle (see Pasta Fresca recipe, for 4, on page 228), do that first. When dough is rolled out thin, dust well with flour, roll into a very loose log, and cut into $1/4$-inch strips. Unravel strips, and place on a linen cloth that is sprinkled with flour.

NOTE It's okay to use frozen porcini mushrooms in this recipe.

1 pound porcini mushrooms (thoroughly washed and dried)

$1/2$ cup extra-virgin olive oil

4 cloves garlic, in their jackets

3 tablespoons chopped nepitella leaves
(if unavailable use fresh mint)

1 cup chicken or vegetable broth

1 tablespoon kosher salt

14 ounces fettuccine

Salt

1. Fill a large stockpot with 3 quarts of water, and bring to a boil.

2. While waiting for water to boil, slice mushrooms into $1/2$-inch strips. Pour oil into a saucepan, add mushrooms, garlic cloves, and nepitella, and cook over medium heat for 5 minutes, stirring occasionally.

3. Add broth, and cook for another 10 minutes, stirring frequently.

4. Add kosher salt to boiling water, toss in fettuccine, and cook until *al dente*. Drain lightly, add to skillet with mushrooms, and sauté for 1 minute, moving everything around with tongs to combine ingredients. Remove garlic cloves. Add salt to taste.

Vitellina ai Carciofi

VEAL WITH ARTICHOKES

1 pound veal

4 small artichokes (make sure they're firm; the firmer the better)

Juice of 1 lemon

2 cloves garlic, finely chopped

$1/4$ teaspoon cracked red pepper

$1/2$ cup + 2 tablespoons extra-virgin olive oil

$1/2$ cup dry white wine

1. Cut veal into 1-inch cubes. Place cubes, about 10 at a time, on a flat surface, sprinkle very lightly with water, cover with plastic wrap, and pound flat with a smooth-surfaced meat mallet. Set aside.

2. Strip off tough outer leaves of artichokes, setting them aside for decorating your serving platter. Slice off tops, where leaves are darker in color. With a paring knife, trim off the bitter outer part of the stem, and remove any fluff or choke from the center. Discard these parts.

3. Add lemon juice to a large bowl of water. Cut each artichoke lengthways into 8 pieces, making sure you include some of the heart in each wedge (otherwise, your wedges will separate into leaves). Place in lemon water.

4. In a sauté pan (don't use an iron one; it will turn the artichokes brown), heat, but don't brown, garlic and cracked red pepper in $1/2$ cup of the oil.

5. Drain artichokes, and add to pan. Cook over medium heat for 5 minutes, stirring constantly with a wooden spoon. Add wine, cook for 2 more minutes, and set aside.

6. Put remaining 2 tablespoons of oil into a large, heavy skillet. Add veal, turn heat to high, and stir-fry (which means continual stir-ring) for 3 minutes. Add artichokes, and stir-fry for another 2 min-utes. Serve on a platter decorated with outer leaves of artichokes.

APPLE TART ALLA NANCY

My friend Nancy loves apple pie with lots of streusel topping. I created this deliciously decadent version for her.

FOR THE PASTRY:

$1/4$ pound (1 stick) unsalted butter, melted

$1/4$ cup confectioner's sugar

$1 1/4$ cups unbleached all-purpose flour, sifted

$1/4$ teaspoon salt

1. Preheat oven to 350 degrees. Using a fork (or your hands), thoroughly combine above ingredients in a bowl to form a pastry dough.

2. Using your fingers, crumble dough evenly into bottom and up sides (crust should go 2 inches up sides) of a 10-inch springform pan, pressing it down well. Make sure your crust comes to a nice right angle where bottom and sides of pan meet; there should be no bunched-up crust forming a curve. Prick crust at 1-inch intervals, bottom and sides, with the tines of a fork. Bake for 15 minutes, or until crust turns the tiniest bit golden. Do not overbake, or it will taste dry. Let cool for 10 minutes, during which time you can prepare filling.

FOR THE FILLING:

5 large Granny Smith apples

Zest and juice of 1 lemon

$5/8$ cup plain whole-milk yogurt (do not use low-fat varieties)

2 tablespoons corn starch

2 tablespoons sugar

1 teaspoon cinnamon

$1/4$ cup dark raisins

1. Peel apples, cut into quarters, and remove cores. Slice apples, lengthways, into $1/4$-inch pieces, and toss in a large bowl with remaining filling ingredients. Gently pour filling into cooled crust.

FOR THE TOPPING:

$1/4$ cup unsalted butter, softened

$1/4$ cup dark brown sugar

2 tablespoons unbleached all-purpose flour

1. Mix ingredients well in a small bowl, and dot topping all over filling. Bake for 1 hour. Let cake rest at least 2 hours in a cool place (room temperature, but away from the stove); do not refrigerate. Open springform pan just before serving.

Chapter 23

CELEBRATING THE BIRTHDAYS OF GIULIANO AND JESUS

December 14, 1998, was Giuliano's sixtieth birthday. Life was good, and I was in a mood to celebrate. I decided to throw a grand birthday and holiday party at Magrittings on Christmas Eve. I sent out invitations to more than a hundred people, and twice that many showed up. Among the guests were Nancy and our friend Giampiero, both of whom had been witnesses at our wedding. They didn't even recognize one another; thirty years had wrought a few changes.

A sixteenth-century palazzo is a wonderful place to throw a party. A blazing fire in the downstairs hearth made for a warm welcome, and everyone looked glamorous by the light of hundreds of candles. Giuliano, in his element as the *festeggiato* (guest of honor), was soon surrounded by a group of friends passionately discussing the state of modern art.

I cooked all night in a kitchen crowded with old friends coming by to say hello. With some difficulty, I managed to carry on a series of conversations as I baked several dozen loaves of focaccia sprinkled with fresh rosemary; prepared mounds of our famous Insalata del Garga embellished with spicy tomato crostini; and stirred vast cauldrons of ribollita (Tuscan bread soup with vegetables), which I served drizzled with newly pressed olive oil. My main course was roast veal sirloin stuffed with white truffles. And, for dessert, there was a seven-tiered lemon cake, topped with sugar glaze and slices of candied orange. Giuliano, surrounded by so many people who love him, had tears in his eyes as he blew out the candles.

Inspired by this orgy of entertaining, we decided to close the restaurant for Christmas week and invite Giuliano's extensive family for a holiday dinner at the palazzo. We felt it would be wonderful for Zoe, then eighty-eight, to spend the day surrounded by all her relatives—in addition to my family, Giuliano's sisters (Gigliola and Anna), their husbands and grown children, their children's children, plus an assortment of boyfriends and girlfriends, even Gargani in-laws. The guest list came to twenty-four people.

The day of the party, I got up at 5 A.M. in order to get an early start preparing the meal. We had invited everyone for dinner at 1 P.M. I was about to leave for the palazzo, when Zoe came shuffling out of her bedroom in nightgown and slippers to inform me that she had a migraine and wouldn't be coming to the party. I knew that she had every intention of coming, but, as of old, wheedling was required.

"Zoe," I implored, "everyone would miss you terribly. Think how disappointed the grandchildren will be."

Deep sigh from Zoe. I continued to plead with her ("You must come; you're the guest of honor").

After close to thirty years, this was a well-worn drama, and we were both letter-perfect in our roles.

"You're the head of the family, we need you," I continued, sticking to the script.

When she asked what I was cooking, I knew she had capitulated, though she only said she'd see how she felt later.

It was a dark wintry day. The first thing I did at the palazzo was start a fire, the crackling blaze boosting my holiday spirit. Then I rolled up my sleeves and began preparing a five-course feast, centering on a roast suckling pig stuffed with fennel, sausages, and apples. After just having cooked for two hundred, I felt like I was making a snack. Giuliano and the boys joined me a few hours later and pitched in.

As the family began arriving, Giuliano popped open a bottle of champagne, and the party was underway. We began with crostini and prosciutto, followed by tortellini in capon broth, a Christmas staple in Northern Italy. Reverting to my Canadian heritage, I made a plum pudding with hard sauce and homemade marzipan fruits for dessert. We dined in front of the fireplace, by a Christmas tree ablaze with candles.

The meal ended in an astounding occurrence: Before her assembled family, Zoe raised her glass of wine to toast Giuliano and me:

"I'm so proud," she said, "to have such an accomplished son and daughter-in-law!"

Dinner over, the boys and their cousins went off somewhere. Then, as after every Gargani family gathering, the older folk, relaxing in a cozy stupor before the fire, began reminiscing about their experiences in World War II. Giuliano recalled sirens in the middle of the night and being hurried from home, with a coat over his pajamas, to the wooded park surrounding Villa Strozzi. There, they'd huddled with other families from the neighborhood. After a series of air raids, the Garganis and four other families fled to the nearby countryside, where they set up house in an abandoned villa. After searching the villa for food, they'd found a cask of wine, but feared it might be poisoned (a common practice to teach the Germans a lesson if they came). The men drew straws, Ferdinando came up with the shortest, and he drank a glass without keeling over; the wine was good. Later, Zoe, foraging for food, stumbled upon a field of potatoes in which farmers had cut off all the green leaves to hide the crops.

There was much more: One time Giuliano, his father, and some other men had been rounded up by German soldiers searching for weapons hidden by the *partigiani* and were forced to sit for over an hour with their hands over their heads. Ferdinando knew that one of the men was sitting right on top of the cache, which was hidden under a pile of wood. Had the Germans discovered it, they might have all been shot.

To Giuliano, these wartime memories were thrilling boyhood adventures; he had been too young to understand the dangers and hardships. As he launched into a particular story about a loaf of bread with a cockroach in it, Anna and I—both born after World War II had ended—slipped out of the room to do the dishes. We had heard all the family's war stories countless times (we could have told them ourselves) and knew that this tale was the opening salvo in the next phase of the evening. According to Giuliano, they were so hungry, they ate the loaf, cockroach and all. Zoe and Gigliola felt this story—no doubt apocryphal—was humiliating to the family and protested that they had never been that desperate. The evening ended as it always did, with a raucous family argument over whose memories were correct. They all enjoyed it tremendously.

Focaccia al Rosmarino

TUSCAN FLAT BREAD
WITH FRESH ROSEMARY

1 packet ($^1/_4$ ounce) active dry yeast

1 teaspoon sugar

$^3/_4$ cup warm water (110 degrees)

1 $^1/_8$ cups unbleached all-purpose flour

$^1/_2$ teaspoon salt

2 tablespoons extra-virgin olive oil

Extra flour for dusting work surface

Unsalted butter for greasing baking sheet

1 teaspoon finely chopped fresh rosemary leaves

1 teaspoon kosher salt

1. Preheat oven to 350 degrees. Place yeast in a small bowl, add sugar, and slowly mix in half ($^3/_8$ of a cup) of the warm water. Let rest for 15 minutes, or until foam covers top of yeast mixture. Stir well.

2. Place flour in a large bowl, and sprinkle with $^1/_2$ teaspoon salt. Push flour to sides of bowl to form a crater. Into this crater, pour yeast mixture, 1 tablespoon of the oil, and remaining warm water. Stir slowly with a wooden spoon, starting from the middle to incorporate all the flour. An uneven ball of dough will be formed.

3. Place dough on a flat work surface that has been dusted with flour. Sprinkle flour on top of dough, and knead for 5 minutes. Dough should now be soft and elastic, but not sticky. Knead for another 5 minutes.

4. Place dough in a clean bowl, and cover with a cloth or dish towel until it's doubled in size; this will take at least an hour.

5. Place dough on a greased baking sheet, and, using the tips of your fingers, spread it out into a $^1/_2$-inch-thick circle (or rectangle, if you prefer). Still using your fingers, dimple surface, and brush with remaining oil. Sprinkle evenly with rosemary and 1 teaspoon kosher salt. Bake for 15 to 20 minutes, until golden-brown. Serve hot.

Ribollita

TUSCAN BREAD SOUP

10 ounces dried cannellini beans

1 leek

1 yellow onion, finely chopped

1 tablespoon fresh thyme leaves, finely chopped

$1/2$ cup extra-virgin olive oil

1 bunch elephant kale, coarsely chopped

2 potatoes, diced into $1/2$-inch cubes

2 carrots, diced into $1/2$-inch cubes

2 celery stalks, chopped into $1/2$-inch slices

Salt

Freshly ground black pepper

9 ounces day-old Tuscan, peasant, or sourdough bread, cut into $1/2$-inch slices

Extra-virgin olive oil

1. Soak beans overnight in 2 quarts of water. Rinse, drain, and place in a pot with another 2 quarts of water. Bring to a boil, then reduce heat to lowest simmer, and cook, covered, for 2 hours. Set aside, retaining cooking water.

2. Wash leek thoroughly, and chop into $1/2$-inch pieces, discarding root and tough dark green leaves.

3. In a large stockpot, on medium-high heat, sauté onion and thyme in $1/2$ cup oil. Reduce heat to medium-low, and add leek, kale, potatoes, carrots, and celery, one vegetable at a time. Cook for 10 minutes.

4. Add cooking water from beans, and half the beans to stockpot. Purée other half of beans, and add to soup. Season to taste with salt and pepper. Cook over low heat for 1 hour.

5. Toast bread, and add to soup, stirring it in well. Cook over medium heat for 10 minutes, stirring occasionally to prevent sticking. Let soup stand for 15 minutes, then drizzle with olive oil, and serve (in earthenware bowls, if you have them).

ROAST PIGLET

1 piglet (about 12 pounds)

Salt

Freshly ground black pepper

2 fennel bulbs

1 Granny Smith apple

2 teaspoons fennel seeds (preferably wild fennel)

$1/2$ pound sausage meat

$1/4$ cup brandy

$1 1/2$ cups dry white wine

1. Preheat oven to 275 degrees. Wash and dry piglet. Salt and pepper cavity.

2. Halve fennel bulbs lengthways, and cut into $1/8$-inch slices, discarding tough outer leaves. Peel apple, halve lengthways, remove core, and cut into $1/8$-inch slices. In a large bowl mix stuffing ingredients—fennel, apple slices, fennel seeds, and sausage meat.

3. Fill cavity of piglet with stuffing, and sew up with butchers' string.

4. Place piglet in a baking pan, cavity side down. Cover pig's ears, snout, and tail with aluminum foil, and bake for 2 hours.

5. Add brandy, and bake for another hour.

6. Add wine, and bake for another hour.

7. Remove from oven, take off foil, and place piglet on a platter. Wait 15 minutes before serving. While waiting for piglet to cool, pass drippings through a sieve, and transfer into a gravy boat.

8. Using a very sharp knife, carve piglet, and serve slices topped with gravy. Serve stuffing on the side.

Torta Glassata al Limone

LEMON CAKE

Unsalted butter

Unbleached all-purpose flour

2 cups cake flour

2 teaspoons baking powder

$1/2$ teaspoon salt

1 stick ($1/2$ cup) unsalted butter, softened

1 cup sugar

3 jumbo eggs, room temperature

$1 1/2$ teaspoons vanilla

$1/4$ cup vin santo (or sherry)

1. Preheat oven to 350 degrees. Butter and flour an 11-inch baking pan, and set aside.

2. Sift cake flour, baking powder, and salt into a bowl. Set aside.

3. In a large bowl, beat butter and sugar with an electric mixer at medium-high speed until pale and fluffy (3 to 5 minutes). Beat in eggs, one at a time, then add vanilla, and beat until all ingredients are thoroughly incorporated (about 5 minutes).

4. Add flour mixture at low speed. Add vin santo, and mix until batter is just smooth. Spread evenly in pan.

5. Bake cake in middle of oven until it begins to pull away from sides of pan and a baking pin comes out clean (20 to 25 minutes). Cool 5 minutes in pan, then invert onto a rack, and cool completely.

FOR THE ICING:

$3/4$ cup confectioner's sugar

3 teaspoons fresh lemon juice

$1/2$ cup candied lemon peel, finely chopped

1. Place sugar in a small bowl. Mix in lemon juice and candied lemon peel. Spread icing evenly on cake with a metal spatula.

Chapter 24

LOOKING BACK, LOOKING AHEAD

Unlike our first disastrous New Year's Eve, we rang in the new millennium with the restaurant filled to capacity with loyal customers and friends. We stayed up until dawn, drinking champagne and singing old Italian songs. And just before closing, Giuliano and I sang a duet: "There's a Place for Us," from *West Side Story*.

Three days later came my fiftieth birthday. I didn't have a big to-do on the actual date. I was waiting to celebrate the event with my twin sister, Karen, who, though I'd visited her occasionally in Canada, was coming to Italy for the first time since 1975.

Karen arrived in February. For about ten minutes, we were awkward with each other, and there was an embarrassing silence. Then we reverted to about age ten, making idiotic jokes and laughing like lunatics. Karen and I have had very different lives. She's stayed in Winnipeg raising her family. I've stepped through the looking glass and made a life and career in another country. But diverse as our lives have been, we share two essentials: We seldom speak seriously of life's tribulations; once over, they always become grist for humor. And we both love to cook. Karen makes the best blueberry pie in the world.

Half a century old! Should I begin summing up my life, or, as I've always done, just keep hurtling forward, never looking back? Optimistically, I think of fifty as a halfway mark in life. I do, in fact, find myself increasingly introspective. And after years of a work-dominated life, in the spirit of "now or never," I've repossessed my body—taken up yoga and swimming.

These days, Andrea pretty much runs Trattoria Garga, though Giuliano is still a vibrant presence in the kitchen—often shirtless, arms flying, imperiously shouting orders, chopping meat, banging saucepans, and belting out arias.

Though I still have a hand in the restaurant—among other things, I bake a big batch of biscotti every morning—the cooking school has become the focus of my work life. As it grew in popularity, running it became too much for me alone, and I took in a partner, my dear friend Mims Walbridge. A sophisticated New Yorker who worked at *GQ* for years, Mims was, like me, swept away by a charming Italian. She married him and has been living here since 1993.

Very athletic and fit, Mims has been a mentor in my physical renaissance; she had, for years, been running weeklong bicycle tours through the Tuscan countryside. When she suggested combining a cy-

Giuliano: prelude to butchering an octopus. Courtesy of Nancy Rica Schiff

cling trip with culinary classes, I thought it was a great idea. We arranged visits to olive groves, vineyards, and a sheep farm (to observe the making of pecorino cheese); meals at local trattorias; and lovely walks in search of seasonal edibles such as wild radicchio and wood mushrooms. My good friends Francesca and Stefano Dalgas invited us to use their eighteenth-century farmhouse, Santa Margherita, near the medieval town of Cetona. In its rustic kitchen, with high-beamed ceilings and a walk-in fireplace, students prepared a four-course dinner, each course paired with local wines.

Another big change: When the lease was expiring at Magrittings, I decided not to renew it. Though I loved the palazzo's charming old-world ambience, it had always been problematical. The place was just too big, and too old, to manage or clean easily. Its ancient wooden rafters were disintegrating, depositing a layer of silt on everything each morning. Giuliano, who'd originally appropriated a Magrittings room for his art studio, as always, preferred to set up shop wherever inspiration struck. Hence, no surface in the cooking school was ever exempt from the paraphernalia of his creative chaos.

Similarly, the proximity of Magrittings to Trattoria Garga cut both ways. Though I loved seeing my family so often, they were also constantly coming in and out with restaurant business—not to mention helping themselves to whatever was needed across the street. One night, without telling me, they'd taken all my dinner plates away; I didn't find out until I was just about to serve the entrée!

Close by, but far enough away to discourage easy platter pilfering, I discovered, on the first day I looked, another sixteenth-century palazzo—one that was not crumbling. On the Via delle Belle Donne (Street of Beautiful Women), it's as light and cheerful as my previous school was darkly atmospheric. Its marble floors, lofty fresco-embellished ceilings, and big French windows with white shutters make me feel like I'm inhabiting rooms in a Matisse painting. I couldn't be more happily transplanted.

In 2001, Andrea married a local girl named Ginerva, who is descended from Tuscan nobility. With her beautiful oval face, dark hair and eyes, she looks like a Florentine Madonna. Giuliano likes her, thank God—unlike the hated Tina—though he sometimes accuses Andrea of having "betrayed his proletarian origins."

Like our own, their wedding took place in the fourteenth-century Palazzo Vecchio, its rather forbidding Gothic exterior belying the Renaissance splendor within, which dates to a later renovation. Ginerva looked dazzling in her red silk gown (it's becoming fashionable here for brides to wear the "color of joy"). Andrea had had his hair cut the day before, and, through a mother's eyes, looked much as he did on his first day of school. The ceremony was followed by a cocktail party at the Café Rivoire, our old hangout in the Piazza della Signoria.

Recently, Andrea and Ginerva had a little girl. They named her Fiammetta, which was the name of Boccaccio's mistress; it means "little flame." Giuliano and I sat in a pew in the church of Santa Lucia during Fiammetta's christening, holding hands, our eyes filled with happy tears. Andrea held his daughter—who was wearing Ginerva's great-grand-mother's christening gown—at the baptismal font. During the ceremony, I flashed back on Giuliano holding Andrea in his arms at our son's baptism in the church of San Pietro a Monticelli, and I thought about how much time had passed since then, about how much had happened in our lives, and about how quickly it all seems to have gone.

Lately, even Zoe, increasingly frail in her nineties, has somewhat grudgingly admitted that she doesn't know how she would have managed without me all these years. She adores Fiammetta, though, with a touch of the old Eve, she did make a point of reassuring me about Ginerva's ability to produce milk, because "Italian mothers never have trouble nursing their babies." In her mind, it's still a miracle that Andrea didn't starve.

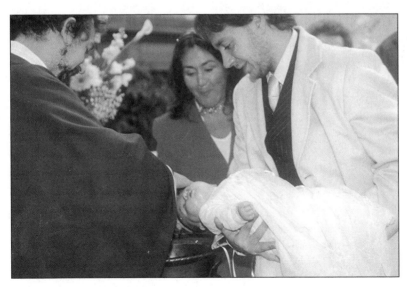

Ginerva and Andrea with Fiammetta

Alessandro recently moved to New York with his beautiful American girlfriend, Elizabeth, and is working as head chef of a SoHo restaurant there. They plan to marry soon. When I last visited, he asked me to help him shop for a diamond engagement ring. Imagine my surprise when the saleswoman assumed I was his fiancé! "I'm his mother," I explained, immensely flattered. With perfect aplomb, she responded: "His mother, too. Well, that's all right, dear." I guess in New York, anything goes.

Sharon and Giuliano at Fiammetta's christening

KAREN'S BLUEBERRY PIE

It seems apt to me to end my tales as they began, with my twin sister and lifelong companion, Karen. We've spent most of our adult life apart, but I still think of her as my closest friend. She's the only person who shares all my childhood memories, and the older I get, the more I cherish that. Like me, an enthusiastic forager, Karen picks her own blueberries in Whiteshell, the lake district of Manitoba.

FOR THE PASTRY:

1 $^1/_4$ cups all-purpose flour

$^3/_4$ stick (6 tablespoons) cold unsalted butter, cut into bits

2 tablespoons ice-cold vegetable shortening

$^1/_4$ teaspoon salt

2 tablespoons ice water (more if needed)

1. Using a pastry cutter, blend flour, butter, vegetable shortening, and salt in a large bowl until mixture resembles coarse meal.

2. Add 2 tablespoons ice water, and toss mixture with 2 spoons until water is incorporated, adding additional ice water if necessary to form a dough.

3. Shape dough into a ball, dust with flour, cover in plastic wrap, and chill for 1 hour.

FOR THE GLAZE:

1 jumbo egg yolk, beaten

2 tablespoons heavy cream

1. Mix egg yolk and cream together, and set aside.

FOR THE FILLING:

6 cups wild blueberries, picked over
(if unavailable, use regular blueberries)

$^1/_4$ cup cornstarch

1 cup sugar

2 tablespoons fresh lemon juice

$^1/_2$ teaspoon salt

1. In a large bowl, mix all ingredients well, and set aside.

ASSEMBLING THE PIE:

1 tablespoon unsalted butter, cut into bits

2 tablespoons sugar

1. Preheat oven to 425 degrees. On a lightly floured surface, roll out half the dough $1/8$-inch thick. Place rolled-out dough in a 9-inch (1-quart) pie pan, and trim edge, leaving a $1/2$-inch overhang. Chill while preparing remaining dough.

2. On a lightly floured surface, roll out remaining dough into a 13- to 14-inch circle.

3. Carefully pour blueberry filling into pie pan with bottom crust, and dot with butter bits.

4. Drape circle of dough over filling, and trim, leaving a 1-inch over-hang. Fold overhang from top crust under overhang from bottom crust. Press edge to seal, and crimp decoratively.

5. Brush crust with glaze. Starting about an inch from the center, cut 4 slits (about 2 inches each) in crust, at $1/4$-pie intervals, to make a cross shape. Sprinkle crust lightly with 2 tablespoons sugar.

6. Bake in bottom third of oven for 20 minutes. Reduce temperature to 375 degrees, and bake 30 to 35 minutes more, or until crust is golden and filling is bubbling. Transfer pie to a rack, and let cool.

Ricette

Giuliano, Sharon, Andrea, *behind Sharon*, Elio, *on left, behind Giuliano*, and restaurant staff

RECIPES

As on the Trattoria Garga menu, I've divided recipes in this section into the four courses (along with subcategories) that comprise a traditional Italian meal:

Antipasto (which literally means "before the meal") is a little something to whet the appetite. It can range from a tantaliizing tidbit (what the French call an *amuse bouche*) to a more substantial offering, such as cold charcuterie, anchovies with lemon zest and olive oil, pickled vegetables, salads, frittati, or, very often, crostini, fettunti, and bruschetti—small slices of toasted Tuscan bread spread with scrumptious toppings.

At dinner parties, antipasti are usually served—along with a glass of white wine, perhaps a fizzy prosecco—before everyone sits down at the table. This wonderfully civilized custom sets a convivial mood for the meal to come, not that Italian dinner parties really need an icebreaker; everyone always arrives in high spirits, anticipating scintillating conversation and great food. And they're seldom disappointed.

Next comes the **Primo Piatto** (first dish), which is a more substantial appetizer, such as soup, risotto, polenta, pasta, or crêpes. Pasta, always freshly made, is served by itself, not with an entrée, so that you can savor its deliciousness without the distraction of competing flavors.

The **Secondo Piatto** (second dish) is the entrée, consisting of meat, fish, or poultry. It is often served with a **Contorno** (side dish), a vegetable or salad.

And **Dolce**, of course, is dessert, usually a sweet, though it could also be a platter of cheese or fruit.

However, even in food-focused Italy, it's the exception nowadays for people to eat so much at one sitting. This style of dining harks back to a more leisurely time, when long lunch hours, often followed by siestas, were the rule, and no one worried about calories, cholesterol, or being fashionably slim. In today's hurried and health-conscious world, lunch is more likely to be a plate of pasta, sandwich, or salad.

That said, it's a poor soul—and not an Italian one—that never rejoices. People here do still linger for hours over four-course Sunday dinners and restaurant meals. And those bountiful blowouts seem like mere nibbles compared to the *ne plus ultra* in overindulgence—an Italian holiday meal. My first experience of such a feast was a Christmas dinner, in 1971, at the home of my sister-in-law, Gigliola. Had I known what was in store for me, I would have fasted the entire week before.

We sat down at 1 P.M. sharp at a table laden with about a dozen varieties of cold cuts, pickled vegetables in oil, and crostini topped with chicken liver paté. As wines were poured, Gigliola's husband, Umberto, explained the various cured meats, telling me their names and the places in the country where he'd gone to purchase them (almost every little Tuscan town has its own specialty, and one of Umberto's favorite pastimes is venturing out in search of exquisite foods).

Plates were cleared, and a steaming cauldron of soup (tortellini in broth) appeared. No sooner had we surrendered our soupspoons, than an enormous platter of bolliti (boiled meats) appeared—capon, beef, tongue, and veal trotter—accompanied by a bowl of salsa verde, a green sauce made of capers, parsley, garlic, anchovies, bread, and vinegar.

By that point I was already more than satiated, but there was more to come. Much more. Boiled meats were followed by umidi (braised meats), in this case beef and chicken. And umidi gave way to arrosti (roasted meats), including an arista (roast pork) and a spiedini di uccellini, (skewers of tiny larks, interspersed with pieces of bread and bay leaves). Side dishes of sautéed greens and other vegetables abounded.

Finally, an enormous salad of wild greens was presented, *per pulire la bocca* (to clean the palate). By now I was bilious, having been forced to taste a little bit of everything (so as not to offend my in-laws), and having washed it all down with considerable amounts of wine. We had been seated for three-and-a-half hours, and all I really wanted was to get into a horizontal position and attempt digestion. No such luck. Out came the dolci, presented on an oval dish the size of a baptismal font. Its centerpiece, tiramisù, was embellished for the special occasion—as if it wasn't already rich enough—with whipped cream and pieces of dark chocolate. There were packets of Ricciarelli (almond cookies), Panforte di Siena (a hard cake full of nuts and candied fruits), and Panettone (a Christmas bread studded with raisins and fruit). Home baking isn't especially popular with Florentines on holidays, but they love ripping open packages of store-bought delicacies. The dolci were served with vin santo, a sweet dessert wine.

Finally, with coffee and liqueurs, the meal culminated around 5 P.M. I'd been amazed at the capacity of my husband's family to consume so much food. Even slender Zoe had eaten every single course, not to mention Umberto's tiny, ancient, blind grandmother, who'd devoured every morsel with great enjoyment.

Zoe and I offered to help with the dishes, which took about an hour, and the women remained gossiping in the kitchen while the men chattered and smoked in the dining room.

When I suggested that it was time to go home, my sister-in-law gazed at me wide-eyed. "You mean you're not staying for dinner?" she gasped.

Antipasti

HORS D'OEUVRES

CAPONATA

5 stalks celery

2 pounds yellow peppers

2 pounds eggplant

Peanut or sunflower oil for frying

1 small red onion

2 tablespoons extra-virgin olive oil

2 pounds fresh ripe tomatoes, diced into $1/4$-inch cubes

$1/2$ cup white wine vinegar

2 tablespoons sugar

Salt

10 fresh basil leaves

1. Cut white parts of celery stalks into $1/4$-inch slices, setting aside green parts. Remove cores of yellow peppers and cut, lengthways, into $1/4$-inch slices. Remove both ends of eggplant, and dice into $1/2$-inch cubes.

2. In a large skillet, heat peanut or sunflower oil until it begins to smoke. In 2 batches, sauté prepared vegetables on medium-high heat, stirring frequently, until golden. Drain well on folded paper towels.

3. Chop onion and green part of 1 celery stalk very fine ($1/8$-inch pebbles). Place olive oil, onion, and green celery in a saucepan, and cook over medium heat for 5 minutes, or until onion is translucent. Add diced tomatoes, and cook for 15 minutes, stirring only a few times.

4. In another saucepan, cook vinegar and sugar on medium heat until sugar is dissolved.

5. Arrange sautéed vegetables from Step 1 on a large platter. Top with tomato/onion/green celery sauce. Salt to taste, sprinkle with vinegar/sugar mixture, and garnish with basil leaves. This dish can be served tepid or cold.

Fagottini di Melanzane
e Zucchine

EGGPLANT AND ZUCCHINI BUNDLES

1 long eggplant

2 long zucchini

3 ripe tomatoes, diced into $1/2$-inch cubes

1 clove garlic, very finely chopped

10 fresh basil leaves

Juice of $1/2$ lemon

Salt

$1/2$ pound soft goat cheese

2 teaspoons very finely chopped chives

3 tablespoons extra-virgin olive oil

1. Slice eggplant and zucchini lengthways into long ribbons, $1/4$-inch thick (obtain 6 of each). Place vegetable ribbons on a hot grill, and cook 3 minutes on each side. Set aside.

2. Place diced tomatoes into a bowl with chopped garlic. Cut 5 basil leaves into thin strips. Add to tomatoes, along with lemon juice, and salt to taste.

3. In another bowl, mix goat cheese with chives. Place $1/6$ of cheese mixture in the middle of a ribbon of grilled eggplant. Fold both ends of eggplant ribbon towards the center, covering the cheese filling. Wrap a zucchini strip crossways around the center of the eggplant package, completing the bundle. Repeat with remaining ribbons and cheese.

4. Create a bed of chopped tomato mixture on a serving platter, and carefully place bundles on it, with loose ends of vegetables facing down. Drizzle with oil, and garnish platter with remaining basil leaves.

Fiori Fritti

FRIED ZUCCHINI BLOSSOMS

Squash blossoms—delicious edible flowers from zucchini, squash, or pumpkin plants—are common ingredients in summer Italian cookery. The ones used for cooking are the male flowers, which are sterile, so in eating them, you're not threatening the life of a future zucchini. Easy to recognize, male flowers connect to the plant on thin stems, while female flowers—from which zucchini will grow—have thick stems. In summer, you can find squash blossoms at farmers' markets and specialty produce shops. Inquire if you don't see them; they're highly perishable and are usually refrigerated.

NOTE You can fry these up ahead of time, and serve them at room temperature. The beer batter will keep the blossoms crunchy.

$1/2$ pound zucchini blossoms

1 cup unbleached all-purpose flour

1 teaspoon salt

1 12-ounce can beer

Peanut oil

Salt

1. Remove prickly green leaves from the base of each zucchini blossom.

2. Combine flour and teaspoon of salt in a large bowl. Add beer, a bit at a time, while beating to a smooth consistency with a wire whisk.

3. Heat enough oil to halfway fill a large skillet. While oil is heating, dip blossoms into batter, and shake off excess.

4. When oil is sizzling, fry blossoms until golden (approximately 3 minutes on each side). Remove blossoms with a slotted spoon, and drain on paper towels. Salt to taste.

Frittata di Asparagi Selvatici

WILD ASPARAGUS OMELETTE

NOTE If you prefer a well-cooked frittata, at the end of Step 4, place omelette pan in a 350-degree oven for 5 minutes.

$1/2$ pound wild asparagus (if unavailable use thin stalks of regular asparagus)

5 jumbo eggs

$1/2$ teaspoon salt

$1/4$ teaspoon freshly ground black pepper

$1/4$ cup extra-virgin olive oil

1 small yellow onion, finely chopped

12 fresh basil leaves

1. Cut tough ends off asparagus stalks, and steam until just tender. Drain, and set aside.

2. Beat eggs with a fork until yolks and whites are barely combined. Stir in salt and pepper, and set aside.

3. Pour oil into an 11-inch cast-iron frying pan, add chopped onion, cover with a lid, and cook over low heat until onion is transparent but not browned (about 5 minutes). Remove lid, and add asparagus to pan, laying the stalks in flat (cut if necessary to fit in pan).

4. Pour beaten eggs over asparagus. As eggs cook, lift edges with a spatula in order to let uncooked egg run under. Cook for 5 minutes over medium heat until all egg is firm. Asparagus spears should be visible.

5. Remove to a warm serving dish, and garnish with basil leaves.

Fritto di Fiori e Gamberi

FRIED ZUCCHINI
BLOSSOMS AND SHRIMP

NOTE Another time, prepare this recipe using other vegetables—broccoli fleurets, zucchini (cut strips $1/4$" wide $\times$ $1/4$" deep $\times$ $1\,1/2$" long), eggplant (same measurements), butternut squash (same measurements), or whole stringbeans. A mix of vegetables is also fun.

$1/2$ pound zucchini blossoms

1 pound medium-sized shrimp, shelled and deveined

1 cup unbleached all-purpose flour

1 teaspoon salt

2 12-ounce cans beer

Peanut oil

Salt

1. Remove prickly green leaves from base of each zucchini blossom. Wash shrimp, and towel dry. Set both aside.

2. Combine flour and 1 teaspoon salt in a large bowl. Add one can of beer, a bit at a time, while beating to a smooth consistency with a wire whisk. (The second can is for you to drink while cooking.)

3. Heat enough oil to halfway fill a large skillet. While oil is heating, dip blossoms into batter, and shake off excess.

4. When oil is sizzling, fry blossoms until golden (approximately 3 minutes on each side). Remove blossoms with a slotted spoon, and drain on paper towels. Repeat battering/deep-frying process with shrimp. Salt to taste.

Insalata di Carciofi e Parmigiano   SERVES 4

FRESH ARTICHOKE
AND PARMESAN SALAD

4 very large artichokes, purple ones if available
(make sure they're firm; the firmer the better)

Juice of 1 lemon

Salt

Extra-virgin olive oil

2 ounces fresh Parmigiano Reggiano

1 ounce pine nuts

1. Remove stems, tops, and tough outer leaves of artichokes (save them for decoration), retaining only tender hearts.

2. Divide artichokes in half, lengthways. (If any of them has a hairy part inside [the choke], gently remove it with the point of a paring knife.) Place artichoke halves on a wooden chopping board, spoon lemon juice over each, and slice very thinly, still lengthways. Toss well with fingers so artichokes absorb lemon juice.

3. Arrange artichokes on a serving dish, which has been decorated with a crown of outer leaves. Salt to taste, and drizzle with oil. With a sharp paring knife, slice Parmigiano into paper-thin shavings. Distribute Parmigiano shavings and pine nuts on top of salad.

Insalata di Zucchine,
Pinoli, e Olio Tartufato

ZUCCHINI, PINE NUT, AND TRUFFLE OIL SALAD

4 small ribbed summer zucchini (approximately 5 inches long)

$1/2$ teaspoon truffle oil

$1/2$ teaspoon salt

$1/4$ cup extra-virgin olive oil

$1/4$ cup pine nuts

1. Wash and dry zucchini. Using third-largest holes of a four-sided hand grater, shred zucchini, and turn out onto a serving platter.

2. Place truffle oil, salt, and olive oil in a small bowl and stir well. Drizzle zucchini with dressing, and top with pine nuts.

Salvia Fritta

FRIED SAGE LEAVES

With a glass of wine, this makes for a great little predinner munchie.

NOTES Frying can be done ahead of time, as the beer batter will keep leaves crunchy.

Leftover batter can be fried. It forms puffy little pancakes, which are called *coccole* (it means "cuddles").

Peanut oil for frying

$^3/_4$ cup unbleached all-purpose flour

6 ounces ($^3/_4$ cup) beer

$^1/_2$ teaspoon salt

12 very large fresh sage leaves (if only smaller ones are available; use more; they can be fried in bunches with stems twined together)

Salt

1. Heat enough oil to fill a large skillet halfway.

2. While oil is heating, combine flour, beer, and $^1/_2$ teaspoon salt. Mix with a wire whisk until batter is perfectly smooth.

3. Dip sage leaves into batter, and shake off excess. When oil is sizzling, fry leaves, turning until golden on both sides. (Don't crowd too many leaves into the skillet; anything deep-frying needs space.) Drain on paper towels, and add salt to taste.

Torta di Carciofi

SERVES 4

ARTICHOKE TART

1. Preheat oven to 350 degrees.

FOR THE PIECRUST:

1 1/8 cups unbleached all-purpose flour

1/2 teaspoon salt

1/2 cup unsalted butter, melted

1. Mix flour, salt, and butter thoroughly. Using your fingers, press crust evenly into a 9 1/2-inch pie pan. Bake for 15 minutes.

FOR THE FILLING:

5 artichokes (make sure they're firm; the firmer the better)

Juice of 1 lemon

1 ounce (1/4 stick) unsalted butter

2 tablespoons extra-virgin olive oil

Salt

Freshly ground black pepper

Zest of 1 lemon

1. Strip off tough outer leaves of artichokes, slice off tops (where leaves are darker in color) and stems, and remove any fluff or choke from the center. Cut each artichoke, lengthways, into 8 slices. Place artichokes in a bowl of water with lemon juice.

2. Put butter and oil in a skillet (don't use an iron one, which will turn artichokes brown), and turn heat to medium. Drain artichokes well in a colander, squeezing out as much liquid as possible.

3. When butter is melted, add artichokes to skillet, and season with salt and pepper to taste. Cook for 10 minutes, and add lemon zest.

ONCE UPON A TUSCAN TABLE

 og 196 go

1 ounce ($^{1}/_{4}$ stick) unsalted butter

2 tablespoons unbleached all-purpose flour

$^{1}/_{2}$ teaspoon salt

$^{1}/_{4}$ teaspoon freshly grated nutmeg

2 cups whole milk

1. Melt butter over very low heat (don't brown it) in a small nonstick saucepan. Add flour, stirring continuously with a wooden spoon. Cook for a few seconds. Add salt and nutmeg. Still stirring, add milk, a little at a time. Cook for 10 minutes on medium-low heat, stirring all the while. Set aside.

ASSEMBLING THE TART:

2 tablespoons grated Parmigiano Reggiano

1. Carefully turn out artichokes into piecrust, and pour Béchamel Sauce over them. Sprinkle evenly with Parmigiano, and bake for 30 minutes.

Bruschetta con
Pomodori Freschi al Forno

SERVES 6

BRUSCHETTA WITH
OVEN-ROASTED TOMATOES

6 ripe plum tomatoes (about a pound)

2 tablespoons extra-virgin olive oil

Salt

$1/4$ teaspoon cracked red pepper

7 garlic cloves, in their jackets

12 slices (about 2 $1/2$-inches wide and $1/2$-inch thick)
Tuscan or sourdough bread

Extra-virgin olive oil for drizzling

2 tablespoons fresh basil leaves, coarsely chopped

1. Preheat oven to 350 degrees. Cut tomatoes in half lengthways, and arrange, cut sides up, in a shallow baking dish just large enough to hold them all without overlapping.

2. Drizzle 2 tablespoons oil over tomatoes, season with salt and cracked red pepper, and scatter garlic cloves around tomatoes. Roast in middle of oven, until tomatoes are tender and skins are wrinkled (about 1 hour). Cool, then transfer tomatoes to a plate, reserving garlic and oil in baking dish.

3. While tomatoes are cooling, place bread slices on a baking sheet. Bake in middle of oven until golden on one side (about 15 minutes).

4. Peel roasted garlic cloves and mash to a paste with oil and juices from baking dish. Spread paste evenly on untoasted side of each piece of toast, and top with a tomato half, cut side up. Drizzle with oil, and top with chopped basil leaves.

LITTLE TOASTS
WITH CHICKEN LIVERS

3 tablespoons ($^3/_8$ of a stick) unsalted butter

1 small yellow onion, very finely chopped

1 small tomato, diced into $^1/_2$-inch cubes

4 large chicken livers, cut into $^1/_2$-inch pieces

Chicken stock or broth

2 tablespoons capers

4 anchovy fillets (rinse in warm water to remove oil and/or salt)

Salt

Freshly ground black pepper

12 small slices Tuscan or sourdough bread

1. Melt butter in a small pan, add chopped onion, and cook over medium heat for 5 minutes. Add diced tomato and cook another 2 minutes.

2. Add chicken livers to onion and tomato. Cook for 10 minutes, carefully adding a little chicken stock or broth as necessary to keep mixture moist, but not soupy (it has to have a spreadable texture).

3. Add capers and anchovy fillets, and cook another 5 minutes. Pass contents of pan through a food mill. Add salt and pepper to taste.

4. Toast bread in broiler on one side only, and spread liver pâté on untoasted side.

Crostini ai Funghi Porcini SERVES 4

LITTLE TOASTS
WITH PORCINI MUSHROOMS

1 pound porcini mushrooms, thoroughly washed and dried
(it's all right to use frozen porcini if fresh ones aren't available)

$\frac{1}{2}$ cup extra-virgin olive oil

4 cloves garlic, in their jackets

3 tablespoons nepitella or fresh mint leaves

1 teaspoon salt

4 large slices Tuscan or sourdough bread

1. Slice porcini mushrooms into $\frac{1}{2}$-inch strips. Pour oil into a skillet. Add mushrooms, garlic, nepitella, and salt, and cook over medium heat for 20 minutes, stirring occasionally. If mushrooms are sticking to skillet, add a little water. Remove garlic cloves from sauce (they're only to provide a nuance of flavor, which shouldn't compete with the porcini), and discard.

2. Cut slices of bread in half, and toast in broiler until golden-brown (keep an eye on them; they can burn quickly). Top untoasted side with mushroom sauce.

Crostini di Scamorza
Affumicata e Salsa Acciugata

SERVES 4

LITTLE TOASTS WITH SMOKED MOZZARELLA AND ANCHOVY SAUCE

NOTE If you want to make extra anchovy sauce, it can be kept refrigerated almost indefinitely.

6 canned anchovy fillets

$1/4$ cup extra-virgin olive oil

4 large slices ($1/2$-inch thick) Tuscan or sourdough bread

$1/2$ pound smoked mozzarella, cut into 8 equal slices (if unavailable, use smoked cheddar or any other smoked cheese that melts)

1. Preheat oven to 375 degrees. Rinse anchovy fillets in warm water to remove excess oil and salt. In a small skillet, heat oil and anchovies, stirring them together until anchovies are dissolved (about 5 minutes).

2. Place slices of bread on a baking sheet, cover each with 2 slices of smoked mozzarella, and spoon anchovy sauce over cheese. Bake for 10 minutes or until cheese is melted and bubbling around the edges.

SHRIMP TOAST

With a glass of white wine, these crostoni make a lovely entrée for a light summer meal.

1 pound large shrimp, peeled and deveined

4 large slices ($\frac{1}{2}$-inch thick) Tuscan or sourdough bread

1 clove garlic

1 pound ripe tomatoes, at room temperature,
diced into $\frac{1}{2}$-inch cubes

Salt

Extra-virgin olive oil for drizzling

12 large fresh basil leaves

1. Bring a large pot of water to a boil. While waiting for it to boil, wash shrimp, and drain in a colander.

2. Toast bread on both sides, cut end off garlic clove, and rub one side of each bread slice vigorously with it. Keep toast warm.

3. Carefully toss shrimp into boiling water (the water will stop bubbling when you do). As soon as water returns to boiling (about 3 minutes), remove shrimp with a slotted spoon, drain well, and set aside.

4. Put slices of toast on individual serving dishes, and pile an equal amount of tomatoes on each. Sprinkle with salt.

5. Pile shrimp on top of tomatoes, so that each piece of toast is completely covered with tomatoes and shrimp. Drizzle with oil, and garnish with basil leaves.

Fettunta

BRUSCHETTA, FLORENTINE-STYLE

This is the classic bruschetta, based on the inimitable quality of our Tuscan bread and our exquisitely fragrant extra-virgin olive oil. As you'll see, there are numerous variations on this pristine original. Use the best bread and highest-quality extra-virgin olive oil available at stores in your area.

NOTE You can also toast the bread in a toaster oven.

4 large slices Tuscan bread, cut into $1/_2$-inch-thick slices (if unavailable, substitute hard-crusted peasant or sourdough bread)

1 clove garlic

Extra-virgin olive oil

Salt

1. Preheat oven to 350 degrees.
2. Divide each slice of bread into 2 pieces, and toast in oven until golden on both sides. Place toasted bread on a serving platter, and rub one side of each piece with garlic clove. Drizzle generously with oil, and salt to taste.

Fettunta con Cavolo Nero

BRUSCHETTA WITH KALE

2 bunches California or elephant kale

4 large slices Tuscan or sourdough bread,
cut into $1/2$-inch-thick slices

1 clove garlic

Extra-virgin olive oil

Salt

Freshly ground black pepper

1. Put up a large pot of water to boil. While waiting for water to heat, discard kale stalks, keeping only fresh-looking leaves that aren't limp or yellowing. Wash leaves well in cold water.

2. Place kale in boiling water, and cook for 30 minutes. Drain well.

3. Toast bread until golden on both sides. Rub one side of each slice with the garlic clove. Pile equal amounts of kale on each slice of toast, drizzle with oil, sprinkle with salt, and season with a twist of pepper.

Fettunta con Piselli
al Prosciutto

BRUSCHETTA WITH
FRESH PEAS AND PROSCIUTTO

2 $\frac{1}{2}$ pounds fresh peas (approximately 1 pound shelled)

$\frac{3}{8}$ cup extra-virgin olive oil

3 $\frac{1}{2}$ ounces prosciutto, chopped into $\frac{1}{4}$-inch pieces

1 scallion, finely chopped

1 teaspoon sugar

$\frac{1}{2}$ cup water

Salt

4 large slices Tuscan or sourdough bread,
cut into $\frac{1}{2}$-inch-thick slices

1 tablespoon fresh parsley leaves, finely chopped

1. Wash peas, drain, and set aside. Pour oil into a skillet. Add pro-sciutto and scallion, turn heat to medium, and sauté for 3 minutes, stirring frequently.

2. Add peas, sugar, and $\frac{1}{2}$ cup water. Cook on medium heat until peas are tender (about 5 minutes). Salt to taste.

3. Toast bread lightly on both sides, and place a slice on each plate. Pile equal amounts of prosciutto/pea mixture on each slice, press-ing gently to make it adhere to toast. Sprinkle with parsley.

BRUSCHETTA WITH BROCCOLI RABE

NOTE Another time, try this recipe with a mixture of spinach and broccoli rabe.

2 bunches broccoli rabe

$3/8$ cup extra-virgin olive oil

2 cloves garlic, finely chopped

$1/4$ teaspoon cracked red pepper

Salt

6 slices Tuscan or sourdough bread, cut into $1/2$-inch-thick slices

1. Put up a large pot of water to boil. While waiting for water to heat, remove stems, and wash broccoli rabe well in cold water.

2. Toss broccoli rabe into boiling water, lower heat to medium, and cook until tender (about 15 minutes). Drain, squeeze out excess moisture, and coarsely chop. Set aside.

3. Pour oil into a skillet, add garlic, turn heat to medium-high, and sauté until garlic is golden. Add broccoli rabe and cracked red pepper, salt to taste, and sauté for another 3 minutes, stirring occasionally.

4. Toast bread lightly on both sides, place a slice on each plate, and pile equal amounts of broccoli rabe on each slice.

Primi Piatti

FIRST COURSES

Cacciucco SERVES 4

FISH SOUP

Though Italians have been making cacciucco for centuries, it's actually a Jewish dish brought over by refugees from the Spanish Inquisition, who settled in Livorno. Its name comes from the Turkish word *kacukli*, which means "bits and pieces."

$1/4$ cup extra-virgin olive oil

2 cloves garlic, finely chopped

$1/4$ pound yellow onion, finely chopped

$1/2$ cup dry white wine

$2/3$ cup water

$1/4$ teaspoon cracked red pepper

$3/4$ pound fresh ripe tomatoes, coarsely chopped, with skins (remove the seeds)

1 teaspoon salt

$1/4$ pound fillet of red mullet, cut into 2-inch slices

$1/4$ pound dogfish (or monkfish), cut into 2-inch slices

$1/2$ pound fillet of sole, cut into 2-inch slices

1 tablespoon finely chopped fresh parsley leaves

4 slices ($1/2$-inch-thick) Tuscan or sourdough bread

1 clove garlic

1. Place oil, 2 chopped garlic cloves, and chopped onion in a large stockpot. Turn heat to medium, and cook until onion softens (about 5 minutes). Pour in wine, and continue cooking for 2 minutes. Add water, cracked red pepper, tomatoes, and salt. Reduce heat, and simmer for 5 minutes.

2. Add red mullet, and continue simmering for another 5 minutes. Add dogfish (or monkfish), and simmer for an additional 5 minutes. Add sole, and simmer another 5 minutes. Sprinkle parsley into soup, stir, and remove from heat.

3. Lightly toast bread, and rub each toasted slice with remaining garlic clove. Place a slice of toast in each soup plate, pour soup on top, and serve.

Pappa al Pomodoro

TOMATO BREAD SOUP

NOTE This recipe should be made only in summer, when fresh, ripe tomatoes are available.

6 large ripe tomatoes

4 cloves garlic

$1/2$ cup fresh basil leaves

$1/4$ teaspoon cracked red pepper

2 teaspoons salt

1 cup extra-virgin olive oil

12 ounces sliced stale Tuscan bread (if unavailable, use a hard-crusted peasant bread), cut into $1/2$-inch slices

2 cups water

Extra-virgin olive oil for drizzling

18 fresh basil leaves for garnish

1. Put tomatoes whole into a pot of boiling water, and keep on high heat until water bubbles again (about 2 minutes). Drain and cool under cold running water. Slip off skins.

2. Put skinned tomatoes in a large stockpot with garlic, $1/2$ cup basil leaves, cracked red pepper, salt, and 1 cup oil. Cook for 10 minutes. Mash tomatoes, and cook 5 minutes longer.

3. Toast bread golden-brown on both sides.

4. Add 2 cups water and toasted bread to stockpot. Cook, stirring frequently with a wooden spoon (so the mixture doesn't stick to the bottom), until bread is dissolved (about 15 minutes). If soup appears too thick, add a little water. Serve in bowls, drizzled with oil and garnished with fresh basil leaves.

Passato di Fagioli con Farro

PURÉED WHITE BEAN
SOUP WITH SPELT

1 cup dried cannellini beans

2 quarts water

2 cloves garlic, in their jackets

3 tablespoons extra-virgin olive oil

1 small onion, finely chopped

1 tablespoon fresh rosemary leaves, finely chopped

$^1/_4$ teaspoon cracked red pepper

1 cup canned puréed Italian plum tomatoes

Salt

$^3/_4$ cup spelt (a cereal grain; look for it in health-food
or specialty stores)

Extra-virgin olive oil

1. Place beans in large stockpot, and add enough cold water to cover them, plus 3 inches. Let stand overnight.

2. Drain beans well, return to pot, and add 2 quarts water and garlic cloves. Bring to a boil, then reduce heat to low, and simmer, stirring occasionally, for 2 hours (or until beans are tender).

3. While beans are cooking, put 3 tablespoons oil in another large stockpot, and turn heat to medium. When oil is heated, add chopped onion, and sauté until golden. Add rosemary and cracked red pepper, and sauté 1 minute more. Add tomatoes, reduce heat to low, and cook for 5 minutes, stirring occasionally.

4. Remove and discard jackets from garlic, returning cloves to pot of beans. Purée beans and garlic in a blender or food processor, add to tomato mixture, and simmer for 5 minutes. Salt to taste.

5. Add spelt to soup, and cook for 30 minutes over low heat, stirring occasionally to prevent sticking. If soup seems too thick, thin it with water. Serve drizzled with oil.

Passato di Pomodoro

PURÉED TOMATO SOUP

3 tablespoons extra-virgin olive oil

1 cup carrots, chopped into $1/4$-inch pieces

1 cup celery, chopped into $1/4$-inch pieces

1 medium onion, chopped into $1/4$-inch pieces

3 cloves garlic, finely chopped

1 large Idaho potato, diced (about 1 cup)

$4 1/2$ cups canned Italian plum tomatoes

$1/4$ cup fresh basil leaves, loosely packed

$1/4$ cup fresh mint leaves

3 to 4 cups water

Salt

Freshly ground black pepper

1. Spoon oil into a large stockpot, and add chopped carrots, celery, onions, and garlic. Cook vegetables over medium-low heat for 10 minutes, stirring occasionally (vegetables should not brown). Add potatoes, and cook for 5 minutes.

2. Add tomatoes, basil and mint leaves, and 2 cups of the water. Simmer, stirring occasionally, for 20 minutes.

3. Remove pot from heat, and cool soup for 10 minutes. Purée soup in a blender (use caution when blending hot liquids; do it in batches), transferring as puréed to a large bowl. Return soup to pot, and thin to desired consistency with remaining water. Season with salt and pepper to taste. Serve with Crostini al Parmigiano (see recipe, page 213).

EGG AND CHEESE
RAGS IN BROTH

Stracciatella are the little "rags" that form when an egg and cheese mixture is dropped into hot broth. This is a classic family soup dish.

2 jumbo eggs

$1/4$ cup finely grated Parmigiano Reggiano

$1 \, 3/4$ teaspoons kosher salt

$1/4$ teaspoon freshly grated nutmeg

1 tablespoon unbleached all-purpose flour

4 cups broth (chicken, beef, or vegetable)

Salt

Freshly ground black pepper

1. Place eggs, Parmigiano, $1 \, 3/4$ teaspoons kosher salt, nutmeg, and flour in a small bowl, and stir (do not beat) with a fork. Set aside.

2. Bring broth to a boil in a pot large enough to support a colander. (The colander—one with widely spaced holes—will have to fit over the pot without touching the broth, so egg mixture can flow freely into the soup to form strings.)

3. Place colander over boiling broth, and pour egg mixture through it. Remove colander, and stir soup once or twice. Remove from heat, and season to taste with salt and pepper.

Crostini al Parmigiano SERVES 6–8

PARMESAN CROUTONS

These croutons are scrumptious in soups and will suffice for up to 8 bowls . . . if you can resist nibbling too many before you serve it.

6 slices ($\frac{1}{2}$-inch-thick) day-old Tuscan, peasant, or sourdough bread

2 tablespoons extra-virgin olive oil

$\frac{1}{2}$ teaspoon salt

1 cup roughly grated Parmigiano Reggiano

1. Preheat oven to 400 degrees.
2. Cut bread into $\frac{1}{2}$-inch cubes, place them on a cookie sheet lined with parchment paper, drizzle with oil, and sprinkle with salt. Evenly distribute grated Parmigiano over bread cubes.
3. Bake for 10 minutes. Turn croutons with a spatula, and bake 10 minutes more, or until golden-brown.

Crespelle al Radicchio Rosso
con Salsa di Gorgonzola SERVES 4

CRÊPES STUFFED WITH RADICCHIO AND GORGONZOLA

FOR THE FILLING:

1 pound red radicchio (about 1 to 3 heads, depending on size)

2 tablespoons extra-virgin olive oil

10 ounces Gorgonzola cheese (dolce) or Dolcelatte

$1/4$ cup heavy cream

$1/4$ teaspoon truffle oil

1. Preheat oven to 350 degrees. Wash each head of radicchio without separating leaves, and towel dry.

2. Slice each head in half lengthways, then again lengthways into $1/4$-inch slices. Place slices in a baking pan, and drizzle with olive oil. Bake for 20 minutes, stirring once after 10 minutes. Remove pan from oven, and set aside.

3. Melt Gorgonzola and heavy cream together in the top of a double boiler. When cheese is melted, add truffle oil. Add half the cheese sauce to the radicchio, and transfer to a small bowl. Set remainder aside. Leave oven on.

FOR THE CRÊPES:

2 tablespoons ($1/4$ stick) unsalted butter

$3/4$ cups unbleached all-purpose flour

2 jumbo eggs

$1/4$ teaspoon salt

1 cup whole milk

Unsalted butter for greasing ovenproof casserole

3 tablespoons freshly grated Parmigiano Reggiano

1. Melt butter over very low heat (don't brown it) in a small saucepan.

2. In a large bowl, mix flour and eggs together with a wire whisk. Add salt and melted butter, and continue mixing. When mixture is smooth, and free of lumps, add milk, a little at a time, continuing to whisk (for best results, toss it into a blender until silky smooth). Refrigerate mixture for 30 minutes.

3. Put a 9- or 10-inch nonstick pan on the stove at high heat. Keep batter bowl near stove and a large plate close by. Spoon some batter into pan, and swirl pan to completely cover bottom with a thin layer, pouring any excess back into batter bowl. When batter becomes opaque, flip crêpe on its other side for 5 seconds, then turn out onto plate. Continue making crêpes until out of batter (it should make 8).

NOTE If you don't have a nonstick pan, melt 1 tablespoon of butter in the pan. Then, with a paper towel, wipe up most of the butter, leaving only a very thin film of it. You can fry all your crêpes without adding extra butter.

4. Place crêpes, one at a time, on a flat surface, lighter side up. Divide radicchio-cheese filling into 8 parts, and place an equal amount in center of each crêpe. Roll crêpes into log shapes.

5. Grease an ovenproof casserole with butter, place crêpes in casserole, and spoon remaining cheese sauce over them. Sprinkle with grated Parmigiano. Bake for 20 minutes.

Polenta con Funghi Porcini

POLENTA WITH PORCINI MUSHROOM SAUCE

$1/2$ cup extra-virgin olive oil

4 cloves garlic, in their jackets

1 pound porcini mushrooms (thoroughly washed, dried, and sliced into $1/4$-inch pieces)

2 tablespoons nepitella (if unavailable use mint leaves), finely chopped

1 cup chicken or vegetable broth

2 teaspoons salt

2 cups polenta corn flour

2 tablespoons unsalted butter

1. Pour oil into a saucepan with garlic cloves, mushrooms, and nepitella. Sauté on medium heat for 5 minutes. At the same time, put $1 1/2$ quarts of water up to boil in a large stockpot.

2. Add broth to mushrooms, and cook, stirring frequently with a wooden spoon, for 10 minutes. Remove saucepan from heat, and discard garlic cloves. Set saucepan aside.

3. Add salt to boiling water, and stir in polenta corn flour with a wire whisk. Reduce heat to low, add butter, and cover with a heavy lid. Cook for 20 minutes, stirring every 5 minutes with a wooden spoon.

4. Serve polenta in bowls topped with mushroom sauce.

POLENTA WITH
SWEET GORGONZOLA

2 teaspoons salt

2 cups polenta corn flour

2 tablespoons unsalted butter

6 ounces Gorgonzola (dolce) or Dolcelatte, divided into 6 slices

1. Bring $1\frac{1}{2}$ quarts water to a boil. Add salt, and stir in polenta flour with a wire whisk. Reduce heat to low, add butter, and cover with a heavy lid. Cook for 20 minutes, stirring every 5 minutes with a wooden spoon.

2. Serve polenta in bowls, each topped with a slice of Gorgonzola.

Risotto ai Carciofi

SERVES 8

RISOTTO WITH ARTICHOKES

FOR THE ARTICHOKE SAUCE:

8 artichokes

Juice of 1 lemon

$1/2$ cup extra-virgin olive oil

2 cloves garlic, finely chopped

$1/2$ cup water

$1/4$ teaspoon cracked red pepper

3 ripe tomatoes, cut into wedges

1. Strip off tough outer leaves of artichokes, and slice off tops (where leaves are darker in color) and stems. Halve artichokes lengthways, and remove any fluff or choke from centers with the point of a paring knife. Cut each artichoke, still lengthways, into $1/4$-inch slices, and place in a bowl of water with lemon juice. Set aside.

2. Pour oil into a large skillet (don't use an iron one, which will turn artichokes brown). Turn heat to medium, and sauté garlic until just golden.

3. Add artichokes to skillet, and cook covered for 10 minutes. Add water, cracked red pepper, and tomato wedges. Cook covered for another 10 minutes, and set aside.

FOR THE RISOTTO:

2 tablespoons unsalted butter

$1/2$ yellow onion, finely chopped

2 cups Carnaroli rice (if not available, use risotto rice)

$1 1/2$ quarts chicken or vegetable broth

1 cup dry white wine

1 tablespoon fresh parsley leaves, finely chopped

Freshly grated Parmigiano Reggiano

1. On low-medium heat, melt butter in a large earthenware pot (or any other heavy nonstick stockpot), and sauté onion until soft and lightly golden in color (about 5 minutes). Turn heat to medium, add rice, and cook for 5 minutes, stirring frequently. At the same time, on another burner, heat broth in a saucepan.

2. Add wine to rice, and stir until it evaporates. Add 1 cup hot broth, and stir until liquid is almost completely evaporated. Add another cup hot broth, and repeat procedure, still stirring constantly. Keep adding broth, stirring, and letting liquid evaporate, until rice is cooked and its consistency is creamy (about 20 minutes). There may be leftover broth.

3. Stir in artichoke sauce, and let rest, covered, for 5 minutes. Top with chopped parsley. Serve accompanied by grated Parmigiano.

SAFFRON RISOTTO

2 tablespoons unsalted butter

$1/2$ yellow onion, finely chopped

2 cups Carnaroli rice (if not available, use risotto rice)

$1 1/2$ quarts chicken or vegetable broth

1 cup dry white wine

$1/2$ teaspoon ground saffron

1. On low-medium heat, melt butter in a large earthenware pot (or heavy nonstick stockpot), and sauté onion until soft and lightly golden in color (about 5 minutes). Turn heat to medium, add rice, and cook for 5 minutes, stirring frequently. At the same time, on another burner, heat broth in a saucepan.

2. Add wine to rice, and stir until it evaporates. Add 1 cup hot broth, and stir until liquid is almost completely evaporated. Add another cup hot broth, and repeat procedure, still stirring constantly. Keep adding broth, stirring, and letting liquid evaporate, until rice is cooked and its consistency is creamy (about 20 minutes). There may be leftover broth.

3. Remove from heat, add saffron, and stir well. Let stand for 5 minutes before serving.

Risotto con Asparagi SERVES 8

ASPARAGUS RISOTTO

16 asparagus stalks

2 tablespoons unsalted butter

$\frac{1}{2}$ yellow onion, finely chopped

2 cups Carnaroli rice (if not available, use risotto rice)

1 $\frac{1}{2}$ quarts chicken broth

1 cup dry white wine

Freshly grated Parmigiano Reggiano

1. Wash asparagus. Using a sharp knife, remove tough ends of stalks. Cut off tips (about 1 inch), and slice remaining stalk in $\frac{1}{4}$-inch rounds. Set aside.

2. On low-medium heat, melt butter in a large earthenware pot (or heavy nonstick stockpot), and sauté onion until soft and lightly golden in color (about 5 minutes). Turn heat to medium, add rice, and cook for 5 minutes, stirring frequently. At the same time, on another burner, heat broth in a saucepan.

3. Add wine to rice, and stir until it evaporates. Add cut asparagus. Add 1 cup hot broth, and stir until liquid is almost completely evaporated. Add another cup hot broth, and repeat procedure, still stirring constantly. Keep adding broth, stirring, and letting liquid evaporate, until rice is cooked and its consistency is creamy (about 20 minutes). There may be leftover broth.

4. Remove rice from heat, stir well, and let stand for 5 minutes before serving. Offer freshly grated Parmigiano on the side.

Risotto con Zucchine
al Pomodoro e Rucola

RISOTTO WITH ZUCCHINI, TOMATO, AND ARUGULA

8 small zucchini

2 tablespoons unsalted butter

$1/2$ yellow onion, finely chopped

2 cups Carnaroli rice (if not available, use risotto rice)

$1\,1/2$ quarts chicken broth

1 cup dry white wine

1 tablespoon kosher salt

$1/2$ cup extra-virgin olive oil

4 large ripe tomatoes, each cut into 8 wedges

3 cloves garlic, sliced thin

10 fresh basil leaves

$1/4$ pound arugula

1. Slice zucchini lengthways, and julienne into $1/8$-inch strips. Set aside.

2. On low-medium heat, melt butter in a large earthenware pot (or heavy nonstick stockpot), and sauté onion until soft and lightly golden in color (about 5 minutes). Turn heat to medium, add rice, and cook for 5 minutes, stirring frequently. At the same time, on another burner, heat broth in a saucepan. On a third burner, put up a large pot of water to boil (for Step 4).

3. Add wine to rice, and stir until it evaporates. Add 1 cup hot broth, and stir until liquid is almost completely evaporated. Add another cup hot broth, and repeat procedure, still stirring constantly. Keep adding broth, stirring, and letting liquid evaporate, until rice is cooked and its consistency is creamy (about 20 minutes). There may be leftover broth.

4. Add kosher salt to boiling water, and blanch julienned zucchini for 3 minutes. Drain, and set aside.

5. Pour oil into a large skillet; add tomato wedges, garlic, and basil, and cook for 10 minutes. Add half the arugula, and cook for another 2 minutes. Add the zucchini, and cook for 1 minute. Serve over rice, garnished with remaining raw arugula.

Gnocchetti di Patate al Gorgonzola
Tartufato Gratinati al Forno

SERVES 6

POTATO GNOCCHI WITH
GORGONZOLA AND TRUFFLE SAUCE

NOTE For quick preparation, use store-bought potato gnocchi.

FOR THE GNOCCHI:

2 pounds Idaho potatoes

$2\frac{1}{2}$ cups unbleached all-purpose flour

1 teaspoon salt

$\frac{1}{4}$ teaspoon freshly grated nutmeg

Flour for dusting

1. Preheat oven to 350 degrees. Cover each potato with aluminum foil, and bake for 1 hour (or until tender). When cool enough to handle, peel potatoes, and pass them through a ricer into a large bowl (if you don't have a ricer, put them through a food mill). Add flour, salt, and nutmeg to bowl of potatoes. Combine, being careful not to overmix.

2. Dust a flat working surface with flour, and, using your hands, quickly roll potato mixture into long logs, approximately $\frac{1}{2}$-inch wide. Cut logs into $\frac{1}{2}$-inch slices, and leave them on a linen towel dusted with flour for 2 hours. (If you want to get fancy—this step is optional—press each gnocco against the back of a floured fork, and push it, with a floured thumb, in a forward motion toward the end of the tines, letting it fall from the fork onto a floured kitchen towel. The idea is to embellish your gnocchi with a striped pattern.)

FOR THE SAUCE:

$\frac{1}{2}$ pound Gorgonzola cheese (dolce) or Dolcelatte

$1\frac{1}{2}$ cups heavy cream

1 teaspoon truffle oil

1. (Before making the Gorgonzola sauce, put up a large stockpot of water to boil; you'll need it for the next step.) Melt Gorgonzola in the top of a double boiler, together with cream and truffle oil. When cheese is melted, reduce heat to very, very low—just enough to keep mixture warm.

ASSEMBLING THE DISH:

Unsalted butter for greasing casserole dish

1 tablespoon kosher salt

1 zucchini, about 5 inches long (coarsely grated, with skin, on the third-largest side of a 4-sided grater)

1 cup freshly grated Parmigiano Reggiano

1. Grease an ovenproof casserole dish with butter. Add kosher salt to stockpot of boiling water, and toss in gnocchi. They're done when they rise to the surface.
2. Remove gnocchi with a slotted spoon as they rise to surface, and place in greased casserole dish. Pour Gorgonzola sauce evenly over gnocchi. Strew grated zucchini on top of sauce, then sprinkle grated Parmigiano evenly on top of zucchini. Bake for 15 minutes.

Gnocchi di Zucca

SQUASH GNOCCHI

1 large butternut squash (approximately 1 $1/2$ pounds), halved lengthways and seeded

Peanut oil for greasing baking pan

$3/4$ pound Yukon Gold potatoes, unpeeled

1 jumbo egg, lightly beaten

$1/2$ cup finely grated Pecorino Romano cheese

$1/2$ teaspoon fresh thyme leaves, finely chopped

$1/2$ teaspoon fresh sage leaves, finely chopped

$1/2$ teaspoon salt

$1/8$ teaspoon white pepper

$1/8$ teaspoon freshly grated nutmeg

$3/4$ cup unbleached all-purpose flour, plus additional for dusting

3 tablespoons unsalted butter

1 tablespoon salt

Freshly grated Parmigiano Reggiano

NOTE Squash-potato purée can be made a day ahead of time, cooled to room temperature, then covered and refrigerated. Return to room temperature before proceeding.

1. Preheat oven to 500 degrees. Arrange squash halves, cut sides down, in an oiled shallow baking pan, and place potatoes alongside. Roast in middle of oven until squash is tender, about 25 minutes. Transfer squash to a cutting board. Continue to roast potatoes until tender, about 12 minutes more.

2. When cool enough to handle, scoop out squash from its skin, scraping it clean. Discard skin, and purée squash through a ricer into a bowl (if you don't have a ricer, put it through a food mill). Measure out $3/4$ cup purée, and put it in a larger bowl (reserve remainder for some other use).

3. Peel potatoes while still hot (obviously not too hot to handle). Discard skins, and rice potatoes into bowl with squash. Spread squash-potato purée in a shallow baking pan, and let cool completely. Put a large wide-surfaced pot of water up to boil.

4. Return squash-potato purée to bowl, and stir in egg, Pecorino Romano, thyme, sage, $1/2$ teaspoon salt, white pepper, and nutmeg. Add flour, and gently knead dough by hand for 1 minute (it will be soft and slightly sticky).

5. Turn dough out onto a floured cutting board, and divide into 3 equal portions. Gently roll each portion into a long log, about $3/4$-inch thick. Cut each log into $3/4$-inch pieces with a floured knife to create individual gnocchi.

6. Press a gnocco against the back of a floured fork, and push it, with a floured thumb, in a forward motion toward the end of the tines, letting it fall from the fork onto a floured kitchen towel. The idea is to embellish your gnocchi with a striped pattern. Repeat with remaining gnocchi.

7. Melt butter in a 12-inch heavy skillet and remove from heat. Add 1 tablespoon salt to boiling water, and cook gnocchi in 3 batches, stirring occasionally, until centers are cooked through (when they rise to surface). Transfer as cooked with a slotted spoon to butter in skillet. When all gnocchi are cooked, transfer to a warm platter, and serve with a bowl of grated Parmigiano.

Gnudi

NAKED RAVIOLI

These are called "naked ravioli," because they don't have pasta skins. Really, they're more like dumplings.

$3/4$ cup cooked spinach

$1\,1/4$ pounds ricotta cheese (freshly made, if you can find it)

3 jumbo egg yolks

1 cup unbleached all-purpose flour

1 cup finely grated Parmigiano Reggiano

1 teaspoon salt

$1/4$ teaspoon freshly grated nutmeg

$1/8$ pound ($1/2$ stick) unsalted butter

4 fresh sage leaves

1 tablespoon kosher salt

1 cup coarsely grated Parmigiano Reggiano

1. Set oven at 350 degrees. Boil 3 quarts of water in large stockpot.

2. While waiting for oven to heat and water to boil, squeeze any excess water from spinach, chop medium-fine, and pulse in a food processor for 10 seconds. Add ricotta, and pulse for another 10 seconds. Turn out spinach-ricotta mixture into a large bowl.

3. Add egg yolks, flour, finely grated Parmigiano, 1 teaspoon salt, and nutmeg. Mix well with a wooden spoon.

4. Place butter and sage leaves in a skillet, and cook on low heat until butter is melted. Pour half the butter into a 9" × 11" baking dish. Set sage leaves aside for Step 6.

5. When water boils, add 1 tablespoon kosher salt. Take a heaping (dinnerware) tablespoon of ricotta mixture in one hand. In the other, using the concave side of another tablespoon, smooth edges of mixture to form an egg-like shape. With the side of your free spoon, scoop out half of the tablespoon of ricotta mixture (half the "egg") and carefully drop it into boiling water. Then scoop out remaining half, and drop into boiling water. (Don't worry if gnudi are imperfectly shaped; another name for them is *malfatti*, "badly made.") Drop in only 10 gnudi at a time. When they float to the surface, remove them with a slotted spoon to baking dish with melted butter. Repeat until ricotta mixture is finished.

6. Drizzle rest of butter on gnudi; top with sage leaves and coarsely grated Parmigiano. Bake for 10 minutes, or until cheese is melted.

Pasta Fresca SERVES 4

FRESH PASTA

This is the basic recipe for homemade pasta dough, which is refer-
enced in many recipes below. Either with a machine, or by hand,
you can use it to create delicious pastas of every shape and size.

$1\frac{1}{2}$ cups finely ground hard-grain semolina flour
(use Rob's Red Mill or Antoine's Pasta Flour)

2 jumbo eggs

2 teaspoons extra-virgin olive oil

1 teaspoon salt

Extra semolina flour for flouring dough-rolling surface

1. On a flat surface, pour out flour in a mound, and make a crater in
   its center. Place eggs (unbeaten), oil, and salt in center of crater,
   and work mixture, kneading with the flats of your hands, until your
   dough is smooth and elastic.

2. Divide dough into two equal parts. Place half the dough on a well-
   floured surface, sprinkle more flour on top, and roll very thin (you
   should be able to see your skin through it). Repeat with remaining
   dough. Either by hand, or using a pasta machine, cut dough to desired shape. Lay pasta on a cloth sprinkled with flour, and set
   aside.

To make the above recipe to serve 6 to 8 people, use the following
measurements:

$2\frac{1}{4}$ cups finely ground hard-grain semolina flour
(use Rob's Red Mill or Antoine's Pasta Flour)

3 jumbo eggs

1 tablespoon extra-virgin olive oil

$1\frac{1}{2}$ teaspoons salt

Extra semolina flour for flouring dough-rolling surface

BUCATINI WITH FRESH
SARDINES AND FENNEL

When people first hear about this traditional Sicilian pasta dish, which combines sardines with raisins, they often look askance. One American friend, to whom I was raving about it, asked if I was pregnant. I can only tell you, I've never known anyone who actually tried it and didn't love it.

1 pound small fennel bulbs with fronds (wild fennel, if available)

1 tablespoon kosher salt

$1/8$ teaspoon crumbled saffron threads

$1/2$ cup dark raisins

$1/2$ cup dry white wine

1 cup onion, finely chopped

1 tablespoon fennel seeds, crushed

5 anchovy fillets, in oil

$1/2$ cup extra-virgin olive oil

1 pound filleted fresh sardines

2 tablespoons extra-virgin olive oil

Salt

12 ounces bucatini

1 tablespoon toasted pine nuts, coarsely chopped

1 tablespoon toasted skinless almonds, coarsely chopped

1 tablespoon breadcrumbs

1. Put up 3 quarts of water to boil in a large stockpot. Preheat oven to 350 degrees.

2. Cut fronds from fennel. Add kosher salt to boiling water, and cook fronds for 4 minutes. Remove fronds with a slotted spoon, chop fine, and set aside. Save water to cook the pasta. Finely chop fennel bulb, and set aside.

3. Combine saffron, raisins, and wine in a bowl, and set aside.

4. In a heavy 12-inch skillet, sauté chopped fennel, onion, fennel seeds, and anchovy fillets over moderate heat in $1/2$ cup oil, stirring, until fennel is tender (about 15 minutes). Add raisin-wine mixture and half of sardine fillets, and simmer 1 minute.

5. In a separate small skillet, sauté remaining sardines in 2 table-spoons oil, 1 minute on each side. Salt to taste, and set aside.

6. Cook bucatini until *al dente* in water you used for cooking fennel fronds. Drain and add to sauce, combining well.

7. Place sauced pasta in a 9" × 11" casserole that can be served at the table. Sprinkle with pine nuts and almonds. Place sardines first, then chopped fronds on top of the bucatini. Sprinkle with bread-crumbs. Bake in oven for 5 minutes, and serve immediately.

LASAGNE AL PESTO

NOTE If preparing fresh lasagne noodles (see Pasta Fresca recipe, for 6 to 8, on page 228), do that first. Cut dough into 3" × 5" rectangles, and place on a linen cloth that is sprinkled with flour. If using prepared lasagne noodles, begin by making pesto.

FOR THE PESTO:

1 cup fresh basil leaves

$3/4$ cup pine nuts

1 cup extra-virgin olive oil

1 large garlic clove

$1/4$ teaspoon salt

6 ounces aged Pecorino cheese (or any other sheep's milk cheese)

1 large white potato

1 tablespoon salt

1. While preparing pesto, boil 3 quarts of water in a large stockpot, and preheat oven to 350 degrees.

2. Place basil, pine nuts, oil, garlic, $1/4$ teaspoon salt, and Pecorino in a food processor, and blend until smooth. Set aside in a bowl.

3. Peel potato, chop into $1/2$-inch cubes, and cook until tender in 2 cups water with 1 tablespoon salt. Drain, purée, and add to pesto. Mix well.

FOR THE LASAGNE:

1 tablespoon kosher salt

1 tablespoon peanut oil

12 lasagne noodles (3" × 5")

$1/2$ cup grated Parmigiano Reggiano

1. When your water is boiling, add kosher salt and peanut oil. Add lasagne noodles, 3 at a time. Cook for 1 minute, carefully remove with a slotted spoon, and place on a damp cloth. Repeat until all 12 are cooked.

2. Place a row of 4 lasagne noodles in a 9" × 11" nonstick baking pan (they'll overlap). Pour $1/3$ of pesto sauce on pasta, and smooth out evenly. Repeat this procedure 2 more times with remaining noodles and pesto. Top with grated Parmigiano, and bake for 20 minutes.

Lasagne alle Verdure

VEGETABLE LASAGNE

NOTE Because this recipe is somewhat labor-intensive, I usually make it only for parties, hence the large quantity. You can, of course, buy prepared lasagne noodles, if you don't want to make your own. Also, all the fillings can be made the night before and refrigerated.

1. Begin by preparing Pasta Fresca recipe, for 6 to 8, on page 228. Cut rolled-out dough into a dozen 3" × 5" rectangles. Lay them out on a linen cloth sprinkled with flour, and set aside.

FOR THE EGGPLANT FILLING:

NOTE Another time, try this filling as a pasta sauce.

$1/4$ cup extra-virgin olive oil

1 clove finely chopped garlic

1 medium-large eggplant (about $3/4$ pound), unpeeled

1 pound ripe tomatoes

$1/4$ teaspoon cracked red pepper

Salt

1 tablespoon finely chopped fresh parsley leaves

1. Pour oil into a large nonstick skillet, add garlic, and sauté over medium heat until golden.
2. Chop eggplant into $1/4$-inch cubes, and add to garlic and oil. Cook, stirring often, for 5 minutes. Cut tomatoes into $1/2$-inch cubes, and add to eggplant along with cracked red pepper; cook for another 10 minutes. Salt to taste, stir, sprinkle with parsley, stir again, and set aside.

FOR THE STRING BEAN FILLING:

NOTE Another time, serve this filling as a side dish.

$1/4$ cup extra-virgin olive oil

$3 1/2$ ounces celery, sliced paper thin
(use the whiter part, closer to the core)

1 cup carrots, peeled and sliced paper thin

1 small ($3 1/2$ ounces) yellow onion, sliced paper thin

$^3/_4$ cup string beans, cut into $^1/_2$-inch pieces

1 cup water

$^1/_4$ teaspoon salt

8 fresh basil leaves

1. Pour oil into a large skillet. Add sliced celery, carrots, and onion. Turn heat to medium-high, and sauté for 5 minutes, stirring occasionally. Add string beans, water, salt, and basil leaves, and cook for 10 minutes. Set aside.

FOR THE SPINACH/RICOTTA FILLING:

$^3/_4$ pound fresh spinach

14 ounces ricotta cheese (freshly made, if you can find it)

$^1/_2$ cup grated Parmigiano Reggiano

$^1/_4$ teaspoon freshly grated nutmeg

$^1/_4$ teaspoon freshly ground black pepper

$^1/_4$ teaspoon salt

1. Wash spinach thoroughly, toss into boiling water, and cook until wilted. Drain, squeeze out moisture, and chop finely. Place spinach in a mixing bowl with ricotta, Parmigiano, nutmeg, pepper, and salt. Mix well, and set aside.

2. At this point, preheat oven to 350 degrees. Also put up 3 quarts of water to boil in a large stockpot. While waiting for oven to heat and water to boil, prepare Béchamel Sauce.

FOR THE BÉCHAMEL SAUCE:

$^1/_2$ stick unsalted butter

$^1/_4$ cup unbleached all-purpose flour

$^1/_4$ teaspoon salt

$^1/_4$ teaspoon freshly grated nutmeg

3 cups whole milk

1. Melt butter over very low heat (don't brown it) in a small nonstick saucepan. Add flour, stirring continuously with a wooden spoon. Cook for a few seconds. Add salt and nutmeg. Still stirring, add milk, a little at a time. Cook for 10 minutes on medium-low heat, stirring all the while. Set aside.

ASSEMBLING THE LASAGNE:

Unsalted butter for greasing baking dish

1 tablespoon kosher salt

2 cups grated Parmigiano Reggiano

1. Grease an 11" × 14" baking dish with butter. When water you put up earlier is boiling, add kosher salt, and cook 3 lasagne noodles for 2 minutes. Carefully remove with a slotted spoon, and drain on a damp cloth (the dampness keeps it from sticking). Line bottom of buttered baking dish with a row of cooked pasta pieces (they'll overlap), and spoon on eggplant mixture, smoothing it on evenly with a spatula. Drizzle with $\frac{1}{4}$ of the béchamel, and top with $\frac{1}{2}$ cup of Parmigiano.

2. Cook another 3 lasagne noodles, drain on damp cloth, and lay on top of eggplant layer. Spoon string bean filling onto pasta, smooth with spatula, drizzle with $\frac{1}{4}$ of the béchamel, and top with $\frac{1}{2}$ cup of Parmigiano.

3. Cook next 3 lasagne noodles, drain on damp cloth, and lay on top of string bean layer. Spread spinach/ricotta filling on pasta, smooth with spatula, drizzle with $\frac{1}{4}$ of the béchamel, and top with $\frac{1}{2}$ cup of Parmigiano.

4. Cook last 3 lasagne noodles, drain on damp cloth, and lay on top of spinach/ricotta filling. Drizzle with remaining béchamel, and top with remaining Parmigiano. Bake for 40 minutes.

Pappardelle al Pollo Scappato

PAPPARDELLE WITH FLOWN CHICKEN

This whimsically named Florentine dish is meatless, because the chicken has flown away. If preparing fresh pappardelle noodles, see Pasta Fresca recipe, for 6, on page 228. Roll dough into a very loose log, and cut into 1-inch strips. Unravel strips, and place on a linen cloth that is sprinkled with flour.

NOTE You can pulse the onions, celery, and carrots to $1/8$-inch pebbles in a food processor. Keep the onions separate. Do not overchop; texture is essential.

$1/2$ cup extra-virgin olive oil

$1 1/2$ cups celery, chopped into $1/8$-inch pieces

1 cup carrots, chopped into $1/8$-inch pieces

2 cups red onions, chopped into $1/8$-inch pieces

1 tablespoon finely chopped fresh rosemary leaves

$1 1/2$ cups Chianti Classico

$14 1/2$-ounce can puréed Italian plum tomatoes (if unavailable, buy a can of whole plum tomatoes and purée them)

4 thin slices lemon peel (use a potato peeler)

2 cups water

$1 1/2$ teaspoons salt

1 tablespoon kosher salt

14 ounces pappardelle noodles

Freshly grated Parmigiano Reggiano

1. Put up 3 quarts of water to boil in a large stockpot. Pour oil into a large skillet, and add celery and carrots. Turn heat to medium-high, and sauté for 5 minutes, stirring occasionally with a wooden spoon. Add onions, and sauté for another 10 minutes, continuing to stir occasionally.

2. Add rosemary and Chianti, stir well, and cook for 3 minutes on medium heat. Add puréed tomatoes, lemon peel, 2 cups water, and $1 1/2$ teaspoon salt, and stir. Set aside.

3. When water is boiling, add 1 tablespoon kosher salt, and cook pappardelle until *al dente*. Lightly drain, transfer to skillet with sauce, and sauté for 1 minute. Serve with freshly grated Parmigiano.

HAND-ROLLED SPAGHETTI
WITH DUCK SAUCE

Nana is the vernacular for *anatra* (duck).

FOR THE PICI:

3 ¹/₂ cups unbleached all-purpose flour

1 jumbo egg

1 ¹/₂ teaspoons salt

1 cup water

1 tablespoon extra-virgin olive oil

¹/₈ teaspoon freshly ground black pepper

1 tablespoon extra-virgin olive oil for brushing

Semolina flour for dusting a linen napkin for the pici to rest on

1. On a flat surface, pour out flour in a mound, and make a crater in its center. Place egg (unbeaten) salt, water, 1 tablespoon oil, and pepper in center of crater, and work mixture, kneading with the flats of your hands, until the dough is smooth and elastic. Cover dough in cling wrap, and let rest for 30 minutes.

2. Place dough on a flat working surface (do not flour surface), and roll to ¹/₄-inch thickness. Brush dough lightly with oil, and cut into ¹/₈-inch strips with a sharp knife. Using the palm of your hand, roll strips into long thin spaghetti shapes. Place pici on a linen napkin sprinkled with semolina flour, and set aside.

FOR THE DUCK SAUCE:

1 small duck (approximately 2 pounds); ask your butcher to chop the duck into 8 pieces, and retain the liver.

3 tablespoons extra-virgin olive oil

1 small yellow onion, sliced

1 small carrot, sliced

2 stalks celery, sliced

1 bay leaf

1 tablespoon fresh basil leaves, finely chopped

1 tablespoon fresh sage leaves, finely chopped

1 tablespoon fresh parsley leaves, finely chopped

3 $1/2$ ounces prosciutto, diced into $1/4$-inch pieces

Salt

Freshly ground black pepper

1 cup dry white wine

1-inch piece lemon peel

1 cup chicken broth

1 tablespoon kosher salt

Pici (hand-rolled spaghetti; see opposite)

Grated Parmigiano Reggiano

1. If your butcher hasn't already done so, chop duck into 8 pieces, setting aside liver. Wash and dry duck pieces.

2. Spoon oil into a large skillet. Add onion, carrot, celery, bay leaf, basil, sage, parsley, and prosciutto, and sauté on medium-high heat for 5 minutes.

3. Add duck to skillet, and brown over medium heat (about 5 minutes per side). Season with salt and pepper to taste.

4. Add wine, and cook for 5 minutes. Reduce heat to low, add lemon peel and broth, and simmer for 30 minutes. Remove duck pieces from skillet, and cool for 10 minutes. On another burner, put up 3 quarts of water to boil in a large stockpot.

5. While duck is cooling, remove bay leaf from sauce, pass the rest through a food mill, and return sauce to skillet. Remove skin from duck pieces, and discard. Pull meat from bones, cut into $1/4$-inch pieces, and add to skillet. If you like liver, cut it into $1/4$-inch pieces, add to sauce, and cook for 5 minutes; otherwise, discard.

6. Add 1 tablespoon kosher salt to boiling water, toss in pici, and cook until *al dente*. Drain lightly, transfer to skillet with sauce, and sauté for 3 minutes over high heat. Serve with grated Parmigiano.

Ravioli con Menta Fresca SERVES 6

FRESH MINT AND RICOTTA RAVIOLI

1. Begin by preparing Pasta Fresca recipe, for 6 to 8, on page 228. Wrap dough in plastic wrap, and set aside.

2. Prepare Pommarola, using recipe, opposite. Set aside.

FOR THE FILLING:

14 ounces ricotta cheese (freshly made, if available)

$\frac{1}{2}$ cup fresh mint leaves, finely chopped

$3\frac{1}{2}$ ounces finely grated Parmigiano Reggiano

$1\frac{3}{4}$ ounces finely grated pecorino cheese

2 jumbo eggs

$\frac{1}{4}$ teaspoon freshly grated nutmeg

1. Place all filling ingredients in a large bowl, and mix well. Set aside.

FOR THE PASTA:

NOTE In Step 3, if you have left-over scraps of pasta, use them for noodles for chicken broth. Leave them in their scrappy form, which Italians call *maltagliati* (it means "badly cut"). You can freeze them in a Ziploc® bag, and toss them frozen into boiling broth. Do not thaw them out before use.

1 tablespoon kosher salt

1. Fill a large stockpot with 3 quarts of water, and bring to a boil.

2. On a floured surface, roll dough until it is thin enough to see your skin through (your sheet of dough should form a rectangle 5 inches wide and at least 24 inches long). Place sheet of dough on work surface with the long side facing you horizontally.

3. On the bottom half of your sheet of dough, place heaping dinnerware teaspoons of filling (horizontally) every 2 inches, leaving a small equal border from bottom of dough to center of dough around each spoonful. Fold other half of dough (like a flap) over filling, and, using a ravioli cutter (the kind that crimps), cut around filling in 2-inch squares or 2-inch diameter circles. If you don't have a ravioli cutter, use a 2-inch diameter glass, and press borders well with the tines of a fork. Left-over scraps can be re-rolled and used again (see also Note above).

4. Add kosher salt to boiling water, and cook ravioli for 5 to 7 minutes (until *al dente*). At the same time, heat Pommarola.

5. Serve ravioli topped with Pommarola.

Pommarola

HOMEMADE FLORENTINE TOMATO SAUCE FOR PASTA

The pasta recipes in this section include a variety of scrumptious sauces. This classic Florentine tomato sauce is also excellent.

1 pound ripe tomatoes, quartered

2 small carrots, sliced into 1-inch pieces

2 celery stalks, sliced into 1-inch pieces

1 small red onion, sliced

$1/2$ cup chopped fresh parsley

$1/2$ cup extra-virgin olive oil

Salt

$1/4$ teaspoon cracked red pepper

10 fresh basil leaves

1. Place all ingredients, except basil leaves, in a stockpot, and cook over medium heat for 30 minutes. Pass sauce through a food mill. Add basil when serving the pasta.

Ravioli di Magro al Burro e Salvia

SPINACH AND RICOTTA RAVIOLI WITH BUTTER AND SAGE

1. Prepare the Pasta Fresca recipe, for 6 to 8, on page 228. Wrap dough in plastic wrap, and set aside while you prepare filling.

FOR THE FILLING:

2 pounds fresh spinach

14 ounces ricotta (freshly made if available)

3 $1/2$ ounces finely grated Parmigiano Reggiano

1 $3/4$ ounces finely grated pecorino cheese

2 jumbo eggs

$1/4$ teaspoon freshly grated nutmeg

1 teaspoon salt

$1/4$ teaspoon freshly ground black pepper

1. Wash spinach thoroughly, but don't drain. Cook on medium heat until wilted, using only the moisture left on leaves after washing. Drain well, squeeze out excess moisture, and chop finely. Add remaining ingredients, and mix well. Set aside.

FOR THE PASTA:

NOTE In Step 3, if you have left-over scraps of pasta, use them for noodles for chicken broth. Leave them in their scrappy form, which Italians call maltagliati (it means "badly cut"). You can freeze them in a Ziploc® bag, and toss them frozen into boiling broth. Do not thaw them out before use.

1 tablespoon kosher salt

1. Fill a large stockpot with 3 quarts of water, and bring to a boil.

2. On a floured surface, roll dough until it is thin enough to see your skin through (your sheet of dough should form a rectangle 5 inches wide and at least 24 inches long). Place sheet of dough on work surface with the long side facing you horizontally.

3. On the bottom half of your sheet of dough, place heaping dinnerware teaspoons of filling (horizontally) every 2 inches, leaving a small equal border from bottom of dough to center of dough

around each spoonful. Fold other half of dough (like a flap) over filling, and, using a ravioli cutter (the kind that crimps), cut around filling in 2-inch squares or 2-inch diameter circles. If you don't have a ravioli cutter, use a 2-inch diameter glass, and press borders well with the tines of a fork. Left-over scraps can be rerolled and used again (see also Note above).

4. Add kosher salt to boiling water, and cook ravioli for 5 to 7 minutes (until *al dente*).

FOR THE SAUCE:

$\frac{1}{4}$ pound (1 stick) unsalted butter

12 fresh sage leaves

2 ounces coarsely grated Parmigiano Reggiano

1. While ravioli is cooking, place butter and sage in a small saucepan, and cook on low heat until butter is melted.

2. Drain ravioli, place on a serving platter, drizzle with sage butter, and top with grated Parmigiano.

THE EMPEROR'S SPAGHETTI

At one time, we had a Japanese chef, Tadashi, training in our kitchen. When a party of six Japanese VIPs came in one night, Tadashi went to their table to help with menu translation. A bit awestruck in the company of these distinguished visitors, he lost his head completely and blurted out: "Giuliano is creating something very special—something exclusively for you—tonight!" Then he sheepishly trotted back to the kitchen to confess what he'd promised. Luckily for Tadashi, Giuliano thrives on challenge. On the spur of the moment, he invented a recipe fit for an emperor.

10 ounces calamari (squid)

1 orange

1 lemon

$\frac{1}{4}$ cup extra-virgin olive oil

$\frac{1}{4}$ teaspoon cracked red pepper

10 large fresh basil leaves

1 teaspoon salt

1 cup dry white wine

4 tablespoons ($\frac{1}{2}$ stick) unsalted butter

2 large very ripe tomatoes

8 ounces large shrimp, shelled and deveined

1 tablespoon kosher salt

10 ounces spaghettini

1. Put up 3 quarts of water to boil in a large stockpot. Wash squid, slice into $\frac{1}{4}$-inch pieces, and set aside.

2. Cut orange and lemon into $\frac{1}{2}$-inch slices, discarding ends of fruit.

3. Heat oil in a large skillet, and add calamari, orange and lemon slices, cracked red pepper, basil leaves, and 1 teaspoon salt. Cook on high heat for 10 minutes, pressing on orange and lemon slices with a fork until they have released all of their juice and pulp. Discard rinds.

4. Reduce heat to medium, add white wine and butter, and cook for 5 minutes.

5. Add tomatoes, squeezing them to pulp with your hands. Add shrimp, and cook on high heat for 3 minutes. Remove skillet from heat, and set aside.

6. Add kosher salt to boiling water, toss in spaghettini, and cook until *al dente*. Drain lightly, add to skillet with seafood, and sauté for 1 minute, moving everything around with tongs to combine ingredients. Add more salt if needed.

Spaghettini dello Zio Alfio

THIN SPAGHETTI WITH VEAL AND TOMATO SAUCE

Giuliano invented this recipe for his close friend, noted Florentine artist Alfio Rapsiardi, who comes into the trattoria almost nightly at 11 P.M. At this late hour, Alfio wants a light meal, and Giuliano always makes sure it is also a healthful one. You'll notice this dish offers a good balance of protein, carbs, and vegetables.

9 ounces thinly sliced veal

$1/4$ cup extra-virgin olive oil

6 ripe tomatoes, each cut into 8 pieces
(or, off-season, 14 $1/2$ ounces canned Italian plum tomatoes)

1 clove garlic, sliced paper thin

16 large sage leaves

$1/4$ teaspoon cracked red pepper

Salt

1 tablespoon kosher salt

1 pound spaghettini

2 small zucchinis, grated on third-largest side of a
four-sided grater

Freshly grated Parmigiano Reggiano (optional)

1. Fill a large stockpot with 3 quarts of water, and bring to a boil. While waiting for water to boil, place veal on a flat surface, sprinkle very lightly with water, cover with plastic wrap, and flatten with a smooth-surfaced meat mallet.

2. Cut veal lengthways into $1/4$-inch strips. Then, in bunches, cut strips horizontally into very small pieces (about $1/8$ inch).

3. Pour oil into a large skillet, and add veal. Turn heat to high, and sauté quickly for about 3 minutes (until veal is translucent).

4. Add tomatoes, garlic, and sage leaves, and lower heat to medium. Add cracked red pepper, and salt to taste. Cook covered for 5 minutes. Mash tomatoes with a fork, and cook, still covered, for another 5 minutes.

5. When water comes to a boil, add 1 tablespoon kosher salt, toss in spaghettini, and cook until *al dente*. Lightly drain, transfer to skillet with veal/tomato sauce, and sauté for 1 minute over high heat, moving everything around with tongs to combine ingredients. Top each serving with grated zucchini and, if desired, grated Parmigiano.

Tagliatelle alla Modi

FETTUCCINE WITH GARLIC AND BUTTER

We named this dish for the artist Amadeo Modigliani (his nickname was "Modi"), at a time when his name was very much in the news. Legend had it that Modi, upon leaving Livorno for Paris as a young man, had thrown a number of his sculptures into a local canal. In 1984, in celebration of Modi's one-hundredth birthday, the City Council decided to dredge the canal. Sure enough, three sculpted heads turned up and were hailed by critics as a major art-world find. It turned out to be a hoax, perpetrated by a group of students, who'd carved one head themselves and had a local dock-worker create the other two. Their aim was to show up the incompetence of art critics.

NOTE If preparing fresh fettuccine (see Pasta Fresca recipe, for 4, on page 228), do that first. When dough is rolled out thin, dust well with flour, roll into a very loose log, and cut into $1/4$-inch strips. Unravel strips, and place on a linen cloth that is sprinkled with flour.

$1/4$ cup ($1/2$ stick) unsalted butter

2 garlic cloves, thinly sliced

$1/4$ teaspoon cracked red pepper

1 tablespoon kosher salt

14 ounces fettuccine

2 tablespoons fresh parsley leaves, finely chopped

1. Put up 3 quarts of water to boil in a large stockpot. While waiting for water to boil, melt butter in a large skillet. Add garlic and cracked red pepper, and sauté on low-medium heat until garlic is golden. Remove skillet from heat, and set aside.

2. Add kosher salt to boiling water, toss in fettuccine, and cook until *al dente*. Drain lightly, add to skillet with garlic, sprinkle with parsley, and sauté on high heat for 1 minute, moving everything around with tongs to combine ingredients.

Tagliatelle alla Bietola

FETTUCCINE WITH SWISS CHARD

NOTE If preparing fresh fettuccine (see Pasta Fresca recipe, for 4, on page 228), do that first. When dough is rolled out thin, dust well with flour, roll into a very loose log, and cut into $\frac{1}{4}$-inch strips. Unravel strips, and place on a linen cloth that is sprinkled with flour.

9 ounces Swiss chard

$\frac{1}{2}$ cup extra-virgin olive oil

2 garlic cloves, sliced into $\frac{1}{8}$-inch pieces

Salt

1 tablespoon kosher salt

14 ounces fettuccine

1. Put up 3 quarts of water to boil in a large stockpot. While waiting for water to boil, cut off tough bottom parts of stems, and wash chard leaves well in cold water.

2. In another large pot, bring 2 inches of water to a boil. Add chard, and cook on high heat until wilted (approximately 5 minutes). Drain, squeeze out excess moisture, and chop coarsely.

3. Pour oil into a skillet, add garlic, turn heat to high, and sauté until golden. Add chard, and sauté for 8 minutes, moving skillet around occasionally. Salt to taste, and set aside.

4. Add 1 tablespoon kosher salt to boiling water, toss in fettuccine, and cook until *al dente*. Drain lightly, add to skillet with chard, and sauté with chard for 2 minutes, moving everything around with tongs to combine ingredients.

FETTUCCINE WITH SPICY TOMATO SAUCE

The first time famed orchestra conductor Zubin Mehta dined at Garga, he ordered our Tagliatelle alla Vigliacca. Before he started his meal, I saw him dig into his pocket and crumble something on top of the pasta. Hopelessly curious, as always, I asked him what he was doing. It seems he loves spicy fare and carries with him, at all times, little chilli peppers he grows in his garden. He exchanged chilis with Garga, who has since planted them on the banks of the Arno with great success.

NOTES Prepare this recipe only in season, when fresh, ripe tomatoes are available.

If preparing fresh fettuccine (see Pasta Fresca recipe, for 4, on page 228), do that first. When dough is rolled out thin, dust well with flour, roll into a very loose log, and cut into $1/4$-inch strips. Unravel strips, and place on a linen cloth that is sprinkled with flour.

$1/4$ cup extra-virgin olive oil

2 cloves garlic, finely chopped

$1 1/2$ pounds ripe tomatoes

$1/4$ teaspoon cracked red pepper

Salt

1 tablespoon kosher salt

1 pound fettuccine

2 tablespoons finely chopped fresh parsley leaves

1. Fill a large stockpot with 3 quarts of water, and bring to a boil. While waiting for water to boil, pour oil into a large skillet, add garlic, turn heat to medium-high, and sauté until golden.

2. Remove skillet from heat, and add tomatoes, squeezing them to pulp with your hands. Add cracked red pepper, and salt to taste.

3. Return skillet (covered) to stove, and cook on medium heat for 2 minutes. Mash tomatoes with a fork, and cook uncovered for another 3 minutes. Set aside.

4. Add 1 tablespoon kosher salt to boiling water, toss in fettuccine, and cook until *al dente*. Drain lightly, and add to skillet with tomato sauce. Sauté for 1 minute, moving everything around with tongs to combine ingredients. Add more salt if needed, and sprinkle with parsley.

FETTUCCINE WITH
FRESH HERBS

NOTE If preparing fresh fettuccine (see Pasta Fresca recipe, for 4, on page 228), do that first. When dough is rolled out thin, dust well with flour, roll into a very loose log, and cut into $1/4$-inch strips. Unravel strips, and place on a linen cloth that is sprinkled with flour.

$1/4$ cup extra-virgin olive oil

1 tablespoon fresh rosemary leaves

8 fresh sage leaves

16 fresh basil leaves

2 fresh bay leaves (optional)

2 garlic cloves, very finely chopped

$1/4$ teaspoon cracked red pepper

1 tablespoon kosher salt

14 ounces fettuccine

Salt

Freshly grated Parmigiano Reggiano

1. Fill a large stockpot with 3 quarts of water, and bring to a boil. While waiting for water to boil, warm oil on medium heat for 1 minute in a large skillet. Remove from heat, and add rosemary, sage, basil, and bay leaves. Then add garlic and cracked red pepper. Set aside.

2. When water is boiling, add 1 tablespoon kosher salt, and cook fettuccine until *al dente*. Drain lightly, transfer to skillet with herbs, and sauté for 1 minute, moving everything around with tongs to combine ingredients. Salt to taste before serving. Top with grated Parmigiano.

Taglierini con Gamberi e Pepe
Verde al Profumo di Arancia

THIN FETTUCCINE WITH SHRIMP, GREEN PEPPERCORNS, AND ORANGE ZEST

NOTE If preparing fresh thin fettuccine (see Pasta Fresca recipe, for 6, on page 228), do that first. When dough is rolled out thin, dust well with flour, roll into a very loose log, and cut into $\frac{1}{8}$-inch strips. Unravel strips, and place on a linen cloth that is sprinkled with flour.

8 ounces shrimp, shelled and deveined

1 tablespoon salt

1 cup heavy cream

1 cup half-and-half

1 tablespoon green peppercorns, packed in brine

Zest of 1 orange

Salt

1 tablespoon kosher salt

14 ounces thin fettuccine

10 large fresh basil leaves

1. Fill a large stockpot with 3 quarts of water, and bring to a boil. On another burner, put up a medium-sized pot of water to boil. While waiting for water to boil, wash shrimp, and drain in a colander.

2. When medium-sized pot of water comes to a boil, add 1 tablespoon salt, and carefully pour in shrimp, removing them as soon as water begins bubbling again. This is very brief; you're just blanching them.

3. Pour heavy cream and half-and-half into a large skillet, and reduce over medium heat for 5 minutes. Rinse peppercorns, drain well, and add to cream mixture, along with orange zest. Salt to taste. Add shrimp and bring to a boil. Remove from heat, and set aside.

4. Add 1 tablespoon kosher salt to large stockpot of boiling water, toss in fettuccine, and cook until *al dente*. Drain lightly, transfer to skillet with shrimp and cream sauce, and sauté for 2 minutes, moving everything around with tongs to combine ingredients. Serve garnished with basil leaves.

Secondi Piatti

SECOND (MAIN) COURSES

Baccalà ai Porri

SERVES 4

SALT COD WITH LEEKS

NOTE Salt cod is a dried fish, preserved in salt. Some specialty shops sell it frozen, with the salt already soaked out. If this isn't available, before use, soak the cod in a large glass pan (do not use plastic or metal) for 2 days, changing the water 3 times a day to get the salt out. Rinse well, and debone (if not already done). Set aside.

2 $1/4$ pounds leeks

$1/4$ pound (1 stick) unsalted butter

1 can (14 $1/2$ ounces) Italian plum tomatoes

2 $1/2$ cups water

$1/4$ teaspoon salt

1 $1/4$ pounds salt cod

2 jumbo eggs

Unbleached all-purpose flour for dredging

$1/4$ cup peanut oil

8 fresh basil leaves

1. Preheat oven to 350 degrees. Wash leeks thoroughly, and chop into 1-inch slices, discarding roots and tough dark green leaves.

2. Melt butter in a large saucepan. Add leeks, and cook over medium heat for half an hour, stirring frequently. Add tomatoes, water, and salt, and cook 15 minutes longer. Set aside.

3. If cod has skin, remove it with a paring knife. Cut cod, lengthways, into sticks (approximately 2 $1/2$" × 1"). Beat eggs in a bowl. In another bowl, pour flour for dredging. Dip cod sticks into eggs, then dredge in flour.

4. Pour oil into a large skillet, and heat to sizzling. Fry cod sticks until golden (no more than 5 minutes on each side), drain on paper towels, and place in a glass or ceramic baking pan. Cover with tomato-leek sauce, and bake for 10 minutes to warm through. Serve garnished with basil leaves.

Gamberi ai Peperoni

SHRIMP WITH PEPPERS

2 large yellow bell peppers

2 large red bell peppers

2 large ripe tomatoes

2 cloves garlic

$1/4$ teaspoon cracked red pepper

$1/4$ cup extra-virgin olive oil

$1/2$ teaspoon salt

1 pound shrimp, shelled, deveined, and washed

Additional extra-virgin olive oil for drizzling

12 fresh basil leaves

1. Preheat oven to 375 degrees. Wash peppers, cut in half length-ways, and remove seeds and cores. Slice peppers, still lengthways, into 1-inch strips, and place in a large baking pan, skin side down, along with tomatoes, garlic, cracked red pepper, $1/4$ cup oil, and salt. Bake for 30 minutes.

2. Remove any blackened skin from peppers and tomatoes, and put everything through a food mill.

3. Transfer sauce into a sauté pan, and heat until boiling. Add shrimp, reduce heat, and simmer for 3 to 5 minutes (depending on size of shrimp). Serve on a warm platter. Drizzle with oil, and garnish with basil leaves.

NOTE The sauce from this recipe is also wonderful on pasta.

SECOND (MAIN) COURSES

CB 253 BO

Gamberi al Pepe Verde

SHRIMP WITH
GREEN PEPPERCORNS

2 teaspoons green peppercorns, packed in brine

1 pound large shrimp, shelled, deveined, and washed

1 cup heavy cream

10 fresh basil leaves

Zest of $\frac{1}{2}$ lemon

Zest of $\frac{1}{2}$ orange

2 tablespoons cognac

Salt

1. Put up a pot of water to boil. Rinse peppercorns, drain well, and set aside.

2. Toss shrimp (carefully) into boiling water for 1 minute, drain, and set aside.

3. Put cream, basil leaves, lemon zest, orange zest, and peppercorns into a skillet. Turn heat to medium, and cook, stirring occasionally, until cream is thickened (about 5 minutes).

4. Add cognac, and cook on medium heat for 2 minutes, stirring constantly. Add shrimp, and cook—still stirring constantly—until sauce is slightly thickened (about 3 minutes). Salt to taste.

Gamberi con Zucchine
al Pomodoro e Rucola

SHRIMP WITH ZUCCHINI, TOMATO, AND ARUGULA

1 pound large shrimp, shelled, deveined, and washed

1 tablespoon salt

8 small zucchini (about 5 inches long),
julienned into $1/8$-inch strips

1 tablespoon salt

$1/2$ cup extra-virgin olive oil

4 ripe tomatoes, cut into wedges

3 cloves garlic, cut into $1/8$-inch slices

$1/4$ teaspoon cracked red pepper

12 fresh basil leaves

$1/2$ pound bunch arugula, thoroughly washed to remove grit

Salt

1. Carefully toss shrimp and 1 tablespoon salt into a pot of boiling water for 1 minute. Drain, and set aside.

2. Carefully toss julienned zucchini and 1 tablespoon salt into another pot of boiling water for 1 minute. Drain, and set aside.

3. Pour oil into a large skillet, along with tomatoes, garlic, and cracked red pepper. Turn heat to medium, cover pan, and cook until tomatoes are softened but still retain their shape (about 10 minutes). Discard any tomato skins that separate from the fruit.

4. Add zucchini and shrimp to sauce, along with basil leaves and half the arugula. Salt to taste, and stir over high heat for 2 minutes. Serve garnished with remaining arugula leaves.

SECOND (MAIN) COURSES

03 *255* 80

Gamberoni con Salsa Vigliacca

SHRIMP WITH SPICY GARLIC AND TOMATO SAUCE

Salsa Vigliacca means "scoundrel sauce," so named because it's hot and spicy.

$1/4$ cup extra-virgin olive oil

2 garlic cloves, very finely chopped

$1 1/2$ pounds ripe tomatoes, halved, with seeds removed

$1/2$ teaspoon cracked red pepper

1 teaspoon salt

1 tablespoon extra-virgin olive oil

2 pounds large shrimp, deveined, washed, and dried
(leave shells and heads attached)

1 ounce cognac

2 tablespoons fresh parsley leaves, finely chopped

1. Pour $1/4$ cup oil into a large skillet. Add garlic, turn heat to medium-high, and sauté until golden. Remove pan from heat. Squeeze tomato halves with your hands into skillet with oil and garlic, add cracked red pepper and salt, cover pan, and cook on high heat for 5 minutes.

2. Uncover, and mash tomatoes with a fork. Cook uncovered on high heat for 5 minutes, stirring occasionally. Set sauce aside (this is your Salsa Vigliacca).

3. Put 1 tablespoon oil into a different large skillet, and place over high heat. When oil starts to smoke, add shrimp, and sauté for 3 minutes.

4. Remove skillet from stove, add cognac, and return to heat. Ignite very carefully with a kitchen match to flambé. When flame dies down, add Salsa Vigliacca from other skillet, and sauté with shrimp for another 3 minutes. Turn out onto a warm serving platter, and sprinkle with parsley.

PERCH WITH LEEKS

2 pounds leeks

$1/4$ pound (1 stick) unsalted butter

$1 1/2$ pounds tomatoes

$2 1/2$ cups water

$1/4$ teaspoon salt

4 perch fillets ($1/2$ pound each)

2 eggs, beaten

Flour for dredging

Peanut oil

Salt

12 fresh basil leaves

1. Preheat oven to 350 degrees, and put up a large stockpot of water to boil. Wash leeks thoroughly, discarding roots and tough dark green leaves. Chop into 1-inch slices.

2. On low-medium heat, melt butter in a large saucepan. Add leeks and cook slowly, stirring frequently, until completely softened (about 30 minutes).

3. Blanch tomatoes by putting them whole into pot of boiling water for 2 minutes. Cool under cold running water, remove skins and seeds, and chop into small pieces. Add chopped tomatoes, $2 1/2$ cups water, and $1/4$ teaspoon salt to leeks, and cook on medium heat for 15 minutes. Remove from heat, and set aside.

4. Cut perch fillets into 1-inch sticks. Dip sticks into beaten eggs, then dredge in flour. Deep-fry perch sticks in oil until golden. Drain on paper towels, and salt lightly.

5. Place fried perch in a glass or ceramic baking dish, and cover with leek/tomato sauce. Bake for 10 minutes to warm through. Garnish with basil leaves.

SWORDFISH, SICILIAN STYLE

1 $\frac{1}{4}$ pounds small new potatoes

2 tablespoons fresh parsley leaves, finely chopped

1 clove garlic, very finely chopped

$\frac{1}{4}$ teaspoon cracked red pepper

$\frac{1}{2}$ cup extra-virgin olive oil

4 swordfish fillets ($\frac{1}{2}$ pound each)

Salt

$\frac{1}{2}$ pound arugula, coarsely chopped

1. Boil new potatoes until tender (approximately 15 minutes). Peel potatoes, slice in half, and set aside.

2. In a small bowl, mix parsley, garlic, and cracked red pepper. Set aside.

3. Spoon $\frac{1}{4}$ cup of the oil into a heavy skillet, and sauté swordfish fillets on high heat, 3 minutes on each side. Salt to taste, turn off heat, and cover to keep warm.

4. In a separate skillet, sauté potatoes in 2 tablespoons of oil for 5 minutes.

5. Arrange chopped arugula on a serving platter, and place swordfish on it. Arrange potatoes around fish. Sprinkle parsley/garlic/cracked red pepper mixture over swordfish, and drizzle with remaining oil.

Polpo Bollito

POACHED OCTOPUS

1 whole octopus (approximately 2 $1/2$ pounds)

Juice of 1 lemon

$1/4$ cup extra-virgin olive oil

1 tablespoon fresh parsley leaves, finely chopped

1. Bring a large pot of water to a boil. Turn off heat. Holding the octopus by one of its tentacles, lower it into the water, then quickly remove it. Repeat procedure 20 times. This process tenderizes the octopus.

2. After dipping octopus, place it in water, and bring to a boil. Reduce heat to medium, and simmer for 45 minutes.

3. Place octopus on a platter, and drizzle with lemon juice and oil. Sprinkle with parsley, and serve.

Petto di Pollo all'Arancio   SERVES 4

CHICKEN BREAST WITH ORANGE SAUCE

4 boneless chicken breast fillets (approximately $1/4$ pound each)

2 tablespoons kosher salt

$1/4$ cup extra-virgin olive oil

1 small yellow onion, cut into $1/4$-inch slices

1 small carrot, cut into $1/4$-inch coins

1 stalk of celery, cut into $1/4$-inch slices

4 oranges, peeled and cut into $1/2$-inch slices

1 tablespoon sugar

$1 1/2$ cups dry white wine

Salt

Freshly ground black pepper

1 orange, cut into $1/8$-inch slices (for garnish)

1. Place chicken breasts in a large bowl of water, and add kosher salt. Set aside while you prepare sauce.

2. Spoon 2 tablespoons of the oil into a skillet, along with onion, carrot, and celery. Sauté over medium heat for 10 minutes.

3. Add 4 sliced oranges and sugar. Cook for 5 minutes. Add wine, and cook another 5 minutes. Pass sauce through a food mill, and set aside.

4. Remove chicken from salted water, and dry well. On medium-high heat, sauté chicken in remaining oil for 3 minutes. Add salt and pepper to taste. Turn chicken and sauté 3 minutes on other side.

5. Place a piece of chicken on each plate, top with sauce, and garnish with orange slices.

Pollo alle Olive Nere e Rosmarino SERVES 4

CHICKEN WITH BLACK OLIVES AND ROSEMARY

1 whole chicken, approximately 2 pounds

1 small yellow onion, sliced paper thin

$3/8$ cup extra-virgin olive oil

1 cup dry white wine

1 tablespoon fresh rosemary leaves, finely chopped

1 clove garlic, finely chopped

$1/4$ pound pitted small black Italian olives (the shiny ones)

1 tablespoon cider vinegar

1. Wash chicken, and dry well. Discard neck and feet. Using poultry shears, cut chicken into 12 pieces. (Alternatively, you can ask your butcher to do this, or purchase a whole chicken in pieces at the supermarket.)

2. Place onion and oil in a skillet. Add chicken pieces, and brown on both sides over medium-high heat.

3. Reduce heat to low, add wine, and cook for 30 minutes. Add rosemary, garlic, olives, and vinegar, and cook for 5 minutes.

DUCK WITH ORANGE SAUCE, FLORENTINE STYLE

1 Long Island duckling, 4 to 5 pounds

Salt

6 oranges

1 tablespoon finely chopped fresh rosemary leaves

1 tablespoon coarsely chopped fresh sage leaves

Freshly ground black pepper

Extra-virgin olive oil

1 ounce brandy

1 small yellow onion, cut into $1/4$-inch slices

1 small carrot, peeled and sliced into $1/8$-inch coins

1 stalk celery, sliced into $1/2$-inch pieces

2 tablespoons sugar

1 cup dry white wine

1. Preheat oven to 450 degrees. Wash duck thoroughly, clean out cavity, and pat dry. Rub salt into cavity. Stuff half an orange (including rind) into cavity, along with rosemary and sage leaves. Tie duck legs together in front of cavity with string.

2. Rub salt and pepper into the skin, and place duck in a roasting pan that has been lightly greased with oil. Bake for 15 minutes, then pour off pan drippings, and discard.

3. Lower oven temperature to 350 degrees. Bake for another 40 minutes, basting with pan drippings at 12-minute intervals.

4. Add brandy to pan juices, and bake 5 minutes more. Remove duck from roasting pan and cover to keep warm.

5. Pour pan drippings into a skillet with sliced onion, carrot, and celery. Cook over medium heat for 10 minutes.

6. Peel 4 of the remaining oranges, and cut into $1/2$-inch slices. Add oranges and sugar to pan drippings and vegetables. Cook for 5 minutes, add wine, and cook for another 5 minutes. Pass sauce through a food mill, and skim off any excess fat.

7. Quarter duck, place a piece on each plate, and top with sauce. Serve on plates garnished with thin slices of remaining oranges.

DUCK BREAST WITH
GREEN PEPPERCORN SAUCE

2 teaspoons green peppercorns, packed in brine

2 tablespoons unsalted butter

4 single duck breasts ($1/_2$-pound each)

Salt

$1/_4$ cup cognac

1 cup heavy cream

1. Rinse peppercorns in a strainer, drain well, and set aside.

2. Melt butter in a large, heavy skillet. When it starts sizzling, add duck breasts. Sauté for 5 minutes (3 minutes if you prefer your duck rare) on high heat, occasionally moving duck breasts around with a fork. Salt, turn duck breasts, and cook for another 5 minutes (3 for rare), still occasionally moving meat around pan.

3. Remove skillet from stove, add cognac, and return to high heat. Ignite very carefully with a kitchen match to flambé. When flame dies down, add cream and green peppercorns. Cook for 2 more minutes, turning once. Arrange duck breasts on serving plates, and pour sauce over them.

Coniglio al Forno con
Pesto di Pomodori Secchi

ROAST RABBIT WITH
SUN-DRIED TOMATO PESTO

Though many Americans have never eaten it, rabbit—yet another "other white meat"—is very popular throughout most of Europe. Extremely digestible (in Italy, it's the first meat most infants are fed after weaning), it's also healthful. Rabbits feed on fresh grasses, and their meat is tender, tasty, and very low in fat. In the U.S., you might have trouble finding rabbit meat. Call around to butcher shops—especially Italian ones—and ask them to order a fresh young rabbit for you.

NOTE You can also prepare this recipe with boneless chicken breasts. If you do, reduce baking time to 30 minutes.

1 young rabbit (approximately 2 to 2 $1/2$ pounds), chopped into approximately 8 pieces (ask your butcher to do it)

5 sun-dried tomatoes

1 cup hot water

$1/4$ cup extra-virgin olive oil

2 cloves garlic, very finely chopped

1 tablespoon fresh parsley leaves, very finely chopped

2 cups dry red wine

Salt

Freshly ground black pepper

1. Preheat oven to 350 degrees. Wash rabbit parts well, and pat dry. Set aside on a platter. Place tomatoes in hot water to soften.

2. Heat oil in a large skillet, and brown rabbit over medium-high heat for 5 minutes on each side. (If your skillet isn't large enough to hold all the pieces without overlapping, do it in batches.)

3. Drain and fine-chop tomatoes, and mix with garlic and parsley. Transfer rabbit to an ovenproof casserole or baking dish, add wine, and coat pieces with sun-dried tomato mixture. Roast for 45 minutes, salting and peppering to taste before serving.

Coniglio Dolceforte

RABBIT IN SWEET-AND-SOUR SAUCE

NOTE See introduction to Coniglio al Forno con Pesto di Pomodori Secchi (opposite) to learn a little about rabbit.

FOR THE DOLCEFORTE SAUCE:

1 ounce bittersweet chocolate

$1/8$ cup golden raisins

$1/8$ cup pine nuts

1 tablespoon candied orange peel, finely chopped

$1/8$ cup red wine vinegar

2 tablespoons sugar

1. Grate chocolate into a bowl. Add raisins, pine nuts, orange peel, vinegar, and sugar, and combine ingredients with a fork. Set aside.

COOKING THE RABBIT:

NOTE You can pulse the onion, carrot, and celery to $1/8$-inch pebbles in a food processor.

$3/8$ cup extra-virgin olive oil

$1/2$ yellow onion, chopped into $1/8$-inch pebbles

1 small carrot, chopped into $1/8$-inch pebbles

2 stalks celery, chopped into $1/8$-inch pebbles

1 ounce prosciutto, very finely chopped

small rabbit, approximately 3 pounds, cut into 8 pieces
(ask your butcher to do it)

Salt

Freshly ground black pepper

1 tablespoon flour

$1 1/2$ cups chicken broth or stock

1 tablespoon fresh parsley leaves, finely chopped

1. Pour oil into a large, wide stockpot, and add onion, carrot, celery, and prosciutto. Turn heat to medium-high, and sauté for 5 minutes, stirring frequently.

2. Add pieces of rabbit, and sauté for 10 minutes, turning over meat as it browns. Season with salt and pepper to taste, and sprinkle flour on top of meat. Pour in broth, and cook 30 minutes.

3. Add Dolceforte Sauce to stockpot with rabbit, and bring to a boil. Serve sprinkled with parsley.

Coniglio Ripieno SERVES 6

STUFFED RABBIT

This is one of my family's (especially Zoe's) favorite recipes, which I started out making at Christmas and Easter. Later, it became a popular selection at catered parties. Though it takes a long time to prepare, it makes for a beautiful presentation.

NOTE See introduction to Coniglio al Forno con Pesto di Pomodori Secchi (page 264) to learn a little about rabbit.

1 young rabbit (approximately 2 to 2 $\frac{1}{2}$ pounds), deboned but whole (ask your butcher to do it, and to be careful to make no holes in the meat)

1 pound ground veal

1 clove garlic

1 tablespoon chopped fresh parsley leaves

$\frac{1}{4}$ pound mortadella

$\frac{1}{8}$ pound prosciutto

$\frac{1}{8}$ pound cooked ham

$\frac{1}{4}$ cup freshly grated Parmigiano Reggiano

2 tablespoons fine breadcrumbs

2 jumbo eggs

$\frac{1}{4}$ cup heavy cream

$\frac{1}{4}$ teaspoon freshly grated nutmeg

$\frac{1}{4}$ cup shelled pistachios

Salt

$\frac{1}{4}$ teaspoon freshly ground black pepper

$\frac{1}{4}$ teaspoon cracked red pepper

$\frac{1}{4}$ cup olive oil

1 tablespoon cognac

1 cup dry white wine

Juice of 1 lemon

1. Preheat oven to 375 degrees. Wash and dry rabbit. Place rabbit on a flat surface, sprinkle very lightly with water, cover with plastic wrap, and flatten to between $1/4$- and $1/2$-inch thick (the meat around the abdomen is thinner) with a smooth-surfaced meat mallet. Set aside, and prepare stuffing.

2. Place veal in a large bowl. Put garlic, parsley, mortadella, prosciutto, and ham in a food processor, and pulse to combine. Add mixture to bowl with veal, along with Parmigiano, breadcrumbs, eggs, cream, nutmeg, pistachios, a pinch of salt, and black pepper. Mix stuffing ingredients well, and shape into a long roll, like a meatloaf.

3. Place roll in middle of flattened rabbit. Gather up end pieces, and pull sides up over filling. To secure filling, close with toothpicks (or skewers), inserted crosswise, about every 1 $1/2$ inches, starting from either end. Take about a yard of butcher's string, and fold it in half. Loop folded part around the first toothpick. Then, holding both ends of the string together, cross doubled string over and around the toothpicks, as if you were lacing a shoe. When you reach the end, secure string with a knot. Sprinkle with salt and cracked red pepper.

4. Pour oil into a roasting pan, and place rabbit on it, toothpick side up. Bake for 25 minutes, carefully turn, and bake 15 minutes more. Baste with cognac, and bake 10 minutes. Baste with $1/2$ cup wine, and bake 15 minutes. Baste again with remainder of wine. Continue roasting for 30 minutes. Add lemon juice, and bake 10 more minutes. Remove rabbit from oven, and let rest for $1/2$ hour before serving.

5. When you are ready to serve, reheat sauce from pan. Remove toothpicks, slice rabbit, and plate slices, spooning sauce over each serving.

Quaglie con Pancetta

QUAILS WITH PANCETTA

8 quails

Salt

Freshly ground black pepper

8 slices pancetta (Italian bacon that is not smoked)

1 ounce ($^1/_4$ of a stick) unsalted butter

3 tablespoons extra-virgin olive oil

1 tablespoon fresh thyme leaves

2 bay leaves (fresh, if available)

1 cup dry white wine

1 cup chicken broth

8 slices of baguette (French bread)

Extra bay leaves for garnish

1. Wash and dry quails, and salt and pepper insides.
2. Wrap a slice of pancetta around each quail, securing it with a piece of string.
3. Place butter, oil, thyme, and 2 bay leaves in a large earthenware pot or Dutch oven, and melt butter on medium heat. When butter starts to brown, turn heat to high, add quails, and sauté, browning all sides. This should take about 10 minutes.
4. Still on high heat, add wine, and cook for 5 minutes. Add broth and continue cooking for 15 minutes.
5. Remove quails from pot, and discard string. Remove bay leaves from sauce, and pass the rest through a food mill.
6. Toast baguette slices, and put two on each plate. Place quails on top of toast, and top with strained sauce. Garnish plates with bay leaves.

Filetto al Pepe Verde

SERVES 4

STEAK WITH GREEN PEPPERCORN SAUCE

2 teaspoons green peppercorns, packed in brine

2 tablespoons unsalted butter

4 beef fillets or New York strip steaks ($\frac{1}{2}$-pound each)

Salt

$\frac{1}{4}$ cup cognac

1 cup heavy cream

1. Rinse peppercorns, drain well, and set aside.

2. Melt butter in a large, heavy skillet. When it starts sizzling, add beef fillets, and sauté on high heat for 5 minutes. Salt to taste, turn fillets, and cook for another 5 minutes. (If you prefer your steak rare, cook 3 minutes on each side.)

3. Remove skillet from stove, add cognac, and return to heat. Ignite very carefully with a kitchen match to flambé. When flame dies down, add cream and peppercorns. Cook for 1 more minute, turning fillets once. Serve on individual plates, topped with sauce.

Filetto alla Parigina

BEEF FILLETS, PARISIAN STYLE

2 anchovy fillets

2 cloves garlic

$1/4$ cup fresh parsley leaves

4 tablespoons unsalted butter, at room temperature

1 tablespoon extra-virgin olive oil

4 beef fillets or New York strip steaks ($1/2$-pound each)

Salt

1. Rinse oil off anchovies in warm water, and dry with paper towel. Chop anchovies, garlic, and parsley leaves extremely fine. Place in a bowl, mix well with butter, and set aside.

2. Pour oil into a skillet, and sauté beef fillets on high heat 3 to 5 minutes (3 minutes for rare, 5 for medium). Salt to taste, turn, and cook another 3 to 5 minutes. Place a fillet on each plate, and spread with butter mixture. Serve immediately.

Agnello Saltato al Rosmarino

LAMB CUTLETS SAUTÉED WITH ROSEMARY

12 small new potatoes

8 lamb chops, $1/4$ pound each
(have your butcher chop them $1/2$-inch thick)

2 tablespoons extra-virgin olive oil

2 cloves garlic, cut into $1/8$-inch slices

1 tablespoon coarsely chopped fresh rosemary leaves

Salt

$1/4$ teaspoon cracked red pepper

1. Boil new potatoes in their jackets until cooked (approximately 15 minutes). Drain, and set aside in a bowl.

2. Flatten chops slightly with a smooth-surfaced meat mallet, being careful not to splinter bones.

3. Spoon oil into a large skillet, add garlic, and turn heat to high. When garlic begins to sizzle, add lamb chops and rosemary leaves. Sauté for 4 minutes. Turn lamb, and sauté for another 2 minutes. Salt to taste, and add cracked red pepper.

4. Remove lamb from pan, and set aside. Slice potatoes in half, and sauté them in pan juices over high heat for 5 minutes, moving them around frequently. Return lamb to pan, and sauté 1 minute more. Place lamb on a warm serving platter, top with potatoes, and serve.

ROAST PORK,
FLORENTINE STYLE

2 cloves garlic, finely chopped

2 tablespoons finely chopped fresh rosemary leaves

1 $1/2$ teaspoons salt

$1/2$ teaspoon freshly ground black pepper

3 pounds (after deboning) sirloin pork
(have your butcher debone it, but keep the bone)

Additional salt

Additional freshly ground black pepper

2 tablespoons extra-virgin olive oil

1. Preheat oven to 350 degrees. Place garlic and rosemary in a small bowl. Add 1 $1/2$ teaspoons salt and $1/2$ teaspoon pepper, and mix well. Spread herb mixture on inside part of the bone (it's V-shaped). Recompose meat around bone, and secure with string.

2. Rub fat on outside of roast with additional salt and pepper. Spoon oil into a roasting pan, and place roast in pan, fat side down. Roast for 30 minutes.

3. Now turn roast, so fat side is facing upward. Roast for another 90 minutes, basting 3 times (at 25-minute intervals) with pan juices. Remove pan from oven, but let roast sit in pan for 10 minutes off heat.

4. Transfer roast to a large cutting board. Remove string, and set bone aside. Carve $1/4$-inch slices. Place bone on a large serving platter, and fan pork slices over it.

Braciola Fritta alla Stinchetti

GOLDEN VEAL CUTLETS
WITH GORGONZOLA SAUCE

This recipe was named for a Mr. Stinchetti, an early customer of Trattoria Garga, who suggested the Gorgonzola sauce to Giuliano. Gorgonzola cheese comes in 2 varieties—*dolce* (sometimes called *Dolcelatte*) and *naturale*. *Dolce* is less marbled and sweeter, *naturale* drier and more piquant. The cheese bears the name of the town where it's made, a town originally called Concordia, in honor of the goddess of harmony. Over centuries of mispronunciation, it evolved into Gorgonzola, which is too bad, since the original name is more lyrical and also more apt: Gorgonzola cheese harmonizes beautifully with other ingredients.

4 boneless veal cutlets, approximately 4 $\frac{1}{2}$ ounces each

2 jumbo eggs

$\frac{1}{4}$ teaspoon salt

12 ounces Gorgonzola cheese (dolce) or Dolcelatte

$\frac{1}{2}$ cup heavy cream

1 $\frac{1}{2}$ cups fine breadcrumbs

Peanut oil for deep-frying

1 teaspoon truffle oil

2 small zucchini (coarsely grated, with skins, on the third-largest side of a 4-sided grater)

1. Place veal cutlets on a flat surface, sprinkle very lightly with water, cover with plastic wrap, and pound to $\frac{1}{4}$-inch thickness with a smooth-surfaced meat mallet.

2. Break eggs into a large, shallow dish, add salt, and whisk well. Soak cutlets in eggs for 30 minutes. While veal is soaking, melt Gorgonzola and heavy cream in the top of a double boiler. Stir and keep warm.

3. Pour breadcrumbs into a large, shallow dish, and dredge cutlets, pressing very firmly with the heel of your hand to make sure breading sticks. Place breaded cutlets on waxed paper.

4. Pour abundant peanut oil into a large skillet, heat to sizzling, lower heat to medium, and fry veal until golden-brown on both sides. Drain on folded paper towels.

5. Place veal on a serving platter, and cover with Gorgonzola sauce. Drizzle with truffle oil, and sprinkle with zucchini.

Braciola Italia

VEAL, ITALIAN STYLE

Veal is white, celery and zucchini are green, tomatoes are red. This dish sports all the colors of the Italian flag.

NOTE Still keeping to the patriotic motif, you can also make this recipe using boneless chicken breasts in place of veal.

4 boneless veal cutlets, approximately 4 $1/2$ ounces each

2 jumbo eggs

$1/4$ teaspoon salt

4 ripe tomatoes

2 small celery stalks

1 $1/2$ cups fine breadcrumbs

Peanut oil for frying

Salt

2 small zucchini (coarsely grated, with skins, on the third-largest side of a 4-sided grater)

Extra-virgin olive oil for drizzling

12 large basil leaves

1. Place veal cutlets on a flat surface, sprinkle very lightly with water, cover with plastic wrap, and pound to $1/4$-inch thickness with a smooth-surfaced meat mallet.

2. Break eggs into a large, shallow dish, add $1/4$ teaspoon salt, and whisk well. Soak cutlets in eggs for 30 minutes. While veal is soaking, cut tomatoes into $1/2$-inch cubes and celery into $1/8$-inch slices, keeping them in separate bowls.

3. Pour breadcrumbs into a large, shallow dish, and dredge cutlets, pressing very firmly with the heel of your hand to make sure breading sticks. Place breaded cutlets on waxed paper.

4. Pour abundant peanut oil into a large skillet, heat to sizzling, lower heat to medium, and fry veal until golden-brown on both sides. Drain on folded paper towels.

5. Place veal on a serving platter, and sprinkle with salt to taste. Layer vegetables on top of veal—first celery, then tomatoes, then zucchini. Drizzle olive oil generously over veal and vegetables, and top with basil leaves.

Osso Buco di Elio

ELIO'S OSSO BUCO

Elio Cotza—whom I affectionately call my little brother—started working as a chef at Trattoria Garga in 1987. A few years later he became our highly valued partner—really our right hand. Since Giuliano's arms are shot, Elio does a lot of the hard physical work these days, not only at the restaurant but also in the Arno garden. When the cooking school was across the street from the restaurant, Elio liked to hang out there, sometimes taking a hand in preparing meals. He said it was a pleasure to work in such a quiet kitchen. Elio's osso buco is better than anyone's.

NOTES You can pulse the celery, carrots, and onions to $1/8$-inch pebbles in a food processor. Keep the onions separate.

Cooked spinach, sautéed for 5 minutes just before serving in a cup of the vegetable-wine sauce, makes a tasty side dish.

$3/4$ cup extra-virgin olive oil

$1 1/2$ cups celery, chopped into $1/8$-inch pieces

1 cup carrots, chopped into $1/8$-inch pieces

2 cups red onions (about 1 pound), chopped into $1/8$-inch pieces

1 tablespoon fresh rosemary, very finely chopped

6 osso buco (veal shanks), each at least $1 1/2$ inches thick

Unbleached all-purpose flour for dredging

$1 1/2$ cups Chianti Classico

$14 1/2$-ounce can puréed Italian plum tomatoes (if unavailable, buy a can of whole plum tomatoes and purée them)

4 thin slices lemon peel (use a potato peeler)

2 cups water

$1 1/2$ teaspoons salt

1. Preheat oven to 400 degrees. Pour $1/2$ cup of the oil into a large skillet, and add celery and carrots. Turn heat to medium-high, and sauté for 5 minutes, stirring occasionally with a wooden spoon. Add onions, and sauté for another 10 minutes, continuing to stir occasionally. Add chopped rosemary, turn off heat, and set skillet aside.

2.   Dredge each veal shank in flour, and shake off excess.

3.   Heat remaining $1/4$ cup oil in a Dutch oven. When oil is hot, brown veal shanks for 5 minutes on high heat. Turn, reduce heat to medium, and brown other side for 5 minutes.

4.   Remove osso buco to a plate. Transfer sautéed vegetables from skillet to Dutch oven (where they will absorb pan juices), add Chianti, and cook on medium heat for 5 minutes. Add tomatoes, lemon peel, water, and salt, and stir well. Return osso buco to Dutch oven, cover, and bake in oven for $1\,1/2$ hours.

5.   Turn osso buco, and bake, uncovered, for $1/2$ hour. Remove osso buco, and serve with vegetable-wine sauce.

Scaloppina ai Carciofi

VEAL CUTLET WITH ARTICHOKES

Juice of 1 lemon

12 artichokes, about 3 pounds total before trimming
(make sure they're firm; the firmer the better)

$1/2$ cup extra-virgin olive oil

2 cloves garlic, finely chopped

$1/4$ teaspoon cracked red pepper

6 large ripe tomatoes (about $1\,1/2$ pounds), cut into wedges

Finely grated zest of 1 lemon

6 veal cutlets (about $4\,1/2$ ounces each) from a tender
hind-quarter cut

2 tablespoons unsalted butter

Salt

12 fresh basil leaves

1 tablespoon fresh parsley leaves, finely chopped

1. Squeeze lemon juice into a large bowl of cold water.

2. Prepare artichokes by stripping off tough outer leaves, reserving the prettier ones for garnish. Slice off tops (about 1 inch), where leaves are darker in color, and trim off bitter green outer part of stems with a paring knife.

3. Cut artichokes in half lengthways, and remove any fluff or choke from centers with the tip of a paring knife. Slice artichokes, still lengthways, into $1/4$-inch strips, and place strips in bowl with lemon water. Set aside.

4. Pour oil into a large skillet (not an iron one, which will turn artichokes brown), add garlic, and sauté over medium heat until golden. Drain artichokes well, and add them to skillet. Cover and cook for 5 minutes

5. Add cracked red pepper and tomatoes, cover skillet, and cook for another 5 minutes. Add lemon zest, remove pan from heat, and set aside.

6. Place veal cutlets on a flat surface, sprinkle very lightly with water, cover with plastic wrap, and pound to $1/4$-inch thickness with a smooth-surfaced meat mallet.

7. On high heat, melt butter in a large, heavy skillet, and sauté veal for 2 minutes. Salt to taste, turn, and sauté 2 minutes on other side, once again salting to taste.

8. Add artichoke sauce, and cook another 5 minutes. Add basil leaves.

9. Place on a warm serving dish, sprinkle with parsley, garnish with artichoke leaves, and serve.

Scaloppina ai Funghi Porcini

VEAL CUTLETS WITH PORCINI MUSHROOMS

NOTE If you can't find fresh porcini mushrooms, look for dried ones. Substitue $1/2$ cup dried mushrooms and 1 pound button mushrooms. Soak dried mushrooms in hot water for 20 minutes before using, in order to soften them.

1 pound porcini mushrooms, thoroughly washed and dried

$1/2$ cup extra-virgin olive oil

4 garlic cloves, in their jackets

3 tablespoons finely chopped nepitella (if unavailable, use mint)

Salt

4 veal cutlets (approximately $1/4$ pound each)

2 tablespoons unsalted butter

1 tablespoon fresh parsley leaves, very finely chopped

1. Slice porcini mushrooms into $1/2$-inch pieces.

2. Pour oil into a large skillet, and add mushrooms, garlic cloves, and nepitella. Sauté over medium heat for 10 minutes, stirring occasionally. Salt to taste, and set aside.

3. Place veal slices on a flat surface, sprinkle very lightly with water, cover with plastic wrap, and pound to $1/4$-inch thickness with a smooth-surfaced meat mallet.

4. In a second large skillet, melt butter, add veal cutlets, and sauté for 3 minutes on medium-high heat. Salt, turn, and sauté 3 minutes longer. Add mushrooms, and sauté for another 3 minutes. Remove garlic cloves. Sprinkle cutlets with parsley, and serve on a warm platter.

SECOND (MAIN) COURSES

℘ *279* ℘

Scaloppina al Dragoncello

VEAL CUTLET WITH TARRAGON SAUCE

4 veal cutlets, approximately 4 to 5 ounces each
$1/8$ pound ($1/2$ stick) unsalted butter
Salt
$1/4$ cup cognac
$3/4$ cup heavy cream
$1/4$ cup finely chopped fresh tarragon

1. Place cutlets on a flat surface, sprinkle very lightly with water, cover with plastic wrap, and pound to $1/4$-inch thickness with a smooth-surfaced meat mallet.

2. On high heat, melt butter in a large, heavy skillet, and sauté veal for 3 minutes. Salt to taste, turn, and sauté 3 minutes on other side, once again salting to taste.

3. Remove skillet from heat, carefully add cognac, return skillet to heat, and ignite very carefully with a kitchen match to flambé. Cook until flame subsides.

4. Once again, remove skillet from heat, add heavy cream and tarragon, return to heat, and cook for 2 more minutes.

5. Place a veal cutlet on each plate, and spoon sauce over it.

Scaloppina al Limone

VEAL CUTLET
WITH LEMON SAUCE

12 small new potatoes

4 veal cutlets, approximately 4 to 5 ounces each

Flour for dredging

$1/4$ pound (1 stick) unsalted butter

Salt

Juice of 2 lemons

Lemon, thinly sliced, for garnish

1 tablespoon finely chopped fresh parsley leaves

1. Boil new potatoes in their jackets until cooked (approximately 15 minutes). Drain, peel, and slice in half lengthways. Set aside.

2. Place veal cutlets on a flat surface, sprinkle very lightly with water, cover with plastic wrap, and pound to $1/4$-inch thickness with a smooth-surfaced meat mallet.

3. Dredge veal in flour. Melt half the butter in a heavy skillet, and brown veal on high heat, 3 minutes on each side. Move veal around pan while cooking.

4. Salt to taste, and add new potatoes. Brown another 2 minutes, still stirring. Add lemon juice.

5. Turn off heat, add remainder of butter, and stir. Serve on plates garnished with thin lemon slices. Sprinkle with parsley.

Scaloppina di Vitella alla Chantal

VEAL WITH ASPARAGUS AND COGNAC CREAM SAUCE

12 large asparagus stalks

1 tablespoon salt

4 veal medallions or fillets, approximately 4 to 5 ounces each

4 tablespoons unsalted butter

Additional salt

$1/4$ cup cognac

1 cup heavy cream

1 tablespoon grainy Dijon mustard

1. Remove tough ends from asparagus spears, and discard.

2. Bring a saucepan of water to a boil, add tablespoon of salt, toss in asparagus spears, reduce heat to a simmer, and cook until *al dente* (about 5 minutes, depending on thickness of asparagus). Drain asparagus, cut off tips, and slice stalks into $1/2$-inch pieces. Set aside in a bowl.

3. Slightly flatten veal with a smooth-surfaced meat mallet (or with the palm of your hand).

4. In a large, heavy skillet, melt butter on high heat. When it starts turning brown, add veal, and brown for 3 minutes, moving it continuously around the pan with a fork. Turn, and brown other side for 2 minutes, still moving with fork. Salt to taste.

5. Add cognac, and cook on high heat for 2 minutes. Add cream, mustard, and asparagus. Cook for another 2 minutes, using fork to combine ingredients.

6. Place veal on a warm serving dish, and spoon sauce on top.

Vitellina al Salvia
con Patate Novelle

VEAL WITH SAGE
AND NEW POTATOES

1 pound veal

$1/2$ cup extra-virgin olive oil

2 cloves garlic, sliced paper thin

$1/4$ teaspoon cracked red pepper

8 fresh sage leaves

12 small new potatoes, boiled in their jackets, peeled,
and cut into $1/2$-inch slices

Salt

1. Cut veal into 1-inch cubes. Place cubes, about 10 at a time, on a flat surface, sprinkle very lightly with water, cover with plastic wrap, and pound flat with a smooth-surfaced meat mallet.

2. Pour oil into a heavy-bottomed skillet. Place flattened veal pieces into cold pan, and add garlic, cracked red pepper, and sage leaves. Turn heat to high, and turn quickly with a wooden spoon (as you would for stir-fry) for about 3 minutes (the veal should not brown). Add potatoes, and cook another 3 minutes. Salt to taste.

Vitellina con Zucchine
al Pomodoro e Rucola

SERVES 4

VEAL WITH ZUCCHINI, TOMATO, AND ARUGULA

NOTE This recipe can also be prepared as a vegetable dish without the veal. To do so, simply skip Steps 1 and 4.

1 pound veal

4 medium-sized zucchini (4 to 5 inches long)

1 tablespoon salt

$1/2$ cup extra-virgin olive oil

4 ripe tomatoes, each cut into 8 wedges

3 cloves garlic, sliced thin

10 fresh basil leaves

$1/4$ pound arugula, coarsely chopped

$1/4$ teaspoon cracked red pepper

Salt

1. Bring a large stockpot of water to a boil. While waiting for water to heat, cut veal into 1-inch cubes. Place cubes, about 10 at a time, on a flat surface, sprinkle very lightly with water, cover with plastic wrap, and pound flat with a smooth-surfaced meat mallet. Set aside.

2. Halve zucchini lengthways. Slice, still lengthways, into $1/8$-inch julienne strips. When water comes to a boil, add 1 tablespoon salt, carefully pour in zucchini strips, and blanch in boiling water for 3 minutes. Drain well, and set aside.

3. Pour $1/4$ cup of the oil into a large skillet, and add tomatoes, garlic, and basil. Turn heat to high, and sauté for 5 minutes. Add $1/2$ the arugula (set remainder aside) and cracked red pepper, and sauté another 2 minutes. Add julienned zucchini, and sauté for 1 minute. Salt to taste, remove skillet from heat, and set aside.

4. Pour remaining $1/4$ cup of oil into a different skillet, add flattened veal pieces, turn heat to high, and turn quickly with a wooden spoon (as you would for stir-fry) for about 3 minutes (the veal should not brown). Salt to taste.

5. Center zucchini/tomato/arugula mix on a serving dish, arrange veal on top, and garnish with remaining arugula.

ONCE UPON A TUSCAN TABLE

Cʒ *284* €ʒ

Contorni

SIDE DISHES

SWISS CHARD SAUTÉED
WITH GARLIC

NOTE This vegetable dish makes a great accompaniment to grilled meats or roast beef.

3 pounds Swiss chard
$\frac{1}{2}$ cup extra-virgin olive oil
3 cloves garlic, finely chopped
$\frac{1}{4}$ teaspoon cracked red pepper
Salt

1. Cut off tough bottom parts of stems, and wash chard leaves well in cold water.
2. In a large pot, bring 2 inches of water to a boil. Add chard, and cook on high heat until wilted (approximately 5 minutes). Drain, squeeze out excess moisture, and chop coarsely.
3. Pour oil into a skillet, add garlic, turn heat to high, and sauté until golden. Lower heat to medium, add chard and cracked red pepper, salt to taste, and sauté for 3 minutes.

Cipolle al Sauternes di Andrea SERVES 6

ANDREA'S ONIONS CARAMELIZED IN SAUTERNES

My son, Andrea, created this side dish during a family ski trip to Abetone, in the Appenine Mountains, north of Florence. We spent a number of Christmas vacations there, renting a cozy accommodation with a fireplace and a complete kitchen. After skiing, we'd invite friends to join us and cook up a storm. Andrea's caramelized onions go especially well with grilled or roasted meats.

2 ounces ($\frac{1}{2}$ stick) unsalted butter

8 medium-sized sweet yellow onions, cut into $\frac{1}{8}$-inch slices

1 cup Sauternes

Salt

1. Melt butter in a heavy pot over medium heat. Add onions, and cook until caramelized (about 10 minutes). Add $\frac{1}{4}$ cup Sauternes at a time, cooking each time until it is evaporated. Salt to taste.

WHITE CANNELLINI
BEANS WITH OIL

This is a classic Tuscan dish, astounding in its simplicity and espe-cially delicious in November when olive oil is newly pressed. One of the ways growers test their new oil is drizzling it over beans.

1 cup dried cannellini beans

2 quarts water

2 cloves garlic, in their jackets

4 sage leaves

Extra-virgin olive oil for drizzling

Salt

1. Place beans in large stockpot, and add enough cold water to cover by 3 inches. Let stand overnight.

2. Drain beans well, and return to pot. Add 2 quarts water, garlic cloves, and sage leaves. Bring to a boil, then reduce heat to the lowest possible, and simmer until beans are tender (at least 2 hours). Do not stir.

3. With a slotted spoon, remove beans to a serving bowl. Discard sage leaves and garlic. Drizzle with oil, and salt to taste.

BAKED FENNEL BULB

Baked fennel makes a great accompaniment to roast pork dishes such as Arista alla Fiorentina, on page 272.

4 large fennel bulbs

1 tablespoon salt

Unsalted butter for greasing baking dish

$\frac{1}{8}$ pound ($\frac{1}{2}$ stick) unsalted butter, melted

1 cup heavy cream

Salt

1 teaspoon fennel seeds

1 cup coarsely grated Parmigiano Reggiano

1. Preheat oven to 400 degrees, and put up a large pot of water to boil. While waiting for water to heat, remove tough outer parts of fennel bulbs, and trim tops and bottoms. Cut bulbs in half, lengthways, then into 1-inch slices, still lengthways. Add 1 tablespoon salt to boiling water, toss in fennel, and cook on high heat for 5 minutes.

2. Drain fennel well, and place in a buttered baking dish. Drizzle melted butter over fennel, pour cream on top, salt to taste, and sprinkle with fennel seeds and grated Parmigiano. Bake for 15 minutes.

Nidi di Radicchio Rosso
di Treviso al Gorgonzola

RADICCHIO NESTS WITH
GORGONZOLA SAUCE

This recipe was created on the spur of the moment when Olympics gold-medal winner Carl Lewis came to Trattoria Garga with a party of thirty. Giuliano—thinking athletes—had devised a menu consisting largely of meat dishes. As it turned out, half of them were vegetarians. I raced to the pantry kitchen in search of available ingredients and, with profound relief, found an entire crate of Trevisan radicchio. Happily, the muses were with me when I invented this vegetarian entrée; everyone loved it! Its been a Garga staple for private parties ever since.

NOTE Radicchio di Treviso have narrow pointed leaves, white ribs, and tight tapered heads.

10 ounces Gorgonzola cheese (dolce) or Dolcelatte

$1/4$ cup heavy cream

$1/4$ teaspoon truffle oil

1 pound radicchio di Treviso

$1/2$ cup extra-virgin olive oil

Salt

2 ounces pine nuts

1. Preheat oven to 350 degrees. Melt Gorgonzola, together with cream, in top of a double boiler. When cheese is melted, add truffle oil. Remove sauce from heat, and set aside.

2. Wash entire heads of radicchio without separating leaves, and dry well. Chop each head in half lengthways, then, again lengthways, into $1/4$-inch slices.

3. Place sliced radicchio in a nonstick baking pan (or one lightly greased with olive oil), drizzle with $1/2$ cup olive oil, and bake for 10 minutes. Stir radicchio, and bake another 10 minutes. Salt to taste.

4. Place a mound of radicchio in the center of each serving plate, spoon an equal amount of Gorgonzola sauce over each, and sprinkle each plate with $1/4$ of the pine nuts.

Patate al Forno
al Rosmarino e Aglio

ROASTED POTATOES WITH ROSEMARY AND GARLIC

3 pounds yellow potatoes

1 teaspoon salt

$1/4$ cup extra-virgin olive oil

1 tablespoon fresh rosemary leaves, finely chopped

2 cloves garlic, finely chopped

1. Preheat oven to 350 degrees.
2. Peel potatoes, wash, and pat dry. Cut potatoes into pieces (approximately 1" × 1" × $1/2$"), place them in a roasting pan, salt evenly, and drizzle with oil. Roast in oven for 50 minutes.
3. With a metal spatula, gently turn potatoes. Evenly distribute rosemary and garlic, and roast for another 30 minutes.

Patate con Noci e Limone

POTATOES WITH WALNUTS AND LEMON

2 pounds medium-sized Idaho potatoes

1 tablespoon ($^1/_8$ stick) unsalted butter

$^3/_8$ cup extra-virgin olive oil

Zest of 1 lemon

1 tablespoon finely chopped parsley leaves

$^1/_4$ teaspoon freshly ground nutmeg

Salt

Freshly ground black pepper

$^1/_4$ cup finely ground walnuts

Juice of 1 lemon

1. Peel potatoes, and cook (whole) in boiling water until tender (20 to 30 minutes, depending on size). Drain, and let cool for 5 minutes. Slice potatoes into $^1/_2$-inch rounds.

2. Place butter, oil, lemon zest, and parsley in a skillet. Cook for 3 minutes over medium heat. Add sliced potatoes, and sauté until golden-brown (8 to 10 minutes), turning over only once. Add nutmeg, and season to taste with salt and pepper.

3. In a small bowl, mix ground walnuts and lemon juice. Arrange potatoes on a serving dish, and top with lemon/walnut mixture.

Patate Novelle Saltate

FRIED NEW POTATOES

16 new potatoes

2 tablespoons extra-virgin olive oil

1 tablespoon fresh rosemary leaves, finely chopped

1 tablespoon fresh sage leaves, finely chopped

2 cloves garlic, finely chopped

Salt

1. Wash potatoes very thoroughly, and cook in their jackets until tender (about 15 minutes). Drain well.

2. Slice each potato in half. Pour oil into a skillet, and add potatoes, rosemary, sage, and garlic. Sauté over high heat, stirring occasionally, until potatoes are golden and crispy. Salt to taste.

Spinaci Saltati

SPINACH SAUTÉED WITH GARLIC

3 pounds spinach

$1/2$ cup extra-virgin olive oil

3 cloves finely chopped garlic

$1/4$ teaspoon cracked red pepper

Salt

1. Thoroughly wash spinach in cold water, and place it in a large pot with 2 inches of water. Cook until wilted (approximately 5 minutes). Drain, squeeze out moisture, and chop coarsely.

2. Pour oil into a skillet, add garlic, and sauté until golden. Add spinach and cracked red pepper, salt to taste, and sauté for 3 minutes.

Dolci

DESSERTS

BISCOTTI DI PRATO

These scrumptious biscotti are a specialty of the Tuscan city of Prato, which is equally famous for its textiles and its *pasticcerie*.

$1/2$ pound almonds, with skins

Parchment paper

$3 1/2$ cups unbleached all-purpose flour

2 cups sugar

1 teaspoon baking powder

$1/2$ teaspoon salt

$1/2$ teaspoon saffron

5 jumbo eggs

1. In a 350-degree oven, toast almonds for 10 minutes on a sheet of parchment paper. Remove paper with almonds, and let cool on a flat surface. Leave oven on.

2. Turn out flour in a mound on a flat working surface covered with parchment paper. Create a crater in its center. Into this crater, place sugar, baking powder, salt, saffron, and 3 whole eggs plus 1 yolk (**HINT:** the unneeded egg white makes a great facial mask). Mix with your hands until ingredients are well blended, add almonds, and continue mixing, brushing your hands with flour if the mixture gets sticky.

3. Divide dough into 8 equal pieces. Still using your hands (slightly dusted with flour) form each of the 8 pieces into a log about 10 inches long and 2 inches wide. Place logs, 2 inches apart (they mustn't be too close together, as they will expand), on a baking sheet lined with parchment paper. You'll need to use 2 baking sheets to fit them all. Beat remaining egg, and brush top of biscotti dough with it.

4. Bake biscotti in the middle of oven for 25 to 30 minutes (until golden). As soon as you remove them from the oven, cut each strip, on a diagonal, into $1/2$-inch slices (as if you were slicing a thin baguette). Return to oven, with cut side up, and bake for 5 more minutes.

Budino di Pane alla Fiorentina SERVES 4

FLORENTINE
BREAD PUDDING

This dish—along with a big bowl of caffélatte—constitutes one of Zoe's favorite evening meals

3 slices (approximately 4" × 4") day-old white bread, such as sandwich loaf or French bread (with crust)

2 tablespoons unsalted butter, at room temperature

2 teaspoons cinnamon

$1/3$ cup dark raisins

Zest of 1 lemon, finely grated

3 jumbo eggs

$1/2$ cup sugar

2 cups whole milk

1. Preheat oven to 300 degrees.
2. Toast bread until golden, and lightly butter both sides of each slice.
3. Place toast slices (without overlapping) in an attractive 9" × 12" ovenproof baking dish (it will become your serving dish), and sprinkle them evenly with cinnamon, raisins, and lemon zest.
4. In a small bowl, whisk eggs with sugar until light and frothy, then gently whisk in milk. Pour mixture over bread, and bake for 30 minutes.

CRÈME CARAMEL

NOTE For this recipe, you'll need half-a-dozen 6-ounce ramekins.

Juice of 1 lemon
1 $^3/_4$ cups sugar
3 cups half-and-half
Finely grated zest of 1 lemon
3 whole jumbo eggs
3 jumbo egg yolks

1. Preheat oven to 325 degrees.
2. Pour lemon juice through a fine sieve into a heavy saucepan, and stir in 1 cup of the sugar. Bring to a boil over medium-high heat, stirring with a wooden spoon until sugar is dissolved. Continue to boil, swirling pan occasionally, until syrup is a deep golden caramel. Immediately divide caramel among ramekins, tilting them if necessary to evenly coat bottoms.
3. In a small saucepan, bring half-and-half and lemon zest to a simmer over moderate heat, then remove from heat and let stand, covered, for 10 minutes.
4. In a large bowl, whisk together whole eggs, extra yolks, and remaining $^3/_4$ cup sugar, until eggs are pale in color. Then whisk in half-and-half/lemon zest mixture a little at a time. Divide custard evenly among ramekins.
5. Arrange ramekins in a small roasting pan, and carefully add enough hot water to pan to reach halfway up sides of ramekins. Bake in middle of oven until custard is just set, but still trembles slightly in center (50 minutes to 1 hour).
6. Run a thin knife around side of each ramekin to loosen custard. Transfer ramekins to a rack, and cool at room temperature for $^1/_2$ hour. Cover ramekins loosely, and refrigerate for at least 2 hours.
7. To unmold, invert plates over ramekins and turn out custards.

Crostata di Limone

LEMON TART

FOR THE PASTRY:

$\frac{1}{4}$ pound (1 stick) unsalted butter, melted

$\frac{1}{4}$ cup confectioner's sugar

1 $\frac{1}{4}$ cups unbleached all-purpose flour, sifted

$\frac{1}{4}$ teaspoon salt

1. Preheat oven to 350 degrees. Using a fork (or your hands), thoroughly combine above ingredients in a bowl to form a pastry dough.

2. Using your fingers, crumble dough evenly into bottom and up sides (crust should go 2 inches up sides) of a 10-inch springform pan, pressing it down well. Make sure your crust comes to a nice right angle where bottom and sides of pan meet; there should be no bunched-up crust forming a curve. Prick crust at 1-inch intervals, bottom and sides, with the tines of a fork. Bake for 15 minutes, or until crust turns the tiniest bit golden. Do not overbake, or it will taste dry. Prepare filling while crust is baking.

FOR THE FILLING:

4 jumbo eggs

1 $\frac{3}{4}$ cups sugar

1 teaspoon baking powder

$\frac{1}{4}$ cup unbleached all-purpose flour

$\frac{1}{4}$ cup lemon juice

Zest of 2 lemons, finely grated

1. Place all ingredients in a bowl, and beat well with an electric mixer. Gently pour filling into hot crust, and bake for 20 minutes. This tart is delicious warm or cold.

Crostatine con Fichi
e Zabaione Chantilly

TARTLETS WITH FIGS
AND WHIPPED SABAYON

NOTE For this recipe, you'll need 12 fluted tartlet forms, each approximately 4 inches in diameter.

FOR THE SABAYON:

3 jumbo egg yolks, at room temperature

$^3/_8$ cup sugar

3 tablespoons Vin Santo or sweet Marsala wine

2 cups heavy cream

1. Fill bottom of a double boiler with water, and bring to a boil. Meanwhile, off the stove, mix egg yolks, sugar, and Vin Santo in top part of double boiler. Beat with a wire whisk until light and frothy.

2. Place pot with this mixture on top of boiling water, reduce heat to medium, and whisk continually until sabayon is light and fluffy (it should stick to the sides of the pot the way custard or pudding does). This will take approximately 10 minutes.

3. Remove sabayon from heat, pour into a bowl, and let cool to room temperature (at least an hour).

4. Whip heavy cream with an electric mixer until it forms very stiff peaks. Refrigerate whipped cream until ready to use.

NOTE For an easier version of this recipe, substitute vanilla gelato or Häagen-Dazs vanilla for the sabayon sauce.

FOR THE PASTRY TARTS:

$^1/_2$ cup sugar

$1^1/_2$ cup unbleached all-purpose flour

$^1/_2$ teaspoon salt

$3^1/_2$ ounces ($^7/_8$ of a stick) cold unsalted butter

2 jumbo egg yolks

Unsalted butter for greasing tartlet pans, at room temperature

Extra flour for dusting

1. Heat oven to 350 degrees. Combine sugar, flour, and salt in a bowl, and pour out in a mound on a flat surface. Create a crater in center of flour mound, and place cold butter (cut into pieces) in it. Using a pastry cutter, cut butter into flour in small bits, until mixture looks like coarse meal.

2. Add egg yolks, and work dough with your hands, until it forms a ball. Do not overwork dough. Cover dough with plastic wrap and refrigerate for 10 minutes. During that time, grease tartlet forms with butter.

3. Dust your work surface generously with flour, and roll dough to $\frac{1}{8}$-inch thickness. Using the top of a tartlet form like a cookie cutter, cut a circle of dough. With a large spatula, scoop up dough with tartlet form, turning it right side up, so dough falls into tartlet form. Center pastry dough, and gently pat into place. Repeat process with remaining dough and tartlet forms. Place tarts in oven, and bake for 15 minutes. Let cool for 5 minutes, then gently unmold tart shells by tipping over forms.

FOR THE FIG JAM FILLING:

12 fresh green figs

6 tablespoons sugar

1. Cut figs in quarters, and place in a pot with sugar. Cook over medium heat for 10 minutes, stirring occasionally.

ASSEMBLING THE TARTLETS:

12 fresh green figs

1. Immediately before serving, fold (don't stir) cooled sabayon carefully into whipped cream, $\frac{1}{4}$ at a time. Arrange tartlets on individual dessert plates, and fill each with $\frac{1}{12}$ of the fig jam. Make a cross incision in each of the 12 remaining figs, and place one, opened in a star shape, on top of jam in each tartlet. Spoon sabayon in center of each fig, letting it flow over jam filling.

Fiorentine al Cioccolato Fondente

BITTERSWEET CHOCOLATE FLORENTINES

NOTE Use the finest quality chocolate you can find. Do not use baking chocolate.

Parchment paper

8 ounces bittersweet chocolate, chopped

2 tablespoons dark raisins

2 tablespoons golden raisins

2 tablespoons pine nuts

Zest of 1 orange, roughly grated

1. Line a cookie sheet with parchment paper.
2. Melt chocolate in the top of a double boiler over barely boiling water.
3. Spoon one tablespoon of chocolate at a time onto parchment-covered cookie sheet, and sprinkle it with dark and golden raisins, pine nuts, and orange zest. Continue until all chocolate is used up.
4. Refrigerate on cookie sheet for at least 2 hours before removing florentines from parchment paper. When hardened, transfer to a covered container, and store refrigerated.

MAPLE ALMOND
LACE COOKIES

This is one of my mother's favorite Canadian cookie recipes, as you may have guessed from the ingredients.

$1/2$ cup dark brown sugar

$1/4$ cup unsalted butter

$1/4$ cup maple syrup

$1/3$ cup unbleached all-purpose flour

$1/2$ cup sliced blanched almonds, finely chopped

$1/4$ teaspoon salt

Parchment paper

1. Preheat oven to 350 degrees. In a small saucepan, on low heat, cook sugar, butter, and syrup until sugar dissolves. Remove from heat, and stir in flour, almonds, and salt.

2. Because they spread a lot when baked, these cookies are made 6 at a time. Spoon out 6 teaspoons of batter on a cookie sheet lined with parchment paper. Bake in middle of oven for 5 minutes, or until cookies are completely flattened out and bubbly. Lift out parchment paper with cookies, and let cool completely (about 15 minutes). Repeat with remaining batter, using new paper each time. When cookies are cooled, place them in an airtight cookie jar.

Pesche con Salsa al Caramello SERVES 4

PEACHES WITH
CARAMEL CREAM

$\frac{1}{2}$ cup sugar

1 tablespoon water

2 cups heavy cream

4 large ripe peaches

Fresh mint leaves for garnish

1. Place sugar and water in a large skillet, turn heat to high, and stir constantly until sugar is caramelized (becomes a dark clear syrup). At the same time, on another burner, bring cream to a boil in a saucepan.

2. Slowly and carefully, stirring constantly, add hot cream to sugar-water mixture. The sugar will harden at first but will then melt. Refrigerate for at least 30 minutes.

3. When ready to serve, peel and slice peaches. Place slices in individual bowls, top with cold caramel cream, and garnish with mint leaves.

PUMPKIN PIE

One Halloween, I bought a big pumpkin to make a jack-o'-lantern for the restaurant, and I used the meat I scooped out for a pumpkin pie. It's been a popular autumn dessert with Garga customers ever since—among them Paloma Picasso, who always calls ahead to request it if she's coming to Florence in October.

1 pumpkin (approximately 4 pounds)

1. Preheat oven to 350 degrees. Halve pumpkin, and remove seeds and stringy center part. Cut in large pieces (about 4 inches), and remove tough outer shell.

2. Place pumpkin pieces in a baking pan, cover with tin foil, and bake until softened (approximately 1 $1/2$ hours). Place baked pumpkin in a colander, and let drain for 1 hour. While pumpkin is draining, prepare your pastry.

FOR THE PASTRY:

$1/4$ pound (1 stick) unsalted butter, melted

$1/4$ cup confectioner's sugar

1 $1/4$ cups unbleached all-purpose flour

$1/4$ teaspoon salt

1. Using a fork (or your hands), thoroughly combine crust ingredients in a bowl.

2. Using your fingers, line bottom and sides of a 10-inch springform pan with pastry dough, pressing it down well. Make sure crust comes to a nice right angle where bottom and sides of pan meet; there should be no bunched-up crust forming a curve. Prick crust at 1-inch intervals, bottom and sides, with the tines of a fork. Bake for 15 minutes, during which time you can prepare filling.

FOR THE FILLING:

2 cups cooked and puréed fresh pumpkin

1 cup heavy cream

3 jumbo eggs

$1/4$ cup bourbon

$^3/_4$ cup brown sugar

$^3/_4$ cup walnuts, ground very fine

1 teaspoon cinnamon

1 tablespoon freshly grated ginger

$^1/_4$ teaspoon freshly grated nutmeg

$^1/_4$ teaspoon ground cloves

1. When pumpkin is drained well, purée it in a blender or food proces-sor, and measure out 2 cups. In a large bowl, combine puréed pumpkin with all other filling ingredients, and mix well with a wooden spoon. Gently pour mixture into piecrust, and bake for 25 minutes or until set like a custard (still a little wobbly).

2. Let pie rest at least 2 hours in a cool place (at room temperature, but away from the stove); do not refrigerate. Open springform pan just before serving.

FOR THE TOPPING:

1 cup heavy cream

1. Whip cream with an electric mixer or wire whisk until thick. Serve each slice with a dollop of unsweetened whipped cream on the side.

Schiaccata alla Fiorentina

FLORENTINE CARNIVAL CAKE

This cake, from an ancient recipe, is traditionally served during Carneval–between Epiphany and Ash Wednesday. Meat fats being prohibited during Lent, people naturally want to use up their lard; hence it shows up as an ingredient. If you prefer, substitute extra-virgin olive oil for lard. Another interesting ingredient here is saffron, one of the oldest flavorings–and coloring agents–in Italian cooking.

1 tablespoon lard (or extra-virgin olive oil)

1 packet ($1/4$ ounce) active dry yeast

1 teaspoon sugar

$1/2$ cup warm water (110 degrees)

3 cups unbleached all-purpose flour

$2 1/2$ ounces lard (or extra-virgin olive oil)

Zest of 1 orange, finely grated

$3/4$ cup sugar

$1/2$ teaspoon salt

$1/4$ teaspoon pure vanilla extract

$1/4$ teaspoon freshly grated nutmeg

$1/4$ teaspoon powdered saffron

1 jumbo egg

Confectioner's sugar for dusting

1. Grease an 11" × 7" × 1$1/2$" baking pan with tablespoon of lard.

2. Place yeast in a small bowl, add 1 teaspoon sugar, and slowly mix in warm water. Let rest for 15 minutes, or until foam covers top of yeast mixture. Add flour, and stir well. Cover bowl with a cloth, and let mixture rise for 1 hour.

3. Transfer batter to a large mixing bowl, and add 2 $1/2$ ounces lard, orange zest, $3/4$ cup sugar, salt, vanilla, nutmeg, saffron, and egg. Beat with an electric mixer for 10 minutes.

4. Using your fingers, press dough evenly into greased baking pan. Cover pan with a cloth, and put it in a warm place for 2 hours to allow dough to rise. About 10 minutes before dough has risen, preheat oven to 400 degrees.

5. Bake until golden (about 10 to 12 minutes). Remove pan from oven, and run a knife around its edge. Let cool for 10 minutes, and remove cake from pan onto a serving platter. Using a sieve, dust cake with confectioner's sugar.

GRAPE CAKE

NOTE This cake should be made only when wine grapes are in season.

1 packet ($1/4$ ounce) active dry yeast

3 tablespoons Chianti Classico (or other dry red wine)

1 teaspoon sugar

$1/2$ cup warm water (110 degrees)

3 cups unbleached all-purpose flour

$1/4$ cup extra-virgin olive oil

$1/2$ teaspoon salt

Additiional flour for dusting work surface

Extra-virgin olive oil for greasing bowl and baking pan

3 $1/2$ cups wine grapes

$1/2$ cup sugar

1 tablespoon ground anise

1. Stir together yeast, wine, sugar, and warm water in a large bowl until yeast is dissolved. Let stand until covered with foam, about 15 minutes.

2. Stir in 1 cup of the flour (mixture will be lumpy). Cover bowl with a cloth and let mixture rise in a warm place for 1 hour (or until doubled in bulk).

3. Add $1/4$ cup olive oil, 1 $1/2$ cups of the flour, and salt. Stir with a wooden spoon until a sticky dough forms.

4. Knead dough on a floured work surface, gradually adding up to $1/2$ cup more flour, if necessary, to keep dough from sticking. Knead until dough is smooth and elastic but still soft. This will take about 10 minutes.

5. Transfer dough to an oiled large bowl, and turn to coat. Cover bowl with plastic wrap and a kitchen towel, and let rise in a warm place for 1 hour (or until doubled in bulk again).

6. Turn out dough onto a floured work surface, and knead for 3 minutes. Take half the dough, and cover remainder with plastic wrap. Roll out dough with a lightly floured rolling pin into a rough 12" × 10" rectangle. Transfer dough to a lightly oiled 15" × 10" × 1" baking pan, and gently stretch to cover bottom. Don't worry if it doesn't fit precisely.

7. Distribute half the grapes over dough, and sprinkle them with $1/4$ cup of the sugar and $1/2$ tablespoon ($1\,1/2$ teaspoons) of the ground anise. Roll out remaining piece of dough as in Step 6, stretching it to cover grapes. Distribute other half of grapes on top, sprinkle with remaining sugar and anise, and press grapes gently into dough. Cover pan with a cloth and let rise in a warm place for 1 hour (until doubled in bulk yet again). About 10 minutes before this process is complete, preheat oven to 400 degrees.

8. Bake in middle of oven until well browned and firm in middle, 40 to 45 minutes. Serve at room temperature.

Semifreddo all'Arancia Candita
con Salsa al Cioccolato Fondente   SERVES 8

FROZEN CANDIED ORANGE MOUSSE WITH BITTERSWEET CHOCOLATE SAUCE

FOR THE MOUSSE:

3 jumbo egg yolks

6 tablespoons sugar

$1/2$ cup candied orange peel, finely chopped

2 tablespoons orange juice

2 cups heavy cream

1. Using an electric mixer at high speed, beat egg yolks and sugar until light and fluffy.

2. Add candied orange peel and juice, and mix well.

3. In a separate mixing bowl, beat cream with an electric mixer until it forms stiff peaks.

4. In small batches, fold whipped cream into egg/juice mixture.

5. Spoon equal amounts of mousse into 8 ramekins, and freeze for at least 2 hours. Prepare sauce just prior to serving.

FOR THE CHOCOLATE SAUCE:

$1/4$ pound fine-quality bittersweet chocolate

1 cup heavy cream

1. In the top of a double boiler, over barely boiling water, melt chocolate and cream. Stir to combine.

2. Unmold mousse by running a sharp knife around the edge of each ramekin. Invert onto individual serving plates, and top with chocolate sauce.

TIRAMISÙ

Almost everyone loves tiramisù. It originated in Treviso, but throughout Italy, there are numerous recipes using mascarpone and biscuits. For me, part of its appeal is that it seems like a fancy dessert but is actually very easy to make.

3 jumbo eggs

3 tablespoons sugar

10 ounces mascarpone cheese

1 ounce light rum

12 Italian ladyfingers (Savoiardi)

1 cup espresso coffee, brewed and cooled

2 ounces bittersweet chocolate, finely grated

NOTE The better the quality of your chocolate, the better your tiramisù.

1. Separate egg yolks from whites, and place in individual mixing bowls.

2. With an electric mixer, whip egg whites until they hold a stiff peak. Set aside.

3. Beat egg yolks with sugar until light and fluffy. Beat in the mascarpone for 1 minute. Add rum and stir. Then, using a rubber spatula, gently fold in egg whites.

4. Lightly dip each ladyfinger in coffee, and place it in a glass baking dish large enough to hold them all without overlapping. Top ladyfingers with mascarpone mixture. Sprinkle evenly with chocolate, and refrigerate for 1 hour.

Tiramisù alla Pesca
e Pistacchio

PEACH AND
PISTACHIO TIRAMISÙ

6 yellow peaches

3 cups water

$1/4$ cup amaretto liqueur

$3/8$ cup sugar

3 jumbo eggs

3 tablespoons sugar

10 ounces mascarpone cheese

1 ounce light rum

12 Italian ladyfingers (Savoiardi)

$1/2$ cup unsalted pistachios, finely chopped

1. Peel peaches, placing skins and pits in a saucepan. Cut peaches into $1/4$-inch slices, and set aside.

2. Add water, amaretto, and $3/8$ cup sugar to skins and pits in saucepan. Turn heat to high, and bring to a boil.

3. Reduce heat to medium, and cook for 10 minutes, stirring occasionally. Strain mixture through a sieve into a bowl, and set syrup aside. Discard skins and pits.

4. Separate egg yolks and whites into two mixing bowls. Beat whites with an electric mixer until they form a stiff peak.

5. Add 3 tablespoons sugar to yolks, and beat with electric mixer until light and fluffy. Add mascarpone, and beat for another 2 minutes. Add rum, and beat for 2 more minutes. Gently fold in egg whites with a rubber spatula.

6. Lightly dip ladyfingers in syrup, and place in a glass dish large enough to hold them all without overlapping. Distribute sliced peaches evenly over ladyfingers. Spoon mascarpone/egg mixture over ladyfingers, and smooth with a spatula. Sprinkle pistachio nuts evenly over top. Refrigerate for at least 1 hour before serving.

Torta di Pesca

PEACH CAKE

5 large yellow peaches

$1/4$ pound (1 stick) unsalted butter, softened

1 cup sugar

3 jumbo eggs

1 cup unbleached all-purpose flour, sifted

1 teaspoon baking powder

$1/4$ teaspoon salt

Zest of 1 lemon, finely grated

Butter for greasing pan, at room temperature

Sugar

2 quarts vanilla gelato
(if unavailable, Häagen-Dazs vanilla ice cream will do)

1. Preheat oven to 350 degrees. Peel peaches, cut in half lengthways, and remove pits. Cut halves, still lengthways, into $1/4$-inch slices, and set aside.

2. In a large bowl, using an electric mixer, cream $1/4$ pound softened butter with cup of sugar. Add one egg at a time, mixing after each addition. Add flour, baking powder, and salt, and beat for 3 minutes with electric mixer. Add lemon zest, and beat for 1 minute.

3. Grease a 10- or 11-inch springform pan with butter, and dust it with sugar. Pour batter into pan, and level with a rubber spatula. Top with sliced peaches, pressing gently, leaving a $1/2$-inch border of batter from the circumference of the pan. Bake for 45 minutes, or until a baking pin inserted into the center comes out clean. Serve warm with vanilla gelato.

RICOTTA CHEESECAKE

FOR THE PASTRY CREAM:

2 jumbo eggs

$^3/_4$ cup sugar

$^1/_8$ cup unbleached all-purpose flour

2 cups half-and-half

Zest of one lemon

1. With an electric mixer, beat eggs and sugar in a large bowl until thick and foamy. Add flour, a little at a time, and mix in well.

2. In a medium saucepan, bring half-and-half to a boil.

3. Slowly add boiling half-and-half to egg/sugar/flour mixture, stirring constantly with a wooden spoon as you pour. Transfer mixture back into saucepan, and, on low heat, continue stirring until it has a pudding-like texture (about 10 minutes).

4. Stir in lemon zest. Let cool for 10 minutes, stirring occasionally so that it doesn't form a skin.

FOR THE PASTRY CRUST:

2 $^1/_4$ cups unbleached all-purpose flour

1 jumbo egg

1 cup sugar

3 $^1/_2$ ounces unsalted butter, at room temperature

$^1/_4$ teaspoon salt

$^1/_4$ teaspoon cinnamon

Butter for greasing pan

1. Preheat oven to 350 degrees. Turn out flour onto a flat surface, forming a mound. Create a crater in the center, and place egg, sugar, butter (cut into small pieces), salt, and cinnamon in it. Work ingredients thoroughly together with your hands to create a ball of dough.

2. Grease a 9 $^1/_2$-inch springform cake pan with butter, place dough in center, and working with the tips of your fingers, line pan evenly, leaving some overlapping the edges.

FOR THE FILLING:

10 ounces ricotta cheese

1 cup sugar

1 jumbo egg yolk

Zest of 1 lemon

1. Mix ricotta, sugar, egg yolk, and lemon zest, and add to bowl with pastry cream. Stir in gently.

2. Gently pour mixture into cake pan, and fold pastry that remains above level of filling over it to form a small border. Bake 40 minutes. Let cool for 15 minutes before serving.

Torta Pinolata

PINE NUT TART

FOR THE PASTRY CREAM:

2 jumbo eggs

$^3/_4$ cup sugar

$^1/_8$ cup unbleached all-purpose flour

2 cups half-and-half

Zest of one lemon

1. With an electric mixer, beat eggs and sugar in a large bowl until thick and foamy. Add flour, a little at a time, and mix in well.
2. In a medium saucepan, bring half-and-half to a boil.
3. Slowly add boiling half-and-half to egg/sugar/flour mixture, stirring constantly with a wooden spoon as you pour. Transfer mixture back into saucepan, and, on low heat, continue stirring until it has a pudding-like texture (at least 10 minutes).
4. Stir in lemon zest. Let cool for 10 minutes, stirring occasionally so that it doesn't form a skin. While letting cream cool, make your crust, and preheat oven to 350 degrees.

FOR THE PASTRY CRUST:

2 $^3/_4$ cups unbleached all-purpose flour, sifted

$^1/_2$ teaspoon salt

2 jumbo eggs

1 cup sugar

5 $^1/_2$ ounces (1 stick, plus 1 $^1/_2$ ounces) unsalted butter, at room temperature

Unsalted butter for greasing pan, at room temperature

1. Combine flour and salt in a bowl, and pour out in a mound on a flat surface. Create a crater in center of mound, and place eggs, sugar, and butter (cut into pieces) in it. Work ingredients thoroughly together with your hands to create a crumbly dough.
2. Take $^2/_3$ of dough, and form a ball. Set remaining dough aside. Roll dough ball between two sheets of waxed paper, creating a circle to fit bottom and sides of an 11-inch springform cake pan. Grease bottom and sides of pan with butter.

3. Remove waxed paper from one side, and place dough circle (remaining paper side up) in cake pan. Then remove other piece of paper. Press gently with your fingers, so dough sticks to sides of pan. If it breaks (it's very soft), just pat it together. Gently pour pastry cream into middle of cake pan, and smooth out with a spatula. Fold overlapping dough onto pastry cream.

4. Take remaining dough, and roll it (between sheets of waxed paper) into an 11-inch circle. Take off one side of waxed paper, and gently place dough over pastry cream. Remove top paper. Crimp edges of pie together with your fingers.

FOR THE TOPPING:

1 tablespoon heavy cream

$1/2$ cup pine nuts

2 tablespoons sugar

1. Brush pastry with cream. Distribute pine nuts evenly over top, and sprinkle with sugar. Bake for 40 minutes. Open springform pan just before serving.

SABAYON WITH CHANTILLY
CREAM AND STRAWBERRIES

3 jumbo egg yolks, at room temperature

6 tablespoons sugar

3 tablespoons Vin Santo or sweet Marsala wine

14 ounces fresh strawberries

1 cup heavy cream

1. Fill bottom of a double boiler with water, and bring to a boil. Meanwhile, off the stove, mix egg yolks, sugar and Vin Santo in top part of double boiler. Beat with a wire whisk until light and frothy.

2. Place pot with this mixture on top of boiling water, reduce heat to medium, and whisk continually until sabayon is light and fluffy (it should stick to the sides of the pot the way custard or pudding does). This should take approximately 10 minutes.

3. Remove pot with sabayon from heat, still whisking continually. Pour into a glass bowl, and let cool to room temperature (at least an hour). Meanwhile, slice strawberries, and divide into equal portions in four dessert bowls.

4. Immediately before serving, whip cream until it forms very stiff peaks. Whisk sabayon again a few times, and fold (don't stir) carefully into whipped cream, $1/4$ at a time. Serve over sliced strawberries.

NOTES For variations on this dessert, substitute dry white wine, amaretto, or Cointreau for Vin Santo. You can also vary the fruit: try fresh figs, apricots, peaches, or any other kind of berry.

Also, it's okay to prepare the whipped cream ahead of time, but don't mix it in with the sabayon until just before serving.

INDEX

∽ A ∼

Anchovy sauce, little toasts with smoked mozzarella and, 201
Andrea's onions caramelized in Sauternes, 287
Antipasti
artichoke tart, 196–197
bruschetta, Florentine-style, 203
bruschetta with broccoli rabe, 206
bruschetta with fresh peas and prosciutto, 205
bruschetta with kale, 204
bruschetta with oven-roasted tomatoes, 198
caponata, 188
eggplant and zucchini bundles, 189
fresh artichoke and parmesan salad, 193
fried sage leaves, 195
fried zucchini blossoms, 190
fried zucchini blossoms and shrimp, 192
little toasts with chicken livers, 199
little toasts with porcini mushrooms, 200
little toasts with smoked mozzarella and anchovy sauce, 201
little toasts with spicy garlic and tomato sauce, 95
shrimp toast, 202
Tuscan flat bread with fresh rosemary, 170
wild asparagus omelette, 191
zucchini, pine nut, and truffle oil salad, 194
Apple cake, Florentine style, 91
Apple tart alla Nancy, 165–166
Apricot tart, country house, 82–83
Artichokes
and parmesan salad, 193
risotto with, 218–219
stewed, 108

stuffed, 57–58
tart, 196–197
thin spaghetti with raw, 135
veal cutlet with, 277–278
veal with, 164
Arugula
risotto with zucchini, tomato, and, 222
veal with zucchini, tomato, and, 284
Asparagus
pasta pillows stuffed with, and taleggio cheese, 155–156
risotto, 221
veal with, and cognac cream sauce, 282
Avocado and truffle cream, veal cutlet with, 114

∽ B ∼

Beans
puréed white bean soup with spelt, 210
stewed green, 75
white cannellini, with oil, 288
Beef entrées
beef fillets, Parisian style, 270
sage-scented beef fillets, 90
steak with green peppercorn sauce, 269
stovetop roast beef, 59
Zoe's pot roast with spinach, 48–49
Biscotti di Prato, 296
Blueberry pie, Karen's, 179–180
Breads
Tuscan flat bread with fresh rosemary, 170
Broccoli rabe, bruschetta with, 206
Bruschetta
with broccoli rabe, 206

Florentine-style, 203
with fresh peas and prosciutto,
205
with kale, 204
with oven-roasted tomatoes, 198
pecorino cheese, 33

⊂ C ∽

Cabbage
black, spaghettini with, 104
red, Grandma Gerda's, 10
Cakes
apple, Florentine style, 91
Florentine carnival, 307
grape, 308–309
lemon, 173
peach, 313
ricotta cheese, 314–315
Calf's liver with sage, 116
Capon, roast stuffed, with sweetbreads and truffles, 130
Caponata, 188
Celery root salad, Madame's warm,
with blue cheese vinaigrette, 17
Chantilly cream, sabayon with, and
strawberries, 318
Cheese
pecorino, bruschetta, 33
smoked mozzarella, little toasts
with, and anchovy sauce, 201
taleggio, pasta pillows stuffed with
asparagus and, 155–156,
Cheesecakes
ricotta, 314–315
della Sharon, 140–141
Chicken entrées
with black olives and rosemary,
261
boneless chicken breasts with fresh
herbs and lemon, 97
chicken breast with orange sauce,
260
grilled baby chickens with rosemary and lemon, 74
grilled chicken with a brick, 32
pappardelle with flown chicken,
235

rehabilitated chicken croquettes,
139
Zoe's chicken breast with vegeta-
bles, 61
Chicken liver, little toasts with,
199
Chocolate
florentines, bittersweet, 302
sauce, frozen candied orange
mousse with bittersweet, 310
tart, 136
Cod, salt, with leeks, 252
Cookies, maple almond lace, 303
Country house apricot tart, 82–83
Crème caramel, 298
Crêpes
Florentine, 34–35
stuffed with radicchio and
Gorgonzola, 214–215
Croutons, parmesan, 213
Custard, panna cotta with strawberry
sauce, 109

⊂ D ∽

Danish meat balls, 21
Danish pork tenderloin with cream
sauce and bacon, 22
Danish rice pudding, 10
Desserts
apple tart alla Nancy, 165–166
biscotti di Prato, 296
bittersweet chocolate florentines,
302
cheesecake della Sharon, 140–141
chocolate tart, 136
country house apricot tart, 82–83
crème caramel, 298
Danish rice pudding, 10
Florentine bread pudding, 297
Florentine carnival cake, 307
frozen candied orange mousse
with bittersweet chocolate sauce,
310
grape cake, 308–309
Karen's blueberry pie, 179–180
lemon cake, 173
lemon tart, 299

maple almond lace cookies, 303

panna cotta with strawberry sauce, 109

peach and pistachio tiramisù, 312

peach cake, 313

peaches with caramel cream, 304

pine nut tart, 316–317

pumpkin pie, 305–306

ricotta cheesecake, 314–315

sabayon with chantilly cream and strawberries, 318

tartlets with figs and whipped sabayon, 300–301

tiramisù, 311

Duck entrées

  duck breast with green peppercorn sauce, 263

  duck with orange sauce, Florentine style, 262

Dumplings, semolina, 50

⊱ E ⊰

Egg and cheese rags in broth, 212

Eggplant

  summer, Parmigiana, 76

  and zucchini bundles, 189

Elio's osso buco, 275–276

Emperor's spaghetti, the, 242–243

⊱ F ⊰

Fennel bulb, baked, 289

Fettuccine

  with fresh herbs, 248

  with garlic and butter, 245

  with porcini mushrooms, 163

  shepherd's style, 96

  with spicy tomato sauce, 247

  with Swiss chard, 246

  thin, with citrus zest, 134

  thin, with shrimp, green peppercorns, and orange zest, 249

Figs, tartlets with, and whipped sabayon, 300–301

Fish and seafood entrées

  baby octopus in tomato broth, 129

  fish soup, 208

  fried zucchini blossoms and shrimp, 192

  grilled squid topped with porcini mushroom cap, 103

  lasagne with fish ragout, 150–151

  perch with leeks, 257

  poached octopus, 259

  salt cod with leeks, 252

  shrimp toast, 202

  shrimp with green peppercorns, 254

  shrimp with peppers, 253

  shrimp with spicy garlic and tomato sauce, 256

  shrimp with zucchini, tomato, and arugula, 255

  swordfish, Sicilian style, 258

  thin fettuccine with shrimp, green peppercorns, and orange zest, 249

  thin spaghetti with lobster, 122

Fish soup, 208

Florentine bread pudding, 297

Florentine carnival cake, 307

Florentine crêpes, 34–35

⊱ G ⊰

Gnocchi

  potato, with Gorgonzola and truffle sauce, 223–224

  squash, 225–226

Gnudi, naked ravioli, 227

Goose, Grandma Gerda's roast stuffed, 8–9

Gorgonzola

  crêpes stuffed with radicchio and, 214–215

  golden veal cutlets with, 273

  polenta with, 217

Grandma Gerda's red cabbage, 10

Grandma Gerda's roast stuffed goose, 8–9

Grape cake, 308–309

Green beans, stewed, 75

Grilled baby chickens with rosemary and lemon, 74

Grilled chicken with a brick, 32

Grilled squid topped with porcini mushroom cap, 103

❧ I ❧

Italian meat loaf with scoundrel sauce, 69–70

❧ K ❧

Kale, bruschetta with, 204
Karen's blueberry pie, 179–180

❧ L ❧

Lamb entrées
    lamb cutlets sautéed with rosemary, 271
    rolled leg of lamb with mint and garlic, 157
Lasagne
    with fish ragout, 150–151
    al pesto, 231
    vegetable, 232–234
Lemon cake, 173
Lemon tart, 299
Lobster, thin spaghetti with, 122

❧ M ❧

Madame's warm celery root salad with blue cheese vinaigrette, 17
Maple almond lace cookies, 303
Meat balls, Danish, 21
Meat entrées
    beef fillets, Parisian style, 270
    Danish meat balls, 21
    Danish pork tenderloin with cream sauce and bacon, 22
    Grandma Gerda's roast stuffed goose, 8
    Italian meat loaf with scoundrel sauce, 69–70
    steak with green peppercorn sauce, 269
    Zoe's pot roast with spinach, 48–49
Minestrone soup, Mrs. Ottavio's, 87–88

Mousse, frozen candied orange, with bittersweet chocolate sauce, 310
Mullet roe, spaghettini with, 105
Mushroom sauce, polenta with porcini, 216
Mushrooms
    fettuccine with porcini, 163
    grilled squid topped with porcini, 103
    little toasts with porcini, 200
    porcini, soup, 81
    veal cutlets with porcini, 279
Mustard, Tuscan, with vin santo, 146

❧ O ❧

Octopus
    baby, in tomato broth, 129
    poached, 259
Omelettes
    wild asparagus, 191
    zucchini and zucchini blossom, 124
Onions, Andrea's, caramelized in Sauternes, 287
Orange mousse, frozen candied, with bittersweet chocolate sauce, 310
Osso buco, Elio's, 275–276

❧ P ❧

Pancetta, quails with, 268
Panna cotta with strawberry sauce, 109
Pappardelle with flown chicken, 235
Parmesan croutons, 213
Pastas
    bucatini with fresh sardines and fennel, 229–230
    the emperor's spaghetti, 242–243
    fettuccine, shepherd's style, 96
    fettuccine with fresh herbs, 248
    fettuccine with garlic and butter, 245
    fettuccine with porcini mushrooms, 163
    fettuccine with spicy tomato sauce, 247

fettuccine with Swiss chard, 246
fresh mint and ricotta ravioli, 238
fresh pasta, 228
hand-rolled spaghetti with duck
    sauce, 236–237
lasagne al pesto, 231
lasagne with fish ragout, 150–151
pappardelle with flown chicken,
    235
pasta pillows stuffed with aspara-
    gus and taleggio cheese,
    155–156
spaghettini with black cabbage, 104
spaghettini with mullet roe, 105
spinach and ricotta ravioli with
    butter and sage, 240–241
thin fettuccine with citrus zest, 134
thin fettuccine with shrimp, green
    peppercorns, and orange zest,
    249
thin spaghetti with lobster, 122
thin spaghetti with raw artichokes,
    135
thin spaghetti with veal and
    tomato sauce, 244
vegetable lasagne, 232–234
Zoe's quill-shaped pasta "dragged"
    with meat sauce, 60
Peach cake, 313
Peaches
    with caramel cream, 304
    and pistachio tiramisù, 312
Peas
    bruschetta with, and prosciutto,
        205
    Florentine style, 158
Pecorino cheese bruschetta, 33
Perch with leeks, 257
Pies
    Karen's blueberry, 179–180
    pumpkin, 305–306
Piglet, roast, 172
Pine nut tart, 316–317
Polentas
    with porcini mushroom sauce, 216
    with sweet Gorgonzola, 217
Porcini mushroom soup, 81

Pork entrées
    Danish pork tenderloin with
        cream sauce and bacon, 22
    pork and squab skewered with
        bread and bay leaf, 68
    roast piglet, 172
    roast pork, Florentine style, 272
Pot roast, Zoe's pot roast with
    spinach, 48–49
Potato gnocchi with Gorgonzola and
    truffle sauce, 223–224
Potatoes
    fried, 293
    roasted, with rosemary and garlic,
        291
    veal with sage and, 283
    with walnuts and lemon, 292
Puddings
    Danish rice, 10
    Florentine bread, 297
Pumpkin pie, 305–306

⋅ Q ⋅
Quails with pancetta, 268

⋅ R ⋅
Rabbit entrées
    roast rabbit with sun-dried tomato
        pesto, 264
    stuffed rabbit, 266–267
    rabbit in sweet-and-sour sauce, 265
Radicchio
    crêpes stuffed with, and
        Gorgonzola, 214–215
    nests with Gorgonzola sauce, 290
Ravioli
    fresh mint and ricotta, 238
    naked, 227
    spinach and ricotta, with butter
        and sage, 240–241
Rice "oranges," 89–90
Rice pudding, Danish, 10
Ricotta cheesecake, 314–315
Risotti
    with artichokes, 218–219
    asparagus, 221

saffron, 220
with zucchini, tomato, and
arugula, 222
Roast beef, stovetop, 59
Roast capon stuffed with sweetbreads
and truffles, 130
Roast piglet, 172
Roe, spaghettini with mullet, 105

ᘓ S ᘒ

Sabayon
with chantilly cream and strawberries, 318
tartlets with figs and, 300–301
Saffron risotto, 220
Sage leaves, fried, 195
Sage-scented beef fillets, 90
Salads
fresh artichoke and parmesan, 193
Madame's warm celery root, with
blue cheese vinaigrette, 17
Trattoria Garga signature, 113
Tuscan bread, 123
zucchini, pine nut, and truffle oil,
194
Sauces
chicken breast with orange, 260
duck breast with green peppercorn, 263
duck with orange, Florentine style,
262
fettuccine with spicy tomato, 247
golden veal cutlets with
Gorgonzola, 273
hand-rolled spaghetti with duck,
236–237
homemade Florentine tomato, for
pasta, 239
Italian meat loaf with scoundrel,
69–70
meat, Zoe's quill-shaped pasta
dragged with, 60
potato gnocchi with Gorgonzola
and truffle, 223–224
rabbit in sweet-and-sour, 265
radicchio nests with Gorgonzola,
290

rice "oranges," with béchamel,
89–90
shrimp with spicy garlic and
tomato, 256
steak with green peppercorn, 269
thin spaghetti with veal and
tomato, 244
veal cutlet with lemon, 281
veal cutlet with tarragon, 280
veal with asparagus and cognac
cream, 282
wine, 145
Seafood. See Fish and seafood
entrées
Semolina dumplings, 50
Shrimp entrées
fried zucchini blossoms and
shrimp, 192
with green peppercorns, 254
with peppers, 253
shrimp toast, 202
with spicy garlic and tomato sauce,
256
thin fettuccine with shrimp, green
peppercorns, and orange zest,
249
with zucchini, tomato, and
arugula, 255
Shrimp toast, 202
Side dishes
Andrea's onions caramelized in
Sauternes, 287
artichoke tart, 196–197
baked fennel bulb, 289
fresh peas, Florentine style, 158
fried new potatoes, 293
Grandma Gerda's red cabbage, 10
potatoes with walnuts and lemon,
292
radicchio nests with Gorgonzola
sauce, 290
rice "oranges," 89–90
roasted potatoes with rosemary
and garlic, 291
semolina dumplings, 50
spinach sautéed with garlic, 294
stewed artichokes, 108
stewed green beans, 75

stuffed artichokes, 57–58
summer eggplant Parmigiana, 76
Swiss chard sautéed with garlic, 286
white cannellini beans with oil, 288
Soups
  egg and cheese rags in broth, 212
  fish, 208
  Mrs. Ottavio's minestrone, 87–88
  parmesan croutons for, 213
  porcini mushroom, 81
  puréed tomato, 211
  puréed white bean, with spelt, 210
  tomato bread, 209
  Tuscan bread, 171
Spaghetti
  the emperor's spaghetti, 242–243
  hand-rolled spaghetti with duck sauce, 236–237
  thin spaghetti with lobster, 122
  thin spaghetti with raw artichokes, 135
  thin spaghetti with veal and tomato sauce, 244
Spaghettini
  with black cabbage, 104
  with mullet roe, 105
Spelt, puréed white bean soup with, 210
Spinach
  Florentine crêpes, 34–35
  and ricotta ravioli with butter and sage, 240–241
  sautéed with garlic, 294
  Zoe's pot roast with, 48–49
Squab, pork and, skewered with bread and bay leaf, 68
Squash gnocchi, 225–226
Squid, grilled, topped with porcini mushroom cap, 103
Steak with green peppercorn sauce, 269
Strawberries, sabayon with chantilly cream and, 318
Strawberry sauce, panna cotta with, 109
Summer eggplant Parmigiana, 76

Sweetbreads
  roast capon stuffed with, and truffles, 130
  veal, with lemon and butter, 115
Swiss chard sautéed with garlic, 286
Swordfish, Sicilian style, 258

ೞ T ೞ

Tarts
  apple, alla Nancy, 165–166
  artichoke, 196–197
  chocolate, 136
  country house apricot, 82–83
  with figs and whipped sabayon, 300–301
  lemon, 299
  pine nut, 316–317
Tiramisù, 311
  peach and pistachio, 312
Toasts
  with chicken livers, 199
  with porcini mushrooms, 200
  shrimp, 202
  with smoked mozzarella and anchovy sauce, 201
  with spicy garlic and tomato sauce, 95
Tomato bread soup, 209
Tomato broth, baby octopus in, 129
Tomato sauces
  fettuccine with spicy, 247
  homemade Florentine, for pasta, 239
  little toasts with spicy garlic and, 95
  shrimp with spicy garlic and, 256
  thin spaghetti with veal and, 244
Tomatoes
  bruschetta with oven-roasted, 198
  soup, puréed, 211
Trattoria Garga signature salad, 113
Truffles
  roast capon stuffed with sweetbreads and, 130
Tuscan bread salad, 123
Tuscan bread soup, 171
Tuscan flat bread with fresh rosemary, 170
Tuscan mustard with vin santo, 146

☙ V ❧

Veal entrées
  Elio's osso buco, 275–276
  golden veal cutlets with
    Gorgonzola sauce, 273
  thin spaghetti with veal and
    tomato sauce, 244
  veal, Italian style, 274
  veal cutlet with artichokes,
    277–278
  veal cutlet with avocado and truffle
    cream, 114
  veal cutlet with lemon sauce, 281
  veal cutlet with porcini mush-
    rooms, 279
  veal cutlet with tarragon sauce,
    280
  veal sweetbreads with lemon and
    butter, 115
  veal with artichokes, 164
  veal with asparagus and cognac
    cream sauce, 282
  veal with sage and new potatoes,
    283
  veal with zucchini, tomato, and
    arugula, 284
Vegetable lasagne, 232–234

Vegetables
  eggplant and zucchini bundles,
    189
  fresh peas, Florentine style, 158
  fried zucchini blossoms, 190
  fried zucchini blossoms and
    shrimp, 192
  stewed green beans, 75

☙ W ❧

Wine sauce, 145

☙ Z ❧

Zoe's chicken breast with vegetables,
  61
Zoe's pot roast with spinach, 48–49
Zoe's quill-shaped pasta "dragged"
  with meat sauce, 60
Zucchini
  bundles, eggplant and, 189
  blossoms, fried, 190
  blossoms, fried, and shrimp, 192
  pine nut, and truffle oil salad, 194
  tomato, and arugula, risotto with,
    222
  tomato, and arugula, veal with,
    284
  and zucchini blossom omelette,
    124